John Waters was born in Castlerea, Co Roscommon in 1955 and has been a journalist for fourteen years. He started in 1981 as a writer with the music magazine, *Hot Press*, subsequently became a columnist and feature writer with the *Sunday Tribune*. In 1985 he became editor of *In Dublin* magazine and in 1988 was appointed editor of the current affairs magazine *Magill*.

He now works for *The Irish Time* as a feature writer and columnist. His first book was the No 1 bestseller *Jiving at the Crossroads* published by Blackstaff Press. His second book entitled *Race of Angels* will be published this Autumn (also Blackstaff) and is about the rock group U2.

EVERY DAY
LIKE SUNDAY?

EVERY DAY
LIKE SUNDAY?

JOHN WATERS

POOLBEG

Published in 1995 by
Poolbeg Press Ltd,
Knocksedan House,
123 Baldoyle Industrial Estate,
Dublin 13, Ireland

A catalogue record for this book is available from the British Library.

ISBN 1 85371 423 2

Cover photography by Gillian Buckley
Cover design by Poolbeg Group Services Ltd
Set by Poolbeg Group Services Ltd in Garamond 10.5/13.5
Printed by The Guernsey Press Ltd,
Vale, Guernsey, Channel Islands.

For my nieces, Lisa and Elaine, and my nephews, Andrew, Barry and Ben, that they may not leave without a fight.

ACKNOWLEDGEMENTS

The author acknowledges a debt of gratitude to *The Irish Times* where most of the material in this book was first published, and especially to the paper's editor, Conor Brady.

CONTENTS

THE LITANY OF THE FUNDAMENTALLY SOUND
(August 1994)

Some weeks ago, writing about our state of economic well-being or otherwise, I quoted from a prayer which I thought pertinent to the subject. In doing so I attracted a number of queries from readers of this column. In response to such enquiries, I have decided to reproduce the prayer in full. It is called *The Litany of the Fundamentally Sound*. I offer it up for the intentions of the 2,000 people who are going to lose their jobs as a result of the new round of rationalisations at Telecom Eireann. Let us pray.

Power of the market. Pray for us. Open market. Pray for us. Internal market. Pray for us. Blessed market. Pray for us. Holy Mother of markets. Pray for us. Market most pure. Pray for us. Market most chaste. Pray for us. Market inviolate. Pray for us. Market undefiled. Pray for us. Market most amiable. Pray for us. Market most prudent. Pray for us. Market most venerable. Pray for us. Market most renowned. Pray for us. Market most powerful. Pray for us. Market most merciful. Pray for us. Market most stable. Pray for us. Market of justice. Pray for us. Market of wisdom. Pray for us. Market of beef. Pray for us. Spiritual market. Pray for us. Market of honour. Pray for us. Singular market of devotion. Pray for us. Mystical market. Pray for us. Market of David. Pray for us. Market of ivory. Pray for us. Market of gold. Pray for us. Human capital. Pray for us. Pricing system. Pray for us. Free trade. Pray for us. Incentives. Pray for us. Anti-inflationary pressures. Pray for us. Invisible hand. Pray for us. Sustainable growth. Pray for us. International trade. Pray for us. Peter Sutherland. Pray for us. Unfair competition. Pray for us. Domestic competition. Pray for us. Stimulation on demand. Pray for us. Free enterprise. Pray for us. Fiscal policy. Pray for us. Privatisation. Pray for us. Monetary controls. Pray for us. Balance of payments. Pray for us. Deregulation. Pray for us. General Agreement on Tariffs and Trade. Pray for us. Wealth of Nations. Pray for us. Macroeconomic policy. Pray for us. Zero inflation. Pray for us. Motivating power of self-interest. Pray for us. Microeconomic policy. Pray for us. Milton Friedman. Pray for us. Marginal cost. Pray for us. General equilibrium. Pray for us. Regulatory power of the market. Pray for us. General Theory. Pray for us. Oligopoly. Pray for us. Indifference curve. Pray for us. Units of output. Pray for us. Price index. Pray for us. Price controls. Pray for us. Gold standard. Pray for us. Studies in the Quantum Theory of Money. Pray for us. Principle of Comparative Advantage. Pray for us. Comprehensive Prices and Incomes Policy. Pray for us. Viability. Pray for us. EU Regulations. Pray for us. Economies of scale. Pray for us. Rational options. Pray for us. International Monetary Fund. Pray for us. Boom and bloom. Pray for us. Central Bank. Pray for us. Sterling. Pray for us. US dollar. Pray for us. Deutsche mark. Pray for us. French franc. Pray for us. Dutch guilder. Pray for us. Belgian franc. Pray for us. Danish krone. Pray for us. Italian lira. Pray for us. Greek drachma. Pray for us. Spanish peseta. Pray for us. Portuguese escudo. Pray for us. Japanese yen. Pray for us. Swiss franc. Pray for us. Swedish krone. Pray for us.

Norwegian krone. Pray for us. Finnish markka. Pray for us. Austrian schilling. Pray for us. Hong Kong dollar. Pray for us. Canadian dollar. Pray for us. Australian dollar. Pray for us. Basket of currencies. Pray for us.

Government stocks. Pray for us. FTSE 100. Pray for us. Closing prices. Pray for us. ISEQ index. Pray for us. Dow Jones. Pray for us. Gilt futures. Pray for us. Interim performance. Pray for us. Healthy indicators. Pray for us. Fiscal reform. Pray for us. Tax amnesty. Pray for us. Offshore funds. Pray for us. Tax buoyancy. Pray for us. Spending cuts. Pray for us. Long-term outlook. Pray for us. Medium-term outlook. Pray for us. Short-term outlook. Pray for us. Expansionary fiscal contraction. Pray for us. Strong fundamentals. Pray for us. Irish Life. Pray for us. National Irish. Pray for us. Irish National. Pray for us. Bank of Ireland. Pray for us. Private sector. Pray for us. Consumer price inflation. Pray for us. Exchequer borrowing requirement as a percentage of gross national product. Pray for us. OECD. Pray for us. NESC. Pray for us. PESP. Pray for us. ICTU. Pray for us. GNP. Pray for us. SIPTU. Pray for us. GDP. Pray for us. EBR. Pray for us. NCB. Pray for us. GATT. Pray for us. NAFTA. Pray for us. DKM. Pray for us. ESRI. Pray for us. Golden circle. Pray for us. Bottom line. Pray for us. Social partners. Pray for us. Corporate bodies. Pray for us. Foreign debt. Pray for us. Domestic debt. Pray for us. Foreign debt as a percentage of GNP. Pray for us. Domestic debt as a percentage of GNP. Pray for us. Total government debt. Pray for us. Total government debt as a percentage of GNP. Pray for us. Star chamber. Pray for us. Department of Economic Planning and Development. Pray for us. Doheny and Nesbitt. Pray for us. Stabilisation of borrowings. Pray for us. Liberalisation of capital. Pray for us. Domestic consumption. Pray for us. Exchequer returns. Pray for us. Balance of payments surplus. Pray for us. Deflationary measures. Pray for us. Theory of demand. Pray for us. Theory of supply. Pray for us. Theory of production. Pray for us. Theory of distribution. Pray for us. Theory of value. Pray for us. Theory of capital. Pray for us. Theory of unemployment, interest and money. Pray for us. Law of diminishing returns. Pray for us. Law of diminishing utility. Pray for us. Marginal utility. Pray for us. Martin O'Donoghue. Pray for us. Trade cycle. Pray for us. Market equilibrium. Pray for us. Real income per head of population. Pray for us. Climate for investment. Pray for us. Retail sales. Pray for us. Elasticity of demand. Pray for us. Regulation of demand. Pray for us. Structure of demand. Pray for us. Moore McDowell. Pray for us. Michael McDowell. Pray for us. Derek McDowell. Pray for us. Entrepreneurial net income. Pray for us. Regulation of output. Pray for us. Business confidence. Pray for us. Fiscal realities. Pray for us. Fiscal rectitude. Pray for us. Commercial realities. Pray for us. Convergence requirements. Pray for us. Structural funding. Pray for us. Cohesion. Pray for us. Seán Barrett. Pray for us. Deficit financing. Pray for us. Global markets. Pray for us. Marketplace. Pray for us. Market of covenants. Pray for us. Ark of the market. Pray for us. Gate of the market. Pray for us. Market of heaven. Pray for us. Morning market. Pray for us. Market of gates. Pray for us. Market of sinners. Pray for us. Market of the afflicted. Pray for us. Market of the sick. Pray for us. Market of Christians. Pray for us. Market of angels. Pray for us. Market of patriarchs. Pray for us. Market of prophets. Pray for us. Market of martyrs. Pray for us. Market of confessors. Pray for us. Market of virgins. Pray for us. Market of towers. Pray for us. Tower of markets. Pray for us. Market assumed into heaven. Pray for us. Heaven assumed into markets. Pray for us. Cause of our joy. Pray for us.

To obtain the plenary indulgence you should recite the prayer over lunch at the Unicorn and drinks at Nesbitt's, having just appeared on *Saturday View* and at least once on either *Morning Ireland* or *Prime Time* during the week.

INTRODUCTION

This book is not intended to be read as a "collection". Although it is certainly a compendium of articles previously published in – almost invariably – *The Irish Times*, it is not an attempt to present in book form either the "best" of such pieces or a "selection" from them. The aim is rather to present the statement which those articles sought to articulate.

When I began writing a weekly column for *The Irish Times* at the beginning of 1991, I did not believe I could continue writing it for much more than a month. It's not that I didn't think I had enough opinions to sustain the column, but rather that those opinions seemed to me to be so unexceptionable as to be axiomatic. I was vaguely conscious that the range of my views seemed to converge on key areas of public affairs, and that there was a reasonably straightforward way of working through the series of points which I supposed were there to be made. I believed that what I had to say could be said in a few columns, and that after that my relatively easygoing approach to the world would make me feel that there was little more to be said. Almost four years later, while I make no claims for the reliability of my own insights, I am increasingly conscious that I am still only scratching the surface. It is as if the subject to be addressed expands rather than contracts when you start to engage with it. Far from being able to complete a picture in a few articles, I have found that every article seems to raise more questions than it provides answers. I have this sense that, rather than shining bright, pointed lights on a subject which is there to be revealed, I have been groping in the darkness to feel a shape which has no limits or knowable outline. All I can hope is that I have been able to communicate occasional hints about the bulk and scale of what I sense to be there.

Writing, over the past few years, about what, on the face of it, seems like a *range* of subjects – rural decline, unemployment, the thrust towards European integration, the soap-operafication of politics, or whatever – I have grown conscious that, all the time, I was chipping away at what seemed to be a single thematic block.

The language we use, and the way we have been brought up to use it, tends to separate and encourage specialised forms of thought: *this* is economics, *that* is poverty, and so on. It is in the nature of mass media to avoid making connections. This in itself does not appear to be a serious problem, since people must be presumed to be intelligent enough to make the connections on their own. But that analysis ignores the extent to which the consciousness of society is being formed, as well as *in*formed, by the media. The omission of connections contains the implicit message that such connections do not exist.

One of the first things you learn when you begin to write about the shape of the world you share with other people is the extent to which language, the tool we have fashioned for understanding that world, is a crude and inefficient instrument of communication. Words do not *describe* things, but at best hint at an understanding between people with similar aspirations and cultural experiences. The more divergence between those aspirations and experiences, the less prospect of any understanding. This observation would be patently true between, say, a Cherokee and a Dutchman, but we tend to discount the extent to which it is also – relatively speaking – true of people from within what is ostensibly the same culture. Words have only loose meanings, and at best you can hope that, by placing them in a proper sequence, you can signal the shape of the idea you wish to communicate. Words, like land, have a tendency to become the property of *somebody*, and there is overwhelming evidence to show that the forces which come to bear on this process are the same as in more obviously economic areas.

Journalism is therefore a form of reclamation. I have had this sense that, in writing about what appeared to be separate subjects in a particular way, I was accidentally rediscovering the subterranean threads which connected them, but which had been obscured by the channels of language in which most public discussions are conducted. That is really why I have brought some of those pieces together in this book: in the hope that the juxtapositioning of diverse strands will suggest, in a manner which no direct statement could achieve, the shape of a whole.

If pushed to explain what it is I wish to communicate, I could try to put it like this: to say that, increasingly, it has seemed to me that all the drifts in the life of modern political society are tending to gravitate towards a single point of convergence. Although we are being conditioned to think about such things in separate boxes, we are still able to catch glimpses of the fact that there is a profound degree of connection between concepts like globalism, environmental destruction, economic and monetary convergence, and the interests and activities of multinational corporations.

To give a single example, I could point to the manner in which the activity of work, which has been a central aspect of human expression through the centuries, is being increasingly removed from the territory of personal responsibility and mediated through technologies and economic systems. The process of production, once one of the most crucial and rewarding of man's activities, is broken up into absurd divisions which make a contorted kind of "economic" sense. Public discussion in western society tends to isolate these things and treat them as separate phenomena, and this desire to isolate is built into the language in such a way as to invite the possibility that the sense of those connections is not something we can take for granted.

There is, in other words, a self-perpetuating process at work. It seems to me that the unseen strategy involves the destruction of nationalities, local cultures and the transformation of human relationships into commercial transactions. The concentration of power in ever more remote and distant power blocs seems to parallel an increasing alienation of the individual human being and the decline of forms of work, culture and communication by which the individual human being has exercised control of his or her life and human activity. I have a sense that the same process is spawning the horrific acceleration in unemployment, which in turn leads to the increase in social problems like crime, drug addiction and so on. But I can, in advancing this argument in the pages of a daily newspaper, suggest only a fraction of the process in which it operates.

Sometimes a word creeps into the frame which seems to contain everything of what is to be said. The word "power" is one such. If I were asked, under pain of death, to state one word which suggests what I write about, then this is the best I could do. The range of meanings which the word can have suggests both the breadth of the problem and the duplicity of language. What I find myself *describing* is a society in which the definition of power converges on the external, removed centre of administration of control. What I find myself trying to *imagine* is the possibility of a society in which the true source of power – the heart of the human person – is acknowledged and celebrated. In trying simultaneously to describe and imagine, there is endless scope for confusion and misunderstanding.

As I write these words, I am conscious yet again of the way that, summarised in the words of a single paragraph, the essence of the idea I wish to communicate is lost between the stepping stones of the language. I have felt this many times since I began in journalism – that each attempt to explain myself had been a failure; but I have been encouraged a little by the idea that, together, there was the chance that my attempts were more successful. In a sense, in making each new part of the argument, I need to be able to summon up all the other parts as well, so as to have even the remotest chance of being half-understood. That is chiefly why I have decided to publish this book.

My Tuesday column in *The Irish Times* has never been, I would argue, an "opinion" column. There is a lot of facile snobbery in journalistic circles about the division between the role defined as "comment" and the role defined as "factual reporting". What I have been doing for four years in *The Irish Times* is factual reporting in the most basic sense of the term. I write what I see, what I hear, and what these things make me feel and think. I don't believe that there is any more journalistic virtue in reporting the time of an accident, the colour of a car or the words of a spokesman than in outlining what I perceive as the hidden agendas or subterranean prejudices underlying a particular public development. A newspaper column which confined its role to opinionating would quickly run out of material. The reality of "opinion writing" is of engaging with the world through living in it, reading about it, listening to other people talking about it. What I write is, in one sense, *my* opinion; but in another sense altogether, it is an attempt to crystallise the sum of perceptions – mine and other people's – which I have encountered on my journey so far.

We are all fumbling towards truth, towards the half-imagined consciousness that all the problems we encounter in a public sense have a common source and a converging set of consequences. It *should* be easier to see these things, but our society has evolved fiendishly clever devices to obscure the truth from its view. "Factual" reporting is utterly inadequate in the face of this process, because it is unable to answer the accusation inherent in the question: "*Whose* facts?"

The question "Whose *opinions*?", of course, contains its own set of accusations. But they are easier to answer. What we call "opinions" suggest, by definition, an acknowledgement of the existence of *various* possibilities and realities. What we call "facts" have a tendency not merely to suggest that there is only *one* reality, but that they, in fact, are *it*.

I

GOD OUT OF THE MACHINE

1. JESUS NOT CAESAR

In the summer of 1990 the playwright Václav Havel was re-elected President of Czechoslovakia.

(July 1990)

On the night of June 9th last, the concluding day of the Czechoslovakian elections, an anti-racism concert, headlined by Paul Simon, was held in the Old Town Square in Prague.

Also on the bill was Michael Kocab, better known outside Czechoslovakia for his work as a member of the Bridge, the two-man negotiating team which liaised between Civic Forum and the communists in the weeks after the revolution. Kocab performed a selection of numbers from what to Western ears is a slightly dated repertoire of pomp rock fused with classical and jazz, and then announced that he was about to introduce a special guest, "President Havel".

The Old Town Square erupted as President Havel, wearing a sports jacket and open-necked shirt, shambled onstage. The Square immediately resounded to a chant of "Havel, Havel." The president took the microphone and, after a few introductory remarks, swept his right arm towards the wings and, with the aplomb of a Czech Dave Fanning, announced, "Paul Simon".

The crowd clapped politely as Simon came on and launched into the opening bars of "The Boxer", but his efforts were for some minutes drowned out by the continuing chant of "Havel, Havel" from the thousands of young Czechs, reluctant to allow their president to leave.

In the case of most western politicians, such an incident would be viewed by the public with a mixture of cynicism and embarrassment, an attempt to cash-in on a photo-opportunity and latch on to the youth vote. But Czechoslovakia is different, and Václav Havel especially so.

For a start, Havel actually *likes* rock music and, to the horror of some conservative elements in Prague, he likes rock musicians, as well. But, altogether more relevant to understanding Václav Havel is the fact that he considers rock music an important mode of expression.

The death of John Lennon for instance, he wrote at the time, was for him, "the death of the century (perhaps more so than the deaths of Kennedy or King)."

Lennon's murder, he believed, was a shot "fired by the reality of the '80s, at one of the departing dreams – the dream of the '60s for peace, freedom and brotherhood, – a shot as it were in face of that existential revolution of the 'third consciousness'."

And just as he allows no distinctions between "high art" and "low art", neither does Václav Havel acknowledge the conventional barriers between the rulers and the ruled. For him there are essentially only two states of being: living a lie and living in the truth. All his writing has been an exposition of what he has identified as "the profound crisis of human identity brought about by living within a lie."

Totalitarianism has taught him to be suspicious of all

systems. Human beings and human values, he believes, should predominate over science, systems and ideologies – not the other way around.

"Science", he said in a recent speech in Prague, "does not have a conscience. It may be beautiful, important, and the great fruit of human knowledge. But the human spirit is not only knowledge; it is also balance, and consideration, and conscience, and civility, and taste, and love for one's neighbour, and responsibility, and courage, and objective distance from oneself, and doubt, and even humour. If Mr Marx had not been an angry, vain man, but a peaceful and merry man, it's possible that his scientific discoveries wouldn't have been so easily misused against mankind and against the very basis of life."

One of the most frequent criticisms of Václav Havel – made particularly in the West – is that he is a creature of opposition, that his ideas, formulated during the years of dissidence, are not geared towards the creation of a viable alternative system now that he finds himself in power.

This is to altogether miss the point of everything Václav Havel has been saying. It is not that he is incapable of putting forward an alternative system, but that he passionately holds that he should not do so.

Havel believes that power should percolate not from the top down but from the bottom up. He also believes that the structures of power – the system for the transmission of power throughout a society – should be allowed to evolve naturally from this process.

This requires, he says, a revolution which is not merely political, nor social, nor even philosophical, but one which takes place within the very centre of human existence – what he calls an "existential revolution".

Politicians, political parties and political thinking, he believes, are there to assist and guide this process, not to lead it or influence it in any particular direction. Only when this "existential revolution" is complete will the alternative political scenario reveal itself.

Two words – "morality" and "responsibility" – have come to be synonymous with the name of Václav Havel. In Western politics, such concepts have been rendered meaningless through overuse, but from the mouth and pen of Václav Havel they seem to acquire a new breadth of meaning.

Much of his work, as a playwright and essayist, has been towards establishing a moral bottom line, what he calls "man's personal horizon", and finding a way of applying this within the political process. This horizon he once described as "the metaphysical vanishing-point of life", which, he acknowledged, "many people experience as God."

Though Havel once conceded that he was "certainly not a proper Christian and Catholic", his message is, nonetheless, essentially a religious one. The German writer Heinrich Böll perhaps put it best when he wrote that Havel was "the manifestation of a new form of religiousness, which out of courtesy no longer addresses God with the name which has been trampled underfoot by politicians."

Though anxious to avoid comparisons, Havel has constantly in his speeches since becoming president invoked the spirit of Thomas Masaryk, president of the first Czech Republic between the two world wars.

Masaryk, a man of great learning and political sophistication, believed that politics should not exist purely on their own terms but had to be legitimated by something which transcends them, that is a higher plane of cultural and ethical values. In his first speech as president, Havel, paraphrasing Masaryk, outlined his approach to his new job as "Jesus, not Caesar."

15

Since his election, while Western politicians have been queuing up to shake Havel's hand and welcome him into "the great family of democracy", they appear oblivious to the fact that for him democracy has come to mean a totally different thing.

His 1984 essay, "Politics and Conscience", for example, characterises Eastern European totalitarianism as a "convex mirror" held up to all Western civilisation, "a harsh, perhaps final, call for a global recasting of that civilisation's self-understanding". "The human failure that it mirrors", he elaborated elsewhere, "is only one variant of the general failure of modern humanity."

In his 1978 essay, "The Power of the Powerless", he wrote: "There is no real evidence that Western democracy, that is democracy of the traditional parliamentary type, can offer solutions that are any more profound."

In Western democracies, he argued, people might be manipulated in a more subtle manner than that employed by the communists, but they were still at the mercy of a "static complex of rigid, conceptually sloppy and politically pragmatic mass political parties run by professional apparatuses, releasing the citizen from all forms of concrete and personal responsibility."

In essence, what Havel aspires to is a system which, in its ideal operation, will cease to exist. The political structures which he wishes to help his people put in place will, in what he ironically describes as his "utopia", disappear like a length of dissolving suture once the process of the "existential revolution" has been completed.

In a sense he is trying to recreate the world in reverse. It is as though he were attempting to create a pearl from the outside in, without the grain of grit or sand – the inbuilt flaw – at the core.

Havel believes in what he calls "anti-political politics", which he defines as "politics not as the technology of power and manipulation, of cybernetic rule over humans or as the art of the useful, but politics as one of the ways of seeking and achieving meaningful lives, of protecting them and serving them."

This "post-democratic" society, he suggested, might be created along lines not altogether dissimilar to the dissident groups which existed under the rule of the communists, and which had as their principal objectives the creation of "an articulate form of 'living within the truth'," and a renewal of "the feeling of higher responsibility in an apathetic society".

Civic Forum represents to a very high degree the realisation of this vision. It is not a formal political party, but a loose coalition of clubs and communities representing a range of viewpoints. It has no fixed ideology, apart from a basic recognition of human rights.

Decisions are arrived at by consensus, usually after prolonged and heated debate, but the concept of democratic centralism familiar in the West, whereby decisions taken collectively are individually binding, does not apply. Each individual, including the individual Civic Forum deputy in parliament, is free to follow his own conscience. The concept of the party whip does not exist.

Thus, though much remains to be done, the first stage of Václav Havel's "utopia" is already in place. The president's chief spokesman, Michal Zantovsky, speaking on radio recently, identified the need to create similar structures for the workings of government as one of the new administration's priorities.

"There have been many politicians before who laid emphasis on morality and ethics. We think how it's implemented into practical politics is more important than the speeches themselves."

Havel has characterised the Civic Forum-led

government of the coming two years as the "government of national sacrifice", and the movement in fact fought the election on a platform of "blood, toil, tears and sweat".

And while the Forum's massive endorsement by the electorate is seen as an indicator that the public is indeed prepared for a period of relative economic hardship, there is also within the movement a degree of concern as to whether people have an adequate grasp of what the imminent switch from a centrally planned to a market economy will mean.

There are times when, from a Western perspective at least, Civic Forum appears to be carrying the Havel concept of "anti-political politics" to an extreme which could threaten the movement's own survival.

The decision, for instance, to place a two-year ceiling on the lifetime of the current parliament seems certain to ensure that the next elections will be held at a time when the negative effects of the economic reforms will be at their most acute, thereby creating the possibility of Civic Forum suffering a major electoral reverse.

The decision to opt for a two-year period, according to the Forum's Jan Kavan, was "a compromise between the length of time necessary for the other parties to build their campaigns and the need to pass important economic and other reforms". He concedes that Civic Forum will almost certainly suffer a setback as a result, but points out that "what would be good for Civic Forum would not necessarily be good for democracy, and vice versa."

Mr Kavan says that for the moment the movement continues to hold true to the ideals of its founder, even though Havel's role as president creates a political and constitutional distance between him and Civic Forum. The problem of evolving structures to cope adequately with the scale of the economic crisis, however, is likely

18

to take the Forum along the road of compromise.

"We're still looking for the optimal structures which will combine both democracy and efficiency. At the moment it seems that we will end up with a combination of some aspects from classical political parties, which can be accountable to their members and which can be more efficient, with a movement in which individuals can have a greater scope for independent thinking. Civic Forum will almost certainly remain a movement for the foreseeable future, and not become a political party, but it will probably move towards more formal structures."

For the moment, then, the more esoteric elements of Havel's "existential revolution" must be put on hold. His speeches since becoming president, while clearly underwritten by his broader views, have tended to deal in the main with more mundane issues, such as problems with the economy and environment.

It's also noticeable that, on the international stage, he appears to have somewhat diluted his views about the shortcomings of conventional democracy, but this is perhaps just his congenital politeness. This does not mean that the president has abandoned his broader objectives.

Only a relative handful of Czechs and Slovaks have read Václav Havel's theories about "the existential revolution" or "anti-political politics", but they know that he is a good man. The Charter 77 signatory and elder statesman of Czech letters, Zdenek Urbanek, has identified what he calls a "responsibility gap" between Havel and the people. This dates from the time ten years ago, when Havel turned down a government offer to leave prison if he agreed to go on a lecture tour of the United States. Václav Havel, they say, has clean hands.

"The people have an idea of Václav Havel, more than an awareness of what it is he is saying," says Mical

Horacek, a rock journalist turned entrepreneur, the other half of the two-man "bridge" negotiating team in the weeks following the revolution. "He is more than a politician; he has the status of demigod. The question is whether any mortal man can do what is expected of Václav Havel: and there is no doubt that when everyday problems begin to emerge, his status won't be as high.

"But it's not really a question of Havel – it's a question of experts. Havel can only supply the philosophical basis; he can only speak about the general direction. We need experts and we are sadly lacking them.

"Many of the people in the upper levels of the country's administration are not up to the task – I know this because I deal with them every day. This is very scary, and there is only so much that President Havel can do."

If Havel has problems, they are certainly not of personal popularity. That, it seems, is assured for a long time to come. In a sense, too, his status is removed from the realm of mere political popularity, since, although president by popular acclaim, he is in practice elected by parliament.

Thus, in not being required to curry electoral favour, Havel is paradoxically, but in a very real sense, able to distance himself from the political process and represent the fundamental aspirations of his people. He is, as Zdenek Urbanek puts it, "the people's guarantor of the political process".

Havel was clearly mindful of this role when he decided, against his earlier pronouncements, to accept the presidency again for the duration of the two-year run-up to full democratic elections in 1992. Whether he will continue beyond that will have to do with the state of the nation's morale after what are likely to be two difficult years.

There have been some snide references in Western

papers to the way Havel appears to be accommodating to power, but anyone who knows him will say that no-one will be happier the day his country no longer needs him. And the irony is that Czechoslovakia will need him only while his vision of a truly democratic society remains unrealised.

Like power, belief – whether in Gods or demigods – is functioning correctly only when it percolates from the bottom up. Genuine faith, Havel wrote in one of those extraordinary letters to his wife from prison, "is faith that animates its object, not the other way around."

Czechoslovakia will truly be free only when Václav Havel is able to stop being a god and go back to being a mere prophet.

2. THE GOD-SHAPED HOLE   (January 1991)

You never know how an artist is going to take it if you say that his life if more important than his art. Most artists tend not to like this very much. It seems now, however, to be incontrovertibly so in the case of Mr Salman Rushdie.

For here is a man whose books are more talked about than read, whose work, in fact, a great number of not insensitive people find, well, unreadable. Not that this necessarily prevents them talking about them, you understand.

If you think I am working up to be cynical about Salman Rushdie's conversion to Islam, then you are wrong. Far from being merely "convenient", as some of even his erstwhile defenders have alleged, his embrace of Islam was courageous, dignified and deeply moving, and he made a statement which may well outlive both himself and his books. In as far, paradoxically, as he distanced himself from *The Satanic Verses* – which he did

– he gave the book a resonance which now makes it essential reading.

Many liberals, predictably, are incensed by what they perceive as Rushdie's "betrayal" of their spirited efforts to defend him from the mad mullahs. Even worse, not only has he embraced these demons; he has also renounced his "liberal" friends. "If they see Islam as an enemy," he told the *Independent on Sunday*, "then they are not my friends. . . . If people want someone to attack the idea of religion, then I'm not your man. I never was."

Rushdie's account of his "conversion" was utterly persuasive. ("Conversion", of course, is not the absolutely correct term, since Mr Rushdie was not a member of another religion, but it is the word which has attached itself to his decision). During his enforced incarceration, he had become increasingly conscious that the sense of the spiritual which he had always expressed in his work was leading him inexorably to Islam. "I have never regarded Muslims as my enemy. When I think of Muslims I think of my grandfather." Islam, sooner or later, would be his spiritual home. "I used to say: 'there is a God-shaped hole in me.' For a long time I stressed the absence, the hole. Now I find it is the shape which has become important."

This is all very unfashionable stuff. An Irish writer, taking a similar line in a remotely comparable situation, would almost certainly be ostracised by the liberal community, which by definition would include many of his fellow artists. To embrace the enemy would be bad enough. To bite the hand that shielded him would be, well, unforgivable. But to *talk about God*. "Can human beings", asked Salman Rushdie, "have access to the spiritual life without having to call that access 'God'? I had 'immortal longings', but I thought of myself as an unbeliever. But I now think it was a stupid argument, because the way human beings have access is by calling it 'God'. It makes the attempt to reach what is spiritual to us easier."

By this time most of the "supporters" of the purative Irish Rushdie would be under the table. Nothing is apt to occasion such embarrassment among liberals as the subject of God.

I have an atheist friend who takes a great interest in Catholic theology, and who appears to know far more about the subject than the majority of Catholics and even the majority of priests. His reasons for being interested are twofold: firstly, religion is all around him and has therefore a daily and direct impact on his life, and secondly, as he says, even atheists have a spiritual yearning, a need to understand the mystical and mysterious, perhaps even more so than those whose faith allows them to take such things for granted. In his experience, he says, it is all but impossible to get Catholics to talk in an intelligent manner about God. When he brings the subject up, he says, people fidget, giggle and make nervous jokes. For such an ostensibly religious country, he says, very few people respond to such promptings in a way which suggests to him they believe in the existence of God.

And yet, he says, he also knows that such people do not share his own lack of belief. In his experience, those who do *not* believe in God have no difficulty in saying so. Those who *do* would rather talk about anything else.

Can there be a single other race in the world which talks so much about religion and yet so little about God? We talk and talk and talk, about "Church/State relations", about "public and private morality", about "the role of the individual conscience". Even sex is discussed in the context of religion.

Virtually the entire national agenda for self-examination is predicated upon the tussle between the forces of liberalism and the representatives of what liberals regard as a reactionary Church. In these discussions however, God, or even the idea of God, is rarely if ever explicit. It is like watching a football match between two equally energetic and determined teams playing without a ball.

I am unable to think of a single "liberal" who has declared him- or herself an avowed atheist. Implicit in everything such people say is the idea of a society which is not only liberal and enlightened, but *Christian* as well. Yet they seem to experience a great difficulty about saying so; about saying, for example, as Salman Rushdie has now done, "By the way, I believe in God." For them, religion is a political issue. It does not appear to occur to them that a simple statement of personal faith could be the most powerful political statement of all.

Let us take, for example, the liberals' attitude to one of the most consistent and forthright defenders of the Church's position, Dr Jeremiah Newman, Bishop of Limerick. Dr Newman, appropriately enough, was once dubbed the "mullah of Limerick" by Dr Conor Cruise O'Brien, and is regarded by his sometime liberal adversaries as a narrow-minded, bigoted defender of a declining Church.

In fact, Dr Newman is a frighteningly learned and thoughtful man, who has written numerous books on theological and philosophical issues, in most of which he displays an acute grasp of the factors affecting the perceived decline of religion in the modern world.

One of Dr Newman's most persistent points is to do with what he regards as the increasing "secularisation" of modern society. By this Dr Newman does not mean the creation of a Godless society, but rather the relocation of religious values in areas of life which he does not regard as sacred. In other words, what the bishop most fears is not that we will cease to believe in God, but that we will cease to regard the Catholic Church as being the sole agency in mediating our belief. "We are Christ," says Dr Newman. "The bishops are Christ."

Liberals do not appear to sufficiently appreciate what Dr Newman's position actually is. Before Christmas, for example, he was denounced for what was described as "a savage and disgraceful attack" on the poor. Dr Newman had suggested that religious groups who make demands on the government for aid to the poor are not necessarily to be regarded as a good thing. However, if one were to look carefully at some of Dr Newman's theological writings, it would become obvious that what he objects to is not the idea of the poor being helped, but the evolution out of such activity of an alternative channel for spirituality and faith.

In short, what Dr Newman appears to fear most is not Catholics who do not conform, or Catholics who do not believe, but those who refuse to conform but continue to believe. By neglecting to assert their belief, the bishop's adversaries therefore yield him the high ground.

It seems to me to be wrong to equate the development of a more progressive model of politics with secular values (and I suspect that, within his own definitions, Dr Newman thinks so as well.) In Czechoslovakia, for example, revolution has been followed by a renewed awareness of spirituality and the sacred. Czechoslovakia's "God-shaped hole" has been filled by Václav Havel and his own, very personal, notion of faith and Christianity. His God is "a horizon without which nothing would have any meaning and without which I would not, in fact, exist – he is by virtue of his essence, and not thanks to some strong-arm tactics that command respect. . . . I accept the

Gospel of Jesus as a challenge to go my own way."

Can you imagine an Irish politician speaking like this about the nature of his personal faith? And is it not bizarre, for example, that the term "Christian Socialist" is regarded almost as one of abuse in political circles in this country, despite the fact that the overwhelming majority of Irish politicians are informed by exclusively Christian values of morality?

A God-shaped hole has opened up in this country in recent years. Its existence stems from a tug-of-war between two sides who have nothing in common, it often seems, except their need to believe in something. To believe, let's fact it, in *God*. One side will not yield up ownership except on its own strict terms; the other seems unwilling to stake a claim in ringing terms. In the end all that will result is a broken rope, a sort of passive agnosticism by default.

We should learn from Salman Rushdie the lesson that, although the mullahs can remove your freedom, only you can hold the key to your soul.

3. DEMONS IN THE MACHINE   (April 1994)

It is nothing short of wondrous how occasionally, when the drift towards disaster appears almost unstoppable, there will arise out of the human condition a sign of the emergence of a consciousness which might serve to prevent that disaster. I have in mind a speech given two weeks ago in the European Parliament in Strasbourg by President Václav Havel of the Czech Republic. If politicians capable of making speeches like this were to become the norm in the European Union, there would be no need for me or anyone else to oppose our membership of that Union.

President Havel was in Strasbourg to make a case for his country's bid for membership of the EU. But he did not go, as so may others have done, with his cap in his hand. He went to say why his country wished to join the community, but also to define what it was that would make such a community worth joining. President Havel believes (as, despite my opposition to the EU, I do myself) in the idea of a single European home. He spoke of the "inner order" of Europe, the way, on the one hand, the "extraordinary variety and diversity" of Europe has been so deeply linked by a common destiny that, on the other, "this continent can accurately be described as a single – albeit complex – political entity."

The President went on to speak of his nation's place at the geographical heart of Europe. He made a case for the expansion of the EU to embrace that heart and beyond, not merely for the benefit of his country but for the betterment of the whole. "There simply is no meaningful alternative to this trend", he said. The "evil demons" which lie in wait must be denied the opportunity to shift the emphasis from consensus to violence.

So far, his speech was both unexceptional and, even for someone as "anti-European" as myself, utterly unexceptionable. But then, President Havel moved into a different groove. He spoke of his "ambiguous response" on reading the Maastricht Treat, which on the one hand he regarded as "a respectable piece of work". However, "into my admiration, which initially verged on enthusiasm, there began to intrude a disturbing, less exuberant feeling. I felt like I was looking into the inner workings of an absolutely perfect and immensely ingenious modern machine. To study such a machine must be a great joy to an admirer of technical innovations, but for me, a human whose interest in the world is not satisfied by admiration for well-oiled machines, something was seriously missing. Perhaps it could be called, in a rather simplified way, a spiritual or moral or emotional dimension. My reason had been spoken to, but not my heart."

All the complex supranational entities we know from history as having contributed something of value to humanity, President Havel elaborated, "were always buoyed by a spirit, an idea, an ethos – and I would even say by a charismatic quality – out of which their structure ultimately grew." To be vital, such entities had to offer "some key to emotional identification, an ideal that would speak to people or inspire them, a set of generally understandable values that everyone could share." It could not be denied, he said, that the EU was indeed based on such a spirit, with its roots in Christian, legal, civil and cultural antiquity.

But "it appears that this spirit is difficult to see". This he surmised, is because it is hidden "behind the mountains of systematic, technical, administrative, economic, monetary and other measures that contain it." I agree with the thrust of this, except to add my own suspicion that the spirit he speaks of may not so much have been hidden as supplanted by the forces he mentions.

The most urgent task facing the European Union today, said President Havel, is the definition and articulation of an identity and the "recreation of . . . its charisma". I could not agree more. If such a lacuna were even to be acknowledged by those who run the EU, opposition to its operations from sensible people would dissolve.

As a practical first step, the President called for the drawing up of a charter of Europe which would define a moral code for all its citizens. "All those hundreds of pages of agreements on which the European Union is founded would thus be brought under the umbrella of a single, crystal-clear and universally understandable political document that would immediately make it evident what the European Union really is."

This was merely a suggestion, he emphasised, and, if I understand his intention, advanced for where it pointed rather than for what it said. "You will certainly understand that at this moment my concern is not so much any particular suggestion, but something deeper. That is, how to make the spirit of the European Union more vivid and compelling, more accessible to all."

We have waited a long time for such a speech by a European leader. The irony of President Havel's speech is that it had to be made by the head of a nation which, for the moment, remains outside the EU. For not merely has no politician from any of the existing EU countries made such telling observations about the absence of a spiritual dimension to the European project, but none of them has even so much as acknowledged that spiritual needs have the least relevance to their work.

There is, I believe, an optimistic message to be found in this. It is as though history has begun to twist in its seating. The norm, whereby the strong bureaucratic powers at the centre issue the conditions and the terms, has begun to be reversed. Suddenly, the irrepressible truth of reality has begun to assert itself. A nation stands and says that the European emperor is a little underdressed. And this nation, it just so happens, has the moral authority of being, as its President rightly points out, at the very heart of Europe. If the vision radiating from Prague could become the guiding light of European unity, no sane person could possibly object to it. I, for one, would be among the first in the queue.

The question is: can it? Having read many of the

President's essays and plays, I suspect that he has glimpsed much more in the present state of the European project than his congenital good manners will allow him to speak. I suspect, too, that he knows that the demons are not all on the outside. "Ladies and gentlemen," he concluded, "I have come from a land that for almost 60 years did not enjoy freedom and democracy. You will perhaps believe me when I say that it is precisely this historical experience that has allowed me to respond at the deepest level to the revolutionary meaning of today's European integration. And perhaps you will believe me when I say that the very depth of that experience compels me to express concern for the proper outcome of this process and to consider ways to strengthen it and make it irreversible."

President Havel was speaking, as he subtly reminded us, as a long-time close observer of well-oiled machines.

II

YABOLLIXYA
(VISITING MIDLAND TOWNS)

1. CATCHPENNY CLIMATE   (August 1990)

Only a fool would try to suggest that all Irish towns are
the same. They are not. Each town has a different shape
or configuration, different geography, different
architecture, more or fewer people than the next one. In
a sense, though, these qualities belong not to the present
but to the far-distant past, to the original impetus of the
individual town, to the dynamic of its initial growth.

There are but brief moments in the life of a modern
town when it is possible, preferably with blinkered, half-
closed eyes, to touch that essential primordial spirit. The
best time is in the early evening of a weekday, between
the time the shops have closed and the pubs begun to
fill or half-fill for the night. Then a town appears as
though suspended in time, without the roar of traffic, the
clatter of tinny pop music, the flashing of neon signs.
Walking through a town in these rare moments allows
one to glimpse a little of its essence, to sense what it was
like before it became invaded by the all-persuasive
Catchpenny Consumer Culture, to feel the reason the
town excites – as all towns do – such loyalty in its
inhabitants.

If you visit first the tourist office at Bridge Street you can take with you a leaflet entitled "Tullamore Town Trail", which details some of the town's more noteworthy buildings and tourist attractions. You can check out the Courthouse, dating originally from 1833 and built, the leaflet informs you, "in the Greek style with a portico of six Ionic columns." Next door to this you will find Kilcruttin Centre where the last public execution in this country was held in 1865.

In the centre of town you can admire the old Market House in O'Connor Square, now the offices of the Irish Nationwide Building Society, or perhaps the premises of Hoey & Denning, solicitors, "designed in the Italianate style in the 1870s and built with a robust façade of Tullamore limestone."

Your trek around the Town Trail's 13 stops will allow you to pass the best part of a day in an enjoyable fashion – provided, that is, you have sufficient imaginative resources to maintain the illusion. Modern life is, for most people, a struggle to preserve their own particular illusion from the encroachment of reality.

There is no mention in the Town Trail leaflet, for example, of the neon-fronted "Bowie" American-style restaurant and takeaway at the corner of High Street and O'Moore Street. This building, dating in its present form from the late 1980s, is a fine example of modern Americana, and, like the "Texas" jean and shirt shop on Columcille Street, or the Yankee Express takeaway further down on the corner with Church Street, is typical of the modern face of Tullamore.

You see what I'm driving at. Or perhaps you don't. This is not about mere aesthetics, about the declining façade of a once-genteel and attractive town, a town which might only slightly ironically be described as the Venice of the Midlands. This, as I say, is about encroachment, the particular world of the town being invaded by the general, homogenising influence of Western consumerism and "popular" culture.

This is not merely about "good taste" and snobbery, but about life and death, because the onslaught of the process defined above has occurred in relentless parallel to the one which has, for several decades now, been sucking the lifeblood out of towns like Tullamore, without hardly a pause for breath.

Tullamore has only comparatively recently become Offaly's capital town. In the early 1700s, for example, Birr was a far more populous centre. It was only with the arrival of an army barracks in 1716, and the extension of the Grand Canal to Tullamore in 1798, that the town began to become a significant population centre. Its progress since then in many ways mirrors that of other midland towns: small industries sprang up in response to local requirements – in particular those connected with food, clothing and housing, but also, of course, distilling and brewing, saddling and harness-making, tobacco and so on.

Tullamore was both a market town and a sort of midlands port, through which goods could be quickly transported to and from Dublin. The two days it took to make the journey between Tullamore and the capital represented a revolution on a par with the arrival of an airport, almost 200 years later, in the west of Ireland.

Thus, like all Irish towns, Tullamore was created from the needs of the people who came and chose to live there. These needs were the product of their time, and while they remained unchanged, the town prospered. They were needs of a particular kind, catered for in a particular way, in a particular setting. This is what made Tullamore what it became.

It is difficult to pinpoint a precise time when things

began to change, but certainly within the past 20 years things have changed beyond recognition. Nearly all the town's long-standing industries came in for the chop, like the Salts Ireland textiles factory, which employed over 1,500 workers and which has been closed since the early '70s. Since then it has been a struggle to attract the occasional factory employing maybe a couple of hundred people. Some factories have come and gone, a few have come and stayed.

Today, there are about 2,000 people, many of them highly skilled, unemployed in Tullamore. Of these, about one-third are under 25: 400 males and 300 females. Against that, there is a total of 400 school-leavers coming onto the market each year, about three girls for every two boys.

These figures tell their own story, a story which is all too easily comprehended. Almost all the girls go; some of the boys stay in hope of getting fixed up – some are lucky, some are not. The net result, somewhere along the line, is a loss of the town's lifeblood and equilibrium.

In the Bridge House in the town centre of a summer's evening, it would be easy to miss the telltale signs. The pub is half-full, and most of those present are young people; many of them in couples and foursomes. But then you notice that almost everyone is drinking the same brand of lager, Budweiser, because it's on special offer tonight: buy a bottle and get another one free. And, when you get talking to a few people you aren't long in reckoning that at least half those present are still at college and will be leaving just as soon as they qualify. Time and again, when you talk to such people, they tell you that the reasons for going will ultimately be economic. "When I qualify I'll be able to earn three or four times as much abroad as I could earn here."

I wish it could seem that simple to me. If it were just

about economics, there would be a prospect of such people returning. There isn't and they won't. For the very forces which have stripped Tullamore of its economic usefulness, have also stripped it of its individuality, its essence, its reason for being.

For Tullamores all over the country, the world has literally turned upside down. From being net producers of goods – catering for much of their own needs as well as selling the odd crate of whiskey to the outside world – they have been reduced to anonymous towns which now seem to exist primarily to absorb the products of mass consumerism. Traditional market towns no longer have markets, industrial towns are devoid of industry. Towns which, were the same natural laws allowed to apply to their deaths as to their births, would fall over and die, are being kept alive on State handouts and the elusive prospect of phantom foreign industry.

And because no one has the heart to turn off the life-support, the life just drains away anyway, and the town, deprived of its identity and self-confidence, falls prey to every whim of the modern Catchpenny Culture. Another branch of the Universal City is born.

And once this process gets a grip, it becomes not just difficult to stay, but also impossible to return. If you have to live with Yankee Express and the Texas jean and shirt shop, you may as well live with them in America where the money is good and you can buy some sort of choice; at home you have the worst of both worlds: consumerism without the means by which to be a consumer. And so you either accommodate or leave; reconcile yourself to a life of spending your life-support wages on Budweiser and batterburgers, or go to where the action is.

It's the "clever" ones, they say, who leave, and to some extent there is truth in this. It's as though the

Market, by some fiendish malfeasance, has created a mechanism to draw those best suited to its purpose to its centre.

But if the corollary of this is that it's the stupid ones who stay, then I'm not so sure. I do know that something happens to make the ones who stay more able to bear their remaining years in a place to which they no longer really belong. People change. They become less confident, less individualistic, less joyous. They become apathetic and fatalistic. They have less to say for themselves. They have fewer opinions of their own and are more open to being swayed by the opinions – usually the more simplistic – of others. They drink a lot, eat lots of southern fried chicken and place regular bets on horses with only slightly more hope than themselves. The Catchpenny Culture rages like a bushfire. The cycle gains speed.

These are things which all of us who remain here are aware of, even if only deep down. Since it requires some measure of blindness to remain in a situation which is essentially unhappy, most of us prefer not to see. This, too, is part of the process, which if it is to prosper, needs to conceal itself from its victims. Thus, if you talk to people in the pubs and shops of a small town, be it Tullamore, Longford or Castlerea, you will find that, although no one is under any illusions about the "reality" of their town's situation, few have anything but the most crude and short-sighted grasp of the true nature of that reality. People talk in received political terms; there are "no jobs", the town is "in a bad way", the politicians should "do something". Most of us see what is happening in the west and midlands as being in the nature of a kind of economic bad weather: when the climate changes, things will improve. We have no difficulty in believing that the destruction of Brazilian rain forests will have catastrophic and irreversible effects on our weather patterns, but we continue to regard the devastation of our country as being in the nature of a bad shower.

2. MORE AND MORE NOISE (August 1990)

The feeling one is left with having visited someplace is hardly ever connected with the things one saw, however interesting, or the weather, however fine, or the things one ate or drank, however pleasant these might have been. To define the essence of a place in such terms would be like painting a landscape by joining up a series of dots. No, when one returns from a place in which one has spent some time, one is left with a feeling – a colour – which is none the less real for being the result of a series of fleeting impressions.

I visited Longford over one of the best weekends we've had in several years. It was also the opening weekend of the Longford 90 Summer Festival, and therefore probably the most exciting weekend, from a social viewpoint, in the town's calendar. I visited St Mel's Cathedral, certainly one of the most impressive buildings in the entire midland region. I spent a fascinating couple of hours in the museum behind the cathedral, admiring an array of relics and artefacts from the town's ecclesiastical past. I did not eat anything which was inordinately disagreeable to my – admittedly uneducated – palate.

But for all that, Longford left me with an overwhelming feeling of greyness. For over a week I racked my brain in an effort to pin this down, to tilt my perspective away from the source of the greyness to something positive – the woman, for example, who so patiently, proudly and passionately recounted the history of the diocese in the museum at St Mel's. But it is to no avail; my impressions of my weekend in Longford are almost entirely bound with a handful of, on the surface, seemingly dissociated impressions.

It is about nine o'clock on Sunday night. I'm sitting in a bar, The Lyons [*sic*] Den, on Main Street, Longford. It is what used to be called a "singing" lounge. Tonight's attraction is one Brian Harkin, whom I remember from the mid-70s when he did a stint as lead singer with The Mighty Avons, then second only to Big Tom in the league table of country 'n' western bands on the ballroom circuit. The poster advertising the gig shows, in fact, a Brian Harkin from that very era.

The Lyons Den is not a large pub. The first time you go in you might be forgiven for thinking that you have strayed into the wrong place. There is room to swing a cat, certainly, but not, one might reflect, to manoeuvre a guitar. A space is annexed off at the back for a pool table, a jukebox and sundry machines of the space-invading persuasion. Having ascertained that this is indeed the location of Brian Harkin's performance, I settle down to wait. I examine my fellow customers, but as I do so, am conscious of a vague feeling of discomfort. It takes a few seconds to pin it down, but gradually the realisation dawns that there are at least three different pop songs being played on three different media to the handful of punters awaiting the arrival of Brian Harkin. There is a jukebox thudding away in the poolroom, a radio blaring behind the bar, and a continuous stream of piped music emanating from somewhere in the ceiling.

Out of this discordant cacophony it proves possible, after some minutes' concentrated listening, to disentangle the strains of a song which becomes recognisable as "Blockbuster", by The Sweet, a British band which operated in the glam rock and bubblegum areas in the early 70s.

At this precise time the bar is occupied by a dozen people or so, all of whom, apart from myself, are aged 40 and over. There are a few middle-aged couples seated around the windows, and a scattering of elderly men along the bar. The couples are engaged in various conversations, the old men for the most part sipping pints in silence. There is no evidence that a single person in the bar is interested in listening to any of the three "tunes" on offer. I am certain that I alone am in possession of the information that, for example, the song "Blockbuster" was written especially for The Sweet by the songwriting duo of Nicky Chinn and Mike Chapman, and that it was a number one hit in Britain and Ireland in 1973. It would have amazed me greatly, in fact, if in the unlikely event of anyone else in the bar having been able to disentangle the song from the general uproar, a single one was able to remember ever having heard it before. In fact, not a single person in the bar was showing the slightest interest in any of the aural delights on offer.

So, for whose benefit was this intended? Who was it supposed to entertain? By what process do we "decide" to surround ourselves with this constant, indecipherable racket? You may protest that it is unfair to single out one pub in one town for something which is universal, ubiquitous. But why not? Isn't it precisely because it happens everywhere else that it happens in Longford? And, doesn't this say at least as much about Longford as it does about the rest of the world? These are genuine questions, rather than assertions of opinion, but before I attempt to answer them, there is my second enduring image from my weekend stay in Longford.

It is Sunday afternoon. Two young men, neither of them yet 20, stand talking in the Main Street, Longford. They are part of a larger group of young people,

39

gathered in the middle of town, the way young people will gather everywhere. The two young men are addressing one another in a playful, good-humoured fashion. Then, making a shouted arrangement to meet later on, they move off in opposite directions. Immediately, one of them turns around and shouts after his departing companion: "Good luck, yebollixye."

The second man then turns around and rejoins: "Yakuntya."

The first man again counters with, "Yebollixye."

"Yakuntya."

"Yebollixye."

This bizarre responsorial psalm continues for what seems like two or three minutes, long after one of the young men has turned the corner onto Ballymahon Street and disappeared.

"Yakuntya."

"Yabollixya."

I scan the dozens of faces around the street for signs of disapproval or distaste. No one appears to be listening.

Nobody would try to suggest that this form of "communication" is unique to Longford, or that it is employed by a majority of people there or anywhere else. But neither is it an isolated incident. If pressed to characterise or quantify it, I would say that, in my experience, an increasing number of people, particularly younger people, are "communicating" with one another in this manner.

I do not believe that this is to do with mere ignorance or yobbery. It is, I believe, just one more symptom of the malaise which besets much of modern Irish life, and each one of us to one degree or another. It is part of the way we protect ourselves from the truth.

Economists will, naturally enough, give an economic

explanation for everything. A leading Irish economist once tried to persuade me that everything that happens in Ireland should be compared only with phenomena in areas with a comparable population and economic situation. Yorkshire, suggested this particular economist, was quite a suitable model for comparison with this country. But when one sees bookshops closing down all over Ireland, to be replaced by American-style video stores, it is precious little comfort to think that we probably still have a few bookshops more than Yorkshire. Bookshops close down, not because people have no money, but because they have no inclination to buy books. Similarly, people address one another in expletives, not because they know no better, but because they are afraid of knowing too much.

The Get Up the Yard Syndrome has always been a strong feature of life in the country. This was the way a community protected itself against deviance and eccentricity, and attacked conceit and insincerity. To return to a country town after a short absence with the merest hint of an accent, or other airs or graces, was to be slagged unmercifully. The Yabollixya Syndrome is simply an escalation of this. There is a belief at large that, in the new wave of emigration, it is the clever who go and the slow who stay. This is a false impression: quite often the factors which decide who goes and who stays have more to do with personal and family considerations than with academic attainment.

A reasonable proportion of those who remain are clever as well – in fact, given the nature of the society in which they remain, far cleverer than they need to be, and certainly far cleverer than it is wise to admit. Being clever in a small Irish town means having to be aware of too much pain, too much unhope, too much despair. And so you accommodate. Those who remain speak in a common language, a language which allows them to relate to one another without having to betray how they really feel. This is the language of the gibe, the cheerful obscenity and the snort of derision. It is a form of self-protection, which allows one to live in a society in which one has little choice and no control.

The tendency of the mass consumer culture to make more and more noise while saying less and less is aped within the society which it invades. The name of the game in much of modern Ireland is to pretend to know as little as possible, to hold no opinions other than on matters of no importance and to use no words which are bigger than "sausages" or "galvanise".

Thus, the community, like a frightened hedgehog, rolls itself into a ball. Nothing's changed. Life goes on. Geddup yabollixya. Nothing of any value originates from within the individual or the community. Everything is received: cultural values, notions of style and sophistication, even analyses of your own situation. Clubs called "Blooms", "Stringfellows" and "Paris" pump out music to audiences comprised mostly of teenage boys who just want to jump up and down to the Waterboys. The girls have either left or are too busy studying so as to ensure that they will not be the ones to stay behind. But nobody notices because the Universal City continues to maintain the semblance of sophistication, and the faculties which would allow society to see what's really happening have begun to atrophy as a result of the same process. People stare at "Neighbours" in smoke-filled bars and imagine themselves to be at the centre of the universe.

Who says the system doesn't work?

III

THE PROMISED LAND

1. THE VALLEY OF TEARS

The Story of the Hanrahan Family of Tipperary
(December 1990)

If a film of this story were made it would have to begin at
dawn on an autumn morning in 1978. A young Richard
Harris as John Hanrahan would be sitting at the kitchen
table of the Hanrahan farmhouse in Ballycurkeen, County
Tipperary. The cock would crow once, twice, three times.
Puzzled by the cockcrow's muffled sound, he would get
up and go to the window. The sunrise in the east would
be obscured by a heavy mist. The theme music, low,
swirling and ominous, would swell.

Cut to exterior and the thick fog overhanging the Suir
Valley. John Hanrahan emerges from the house and
walks across the yard, perplexed and bothered at the
brown haze that enshrouds him. He notices that his
dog's eyes are red and watering heavily. He himself has
difficulty breathing.

The camera travels across the country, past choking
and weeping cattle, past trees with their leaves pointed
in the wrong direction, past the corpses of wildlife, to
the looming factory of the US pharmaceutical company,

Merck Sharp and Dohme, nestled in a hollow in the valley, about a mile distant in the village of Ballydine. Inside, a telephone rings. It is John Hanrahan.

That late August morning in 1978 was just the beginning of a twelve-year nightmare which is only now reaching something of a conclusion; and, in the absence of an expert authority such as the Environmental Protection Agency proposed this week, John Hanrahan and his family convey no sense of certainty that the nightmare has truly ended. For the moment, though, John Hanrahan has achieved a total vindication of his struggle to prove that the disintegration of his farming business was indeed the result of toxic emissions from the Merck factory. Within the last fortnight he has received payment of an undisclosed sum of damages (believed to be in the region of £2.3 million) following a 1988 Supreme Court judgement in his favour.

A spokesman for Merck says that the company has nothing further to add to a 1988 statement in which they emphasised the "rigorous safeguards and high quality standards with which we conduct our operations".

The story of the Hanrahan family's battle against the US multinational is a nightmare of Kafkaesque proportions. The first inkling they had of something wrong was the death of their son's pet rabbit. The vet said the cause was toxic poisoning. Since the rabbit had been fed only on greens from the kitchen garden, kept with great care and pride by John's mother, Mary, they decided to have some of the vegetables tested. The tests indicated the presence of toxic chemicals.

The Hanrahan cattle began to die in early 1981. That year alone, 67 cattle died. The local vet, Tom de Lacy, had to call almost daily. Hanrahan's own health, and that of his wife, Seline, was adversely affected. The Hanrahans, and others in the area complained of burning sensations in the throat and chest, of reddening of the skin, as with a constant and unseasonal sunburn, of irritation and streaming of the eyes and a smothering feeling in the nose, throat and chest. When clouds of emissions came from the Merck factory, Hanrahan noticed that the symptoms became worse. Over the next few years, Hanrahan would suffer constantly from trouble with his lungs. In September 1982 his wife underwent a hysterectomy.

And all the time there was the *smell*, varying from sickly sweet to what Mrs Mary Hanrahan described as being like the smell that occurs when a blacksmith puts a hot iron to a horse's hoof. The smell followed them everywhere, seeped into their lives. The smells were at their worst following emissions from the Merck factory.

The Hanrahans complained to the factory, to South Tipperary County Council, to everybody who would listen and quite a number who would not. Merck Sharp and Dohme gave them apologies and assurances; and County Council commissioned studies and reports. The smells continued; the cattle continued to die. The reports found the level of chemicals on the Hanrahan farm, and of air pollution in the surrounding valley, to be within "acceptable levels". The cattle went on dying. Cows gave birth to stillborn and deformed calves.

At times it almost seemed as though the emission of chemicals from the factory, and the damage they were causing, had become a metaphor for what was happening to the Hanrahans. The evidence of their own eyes, and ears and noses told them that the problems they were experiencing were connected directly with the factory, but Merck refused to accept responsibility. The County Council, though initially sympathetic, became less helpful as time wore on. The factory employed 250 people in an area of high unemployment. The

Hanrahans were rocking the boat. Fogs of obfuscation and verbosity descended on the family's every attempt to have the problem addressed. It was as though some strange slip of logic had occurred: that A had suddenly and mysteriously come to be followed by C, and B had gone missing.

John Hanrahan talks about his battle with Merck Sharp and Dohme as though he does not know where to begin. He tells the story in fits and starts, punctuated with mild diatribes against the perniciousness of the media. "You could talk about this until the cows come home," he says, "and then you could let them out again and keep on talking. But at the end of the day it comes down to the silence. Why is there such a silence about this case?"

But it was a silence marked by activity, verbosity and noise. There was no shortage of opinion, of interest, of reports and investigations. An Foras Forbatha, the IIRS, the IFA and the Departments of Health and Agriculture became involved. There were scientists and engineers by the busload, all offering views and opinions. But nobody seemed able to find the key. At times it seemed as though there was a gigantic conspiracy, unseen and unacknowledged, between forces which ostensibly seemed to have opposite interests and objectives. John Hanrahan's sense of helplessness led to his being characterised as obsessive, vindictive, a bad farmer and gone in the head. The process of investigation seemed to become a system of obfuscation, a way of concealing the reality in jargon and technicality, a process which contaminated the truth, polluted the freshness of commonsense observation and suffocated every attempt to re-establish a sense of reality.

This process became contagious. By 1983, the Hanrahan case had come up for mention at the highest level of government, but even here the labyrinth yielded little but further questions. A seven-page letter in July 1983 from the then-Taoiseach, Garret FitzGerald, to his Minister for Labour, Liam Kavanagh, posed question after question, not just about the nature of the problem, but about the methods of the investigation and the absence of particular pieces of information. The Taoiseach, too, appeared to have been tied in knots. "Is it the case", he wrote, "that Jamieson on page 18 of the first survey report found monochlorobenzene coming off the process stack in July 1981? Is this not something that should not have happened?"

The Hanrahan's darkest day was yet to come. On 19 August 1985, after a hearing of 47 days in the High Court, they sat and heard Mr Justice Ronan Keane deliver a verdict in favour of the US multinational, a judgement which flew in the face of everything they believed. There was, it said, "virtually no evidence in this case of injury to human beings or animals which has been scientifically linked to any chemicals emanating from the defendants' factory."

But in their darkest hour, the Hanrahans found strength in their legal team, their solicitor Tom Menton, and barristers like Dermot Gleeson. If men of such calibre were still behind them, said Mary Hanrahan, they knew they must still have right on their side. They would appeal to the Supreme Court, a gamble which would mean risking everything they had. John Hanrahan sold off his herd and his farm machinery to offset the £0.5 million legal bill he now faced.

Suppliers of grain and feedstuff told him that they could no longer supply his needs. The co-op to which he sold his milk cut off his credit. He put his farm on the market but the bidding was derisory. "They pulled the plug on us," says John Hanrahan. "The wheels came over us: 'Get them out of the way', 'Break them', 'Do everything you can to them', Drive them off their heads if possible . . . '

"We kept our sanity, thanks be to God, but it did become intolerable. In a normal way we had a case: we had the evidence, we had the legal right. We were given the right to appeal. But the right was nearly removed because of the pressures that were put on us."

Another three years would pass before the legal fog would finally be lifted. But on 5 July 1988, the Hanrahans were vindicated by the Supreme Court judgement of Mr Justice Seamus Henchy, which told them that they were not mad. To decide, as Mr Justice Ronan Keane had done, that there was no causative relationship between the factory emissions and the Hanrahan's catalogue of misfortune, would, according to Mr Justice Henchy, be "to allow scientific theorising to dethrone fact". The letter B had been restored to its proper place.

Mr Justice Henchy's judgement has been the subject of a degree of comment among the legal profession. The most objective analysis, perhaps, was summarised in an editorial in *The Irish Law Times* of August 1988, wherein the writer, while noting what he called "Henchy J's rather cavalier attitude to scientific truth", opined that the judgement was "as just as it is courageous . . . loose though some of its law may be, it is in many ways the judgement of Solomon."

The writer of that editorial, Longford-born Dr Conor Gearty of King's College, London, says that, much as the judgement is to be welcomed in the Hanrahan case, it does not go far enough to be of much benefit to future plaintiffs with similar complaints. The common law on which the judgement was based is inherently biased, he says, against such people, because it requires the plaintiff, who is likely to be least able to obtain the necessary information about the operations of the defendant's activities, to provide proof of causation. The law, says Dr Gearty, dates from the nineteenth century when it was established to accommodate the industrial revolution, and was therefore biased in favour of the "men of action" of that time.

"The Supreme Court in Hanrahan", he says, "had a chance to restructure the law in a way which would have favoured individual plaintiffs against big multinational polluters. It failed to do so. So the law remains structured in favour of such defendants. The Supreme Court did *interpret* that law in a way very favourable to the plaintiffs, but as is applied to the old law, its precedent value is less good than if it had transformed the law.

"But," he continues, "if Hanrahan is important, I suppose it is a signal from the highest court in the land that it's prepared, in the right situation, to interpret the law in a way favourable to the plaintiffs in order to achieve a result that accords with justice and fairness."

For the Hanrahans, meanwhile, the resolution, though obviously welcome, is inconclusive. Cattle are no longer dying, but despite their judicial victory, the Hanrahans feel the information available to them is inadequate reassurance that their problem will not recur. Moreover, though they achieved justice in the end, they achieved it in a manner which allowed the truth of what was happening to remain hidden. Mr Justice Henchy righted the injustice without, in a sense, breaking the silence. John Hanrahan says that nothing short of a public inquiry will suffice to fill in the gaps in the story.

His mother, Mary, though sharing her son's sense of hurt and injustice, is anxious that the matter be brought to an end for once and for all. She knows what they were up against, and that although they won in the end, life goes on as before. The Hanrahans lost twelve years of their lives, but Merck Sharpe and Dohme lost the equivalent of a month's profit from their Ballydine plant. There is no point in looking back, she says, no point in crying over spilt milk.

People would laugh at her, she says, if she told them what kept her going through it all, kept her determined to live on the farm where she had been reared when her son and his family moved out at the height of the nightmare.

"I'm a great believer in prayer. I never really got hetted up. My dad used always say, 'Whatever you do, you should always keep inside the law.' In other words, as he used to say, play the game. But if anyone had told me that a body of officials would stand up and do the things that were done to us, I would just not believe it – until we actually went through it ourselves.

"This is the Valley of Tears. You get good and you get bad. But you must always remember that there's another judge up there. If you're telling the truth, you have nothing to fear. Our story was true, you see. John, or any of them, will tell you that I had great strength through all this. I got my strength from God. I wouldn't sell my soul for my farm. If we had lost the farm, we wouldn't have died of hunger either."

In the final analysis, what drove the Hanrahans on was the desire to clear the family name, to establish that they were not bad farmers, to prove that they were not mad.

"We would have gone to Europe if we had to," says John Hanrahan. "I'll tell you this: thanks be to God, I have the greatest faith in justice, in the legal system, in this country – provided that you have the funds to go the whole way if you have to. We had only one judge that went against us. We have been treated with respect and honour. Anything we asked for from the court, we got, because we told the truth. I don't, for one minute, want to criticise the judiciary in this country.

"We were very pleased that in the end we got . . . I suppose you could say *justice*. But at what price? That is something none of us can say."

2. The Promised Land

Government Policy and the Environment
(July 1991)

There was a slight hint of perplexity in the Taoiseach's statement last month when he announced the formation of a new task force on unemployment. Mr Haughey spoke of his impatience for a solution to "this central core problem" of why economic policies which were so successful in other areas were not working with regard to unemployment.

A new feature which had to be dealt with, he continued, was the opposition to particular development projects by local communities which had previously sought projects of *any* kind to provide local employment. Such opposition, he said, had caused several such projects to be delayed and in some cases aborted. "We have to find out why that is happening," he concluded.

It is significant that such a rare confession of prime-ministerial bafflement should coincide with the setting up of a national review of industrial policy, the first such initiative since the Telesis Report, also commissioned by a Haughey government, published almost a decade ago. Perhaps the fate of that report also hold the key to the current bewilderment.

Telesis, published in February 1982, sharply criticised

the thrust of national industrial policy up to then. Running in the face of the conventional wisdom of the time, the report found that the pattern of dependence on foreign investment in the 1970s, in the form of chemical and electronic industries, had not been an overall success.

Contrary to the much trumpeted claims of the Industrial Development Authority, the foreign sector was failing to provide even a third of the jobs it had promised, failed to feed profits back into the national economy and represented a drain on resources which might be better utilised in stimulating Irish enterprises.

Unfortunately, the report was published during the most unstable period in recent political history and was finally shelved during the Coalition government of 1982-1987. Almost ten years on, its lessons remain largely unheeded.

The community protests which so bemuse the Taoiseach can be seen as just another symptom of a growing public impatience with the political failure to deal decisively with an industrial policy which has failed on practically every level, and in whose failure lies the key to our overall economic stagnation. Over the past four or five years, attempts to install new industries of a particular kind at various locations have been dogged by local protests about their environmental unsuitability.

For some time now, politicians and IDA executives have been given to making puzzled and disparaging remarks about the "problem" of community opposition. Much has changed since the mid-1980s, when Tipperary farmer John Hanrahan fought a solitary battle against the US pharmaceutical company Merck Sharp and Dohme, for damage to both his personal health and that of his livestock herd, culminating in an historic Supreme Court judgement in his favour in 1988.

Perhaps learning the lessons of the Hanrahan

experience, communities proposed as hosts for similar industries since then have been much better organised and remarkably effective. The cool reception for multinationals such as Merrell Dow in East Cork and Sandoz in Ringaskiddy has focused attention on existing industries of a similar nature.

The past two or three years have seen an escalating awareness and controversy about a range of industries – from fish-farming in Clare, via fibre-board manufacturing in Tipperary, to gold mining in Mayo.

There have been official insinuations that the opposition to such initiatives comes not from within the host communities but through their infiltration by environmentalists. Two years ago, the IDA's chairman, Padraic White, expressed concern about "small undemocratic groups" which were frustrating attempts at industrial development.

Such suggestions are put in doubt by an examination of the nature of the latest and most emphatic protest so far, the opposition by local communities in both Derry and Donegal to a proposed toxic waste incinerator at the Du Pont factory on the outskirts of Derry city.

The objections are not only an eloquent reassurance of the health of democracy at grassroots level, but have been spurred, too, by fears that the current proposal could be the thin end of the wedge which would thicken rapidly to become a National Incinerator for toxic waste.

The protest represents a unique expression of unanimity from practically every imaginable shade of Irishness from Sinn Féin to the DUP, from Presbyterians in Moville to the Catholic Bishop of Derry.

In terms of the climate currently facing industrial policy in the Republic, a national toxic waste incinerator would be a pearl beyond price. For the Dublin Government, the prospect of an incinerator serving the entire island from over the Border in Derry must have seemed too good to be true. In the words of one Donegal community activist, "The Irish Government must have thought that all its Christmases had come together."

Last January, the Minister for the Environment, Padraig Flynn, confirmed that he had visited the Du Pont factory "at their invitation", to discuss the disposal of toxic waste. In the Dáil he later confirmed that he had spoken about a waste incineration facility with his Northern counterpart, Richard Needham, "having regard . . . to the unlikelihood of the whole of Ireland being able economically to support more than one such facility". The present state of play is that a public inquiry into the Du Pont proposal is to be held by the Northern Ireland Office, and the Government here is "waiting for the situation to clarify itself".

Without a national toxic incinerator, the thrust of industrial policy in the current climate appears to have run out of road. In a sense, there was a historical inevitability about this which has to do with the nature of such policy.

As a response to the economic stagnation of the 1950s and the relative failure of mainstream industry to redress the balance in the 1960s, the Irish State has relentlessly pursued a policy of encouraging foreign-owned multinationals to establish high-skilled, labour-intensive, high value-added, strong growth-potential industries – which in the main turned out to be in the chemical and electronic sectors.

The bait was in the fact that relatively high Irish labour costs would be offset by other factors – the availability of a well-developed infrastructure, an expanding technologically literate workforce and the "assimilative capacity" of the Irish environment.

This latter point was of no small significance.

Economic theorists hold that the quality of the environment and its "assimilative capacity" can be viewed as a "natural factor endowment" in the process of international resource allocation. This is to say that the capacity of the landscape to absorb industrial waste should be a critical factor in deciding where to locate.

By this logic, the IDA had a whole hand of aces – the virginal fields of the Irish countryside – with which to lure foreign multinationals. Included in that are factors such as high social tolerance to pollution, a relative lack of pollution-control regulations, natural "self-cleansing" systems and the unused absorption capacity of the landscape. For US-owned pharmaceutical corporations in particular, on the run from tightening environmental legislation at home in the 1970s, Ireland was literally a promised land.

The trend of such industries relocating in underdeveloped countries during this period has in retrospect all the appearance of a carefully devised strategy – with the aim at the time, perhaps of rolling back the tide of legislation in the US by operating openly and freely in less restrictive climates. American environmentalists were soon warning of the emergence of "foreign pollution havens" in underdeveloped countries prepared to barter their "natural factor endowment" in return for desperately needed employment.

In Ireland, although the regulations were tighter than in many Third World countries, US chemical factories were allowed to be located here under considerably less stringent conditions than obtained in either the US or mainland Europe. Industries arriving in the Cork region, for example, received permission to dump untreated organic waste into Cork harbour. The policy has been described – by H. Jeffrey Leonard in his book, *Pollution and the Struggle for the World Product* – as "a dustbin strategy for development".

An Taisce's chairman at the time, Philip Mullaly, wrote that it was "worth noting that permission to pollute may well be more valuable in economic terms than any IDA grant". Because of the growing unemployment problem (already five per cent in the early seventies), such concessions were not otherwise controversial at that time.

The policy represented more than one type of sell-out, critics argue. The Irish economy, as Telesis pointed out, had become excessively dependent on this form of industry. By 1985, over 850 subsidiaries of foreign multinationals were operating in Ireland, accounting for more than one-third of the entire manufacturing workforce. More than half such industry was in the chemical and electronics sectors, accounting for over 50 per cent of (non-food) manufactured exports of the Irish economy.

Because of repatriation of their profits, however, these companies were not making a contribution to economic growth commensurate with their slice of economic activity. US firms were able to achieve profit levels in Ireland three times their worldwide batting average – around twice the return possible in Britain or Japan, and three to four times the average in mainland Europe.

In most cases, US multinationals were able to recoup their investments in Ireland in under two years. They did this by repatriating profits in vast amounts: £1,346 million in 1986, an estimated £4 billion by 1995. Even the most conservative of estimates indicates that over two decades, this haemorrhaging has cost the Irish economy an amount in excess of the current national debt. This accounts, in large measure, for both the Government's inability to influence unemployment levels and the Taoiseach's puzzlement over escalating protests about new developments.

It is arguable that not only has control of employment been given out of the hands of the Irish government, but so too has control of the overall growth potential of the Irish economy. Both have been surrendered to multinational corporations.

Meanwhile, a combination of factors has served to steer the foreign-owned model for industrial development into a cul-de-sac. In the first place, as Telesis outlined, such industry was failing to deliver on its job targets by a long chalk. By 1981, the report calculated, only 30 per cent of the aggregate number of jobs promised by the IDA for the foreign-owned sector had materialised.

Since 1981 was the peak year for US company investment in Ireland ($1,121 million that year and declining steadily thereafter), it is likely that the forthcoming Industrial Policy Review will paint an even less rosy picture.

In these circumstances, escalating community objections to new developments were the last thing the Government needed. The environmental aspects, combined with the obvious lack of benefit to the Irish economy, were gradually eroding the climate of acquiescence which greeted the advent of such industry two decades ago. The balance to be weighed between the benefits of immediate employment and the danger to the environment began to lean more and more in one direction.

This trend now threatens to throttle Government policy altogether if a way is not found soon to deal with toxic waste on a national basis. About 15,000 tonnes of waste are currently produced annually in the entire island of Ireland, of which one-third is produced by the Du Pont factory. This waste is exported for disposal at incinerators abroad, but Du Pont fears that stricter EC regulations will shortly restrict the transport of toxic waste and compel member states to burn their own.

At the moment, the Du Pont proposal is for a small incinerator to cater for the company's own waste; but the franchise for a national incinerator, to cope with toxic waste from all over the island, would be a commercial proposition as well. It would also provide a lifeline for the Irish Government, freeing it to woo further industry while reassuring local interests that their immediate environments would not be despoiled.

This would enable the current industrial policy to limp along until an alternative strategy is framed. It is clear that Mr Flynn will be watching the progress of the Du Pont controversy with extreme interest.

IV

OCTOPUS-SHAPED TOWN

THE SLOW DEATH OF THE RAILWAY   (July 1991)

Having a railway in the town, says the stationmaster in
Claremorris, is a bit like having a clock in the house.
Michael O'Reilly always has a few clocks in the house:
he collects and restores them as a hobby. When he
started first, the noise of the chiming and ringing kept
him awake at nights; but now he finds that it helps him
to sleep. There is something reassuring, he says, about
the noise they make, and the dependability of their
rhythms.

So it is with trains. Whenever a new train is added to
the night schedule, he has noticed, they get complaints
from people along the line that the noise is disturbing
their sleep. After a while, the complaints die away. Then
one night when the train doesn't run, people ring in to
ask what has happened. They couldn't sleep, they say,
because they didn't hear the train passing.

Michael will acknowledge that he is a sort of
honorary railwayman rather than the totally genuine
article. Like most stationmasters, he came in as a clerk,
answering an advert in the *Railway Circular* shown to
him by a railwayman over 35 years ago. The genuine
article is getting harder and harder to locate.

A railwayman was a special sort of man, a man with a fierce love of something that few outsiders could comprehend, an almost obsessional pride in "the job" that made him seem like a crank, a language and folklore all of his own, a social life that jarred with those of other workers, and an odd propensity for looking as unsuited to uniform while wearing it as he looked uncomfortable without it. Railwaymen were not just men who worked on the railways – they were the railways; they brought the railways to life and earned their own livings in return, and the lives and fates of the railway and its people intertwined and became as one.

They spent their days and nights alongside the permanent way, in the shadow of signal cabin, amidst the roar of locomotive engines, breathing in that unique railway concoction of yeast and grease, their hands always black from the newsprint of that morning's papers. They lived alongside the engineering miracle of rail on sleeper, and grew towards it like climbing roses to a trellis.

The railways tended to run in families, with sometimes the entire male complement of brothers, uncles and sons belonging to one or other division of the standing armies of drivers, shunters, signalmen, porters, guards, milesmen, gatekeepers, checkers and other workers who combine, minute by minute, to make the trains run on time.

There was something uniquely distinguishable and unmistakable about a railwayman, something about the way he moved in time – conscious of its passing but fully cognisant of its dimensions – which made him both the child and the prisoner of his calling. But even if you did not belong to the elite corps of warriors who operated the railways (and I, too, was for a time an honorary railwayman), it was impossible to live close to a station or a line and remain oblivious to its mystery. You did not understand quite how the clock functioned, but you could not escape its incessant tick and tock and its unerring ding and dong.

Railways were – are – more than methods of transportation; they are both a way of life and a metaphor for it. They snake through the countryside like arteries, propelling the lifeblood from the centre to the peripheral regions. They throb through the night while the country sleeps. They provide the assurance of normality but are not boring.

Close your eyes and see again the steam cloud up from the leaky heater hose as the guard sweeps open the doors of the paper train, the bales of *Press*es and *Independent*s piled up high inside, with the rolled bundles of *Irish Times* balanced perilously on top. The driver tall in his engine as Clint Eastwood in the saddle, above the frenetic order of the next two minutes.

Two minutes of unloading, swift but unhurried; haste making no concession to carelessness as the papers are thrown out to be sorted on the platform. The talk of politics or football as the labels are scrutinised and the bales cast this way and that with the facility of basketball players. The ritual telling of legends of great railwaymen, spoken as though of battlescarred warriors; the milesman who never went home, but lived in a sleeping car in a siding at the station; Dostoyevskian stationmasters who stalked their platforms in the early hours looking for someone to report or sack.

Railwaymen know what to say to one another no matter where they go. The railways are at once a universal village and a closed universe.

"The railways", says one railwayman – Eneas MacNally, a depot man at Westport Station – "are an octopus-shaped town, its tentacles spread all over the country. No matter where we come from, we all belong to the same place."

But here in the fiscally conscious Ireland of the 1990s, a more malign metaphor asserts itself. The railway town, like many more conventional towns, is dying – of financial starvation and economic neglect. Though Iarnród Eireann management are anxious to put a confident gloss on what they describe as the "rationalisation" of the railway, talking up their stewardship in the hope of a few more crumbs from the political table, the evidence of decay is everywhere: slimmed-down services, closed goods stores, silent yards, speed limits because of reduced maintenance, railwaymen who talk more and more about the good old days.

As with so many things, the decay is most visible in the west of Ireland. Many western towns, of course, like Ballaghaderreen, Tuam, Kiltimagh, Swinford and Charlestown, have long since been taken off the railroad network – for many years now – with only the Ballina branch, along with the main lines to Galway, Sligo and Westport, remaining. But the fiscal tightening grows ever more insistent – and much of the talk around the remaining stations has to do with how much longer can their stations go on.

Over the past twenty years, most stations in the west have been reduced to the status of halt, with no functions other than as stopping points for passenger traffic. Michael O'Reilly is one of just six stationmasters remaining in the west, where once there were twenty. Many feel that what is happening in the west offers a glimpse of the future of Irish railways, and that the end-product of the rationalisation process will be a railway system comprised entirely of the Dublin to Cork line.

The cutbacks in some stations have stopped only just short of total closure. In Westport, once a thriving freight depot, with enormous traffic throughflow, nothing remains except the passenger service. Most of the remaining freight is delivered by road from Ballina; Guinness deliveries are made from Claremorris. The liner train, which ran nightly to Westport, carrying unit-load containers for the several factories around town, has been diverted to Ballina.

In Castlebar, Mayo's county town, only one man is now employed at the railway station, all operating functions having been transferred to the Manulla Junction down the road. The "loop" line through the station, which allowed trains to be turned and crossed there, has been taken up for use as spares for much-needed repairs in other parts of the rail system.

Eneas MacNally has worked on the railways for almost 22 years. His brother Willie also works at Westport Station. They belong to a railway family. Their father before them worked at the CIE garage on Westport Quay. In his two decades on the job, says Eneas, the railways have declined "to the point of extinction". Twenty years ago, they were carrying the bulk of the freight traffic in and out of Westport, serving the town and its hinterland, from Tourmakeady to the south to Achill in the north-west: cement, fertilisers, Guinness, oil, cornflakes, leather for the local shoe factory, new cars on flat trucks, cigarettes, live chickens . . . Today, he says, hardly anything remains.

Eneas carries out seven distinct functions on the railway. He is a trained guard, signalman, shunter and checker, but he also functions as a station porter and cleaner, and has the overall title of senior depot man. He works six hours and 40 minutes per day, six days a week, on various shifts. He has to submit himself to examination on the company rulebook once a year. His basic pay is £154, plus a shift allowance of £22. The only overtime now available is four hours on a Sunday, which means that, to make a decent living, he must work without a break for months on end.

He has always loved working on the railway, but with each new "rationalisation" wonders if he did the right thing in giving up his job as head porter in a Castlebar hotel all of 22 years ago. "If I had my time over again, I wouldn't be working on the railways," he says. He blames government, who have "screwed CIE to the wall", forcing the company into more and more cutbacks and closedowns while operating a bias in favour of road transport.

Like many of those railwaymen in the "rationalised" stations, Eneas MacNally hold that the changes do not make economic sense. The company abolishes jobs in Westport and Castlebar and must pay overtime to men in Ballina and Claremorris to do the same work. Iarnród Eireann management repudiate this argument; district operating manager Gerry Glynn says that while, for example, the company abolished three jobs in the most recent rationalisation of Castlebar, no extra jobs were required by the transfer of functions to Ballina.

Dave McKeon, the now-retired chief clerk at Westport Station, maintains that this is a red herring. Because the increasingly centralised service is less efficient and lacking a personal touch, the volume of traffic diminishes with each round of cutbacks, he says.

Since the introduction of containerisation for sundry traffic in the mid-70s, followed shortly afterwards by a system of caged pallets organised centrally from the North Wall, says Dave McKeon, the reduced flexibility and carrying capacity, allied to the high levels of pilferage at the central depot, have caused this form of traffic to all but disappear. "That was the start of the rot," he says. Twenty years ago, he recalls, there were over 40 people employed at Westport Station; today there are 15. "The only way they seem to be able to make money nowadays", says Dave McKeon, "is by laying off staff and reducing services."

The more benign among railwaymen speak about the lack of a national policy on transport as being the root of the problem. Others believe the cuts have been imposed for political reasons – to debilitate the railways so as to reduce their ability to compete with private transport. CIE management, most workers acknowledge, has been caught between a rock and a hard place: they must continue to "rationalise" in order to placate their political masters; but each round of cutbacks, while making moderate savings in the short term, only further reduces traffic and the company's overall ability to recover lost ground. The approach, they point out again and again, is doubly uneconomic: the roads disintegrate because of the volume of traffic, while the railways rot away from neglect.

Although staff speak of a much improved relationship between themselves and the new generation of management since the split-up of CIE into three different companies, there are widespread fears that the iron horse may already have bolted. For years, there has been profound demoralisation at practically every level of the national transport company. What is regarded as the disastrous management policy, implemented over many years by a petty and vindictive middle-management, has resulted in many workers losing their sense of identification with their source of employment.

The close bond which once existed between railway workers everywhere has been fatally weakened. There is no longer the same pride in belonging.

"There was a time when you would go out and proclaim that you belonged to the railways," says a clerk in Galway. "It was more than a job: it was your life. But not any more. Now you go out and when someone asks you where you work, you hum and you haw. You come in to work and put in your time, and count the months to your pension."

V

The Land Where Every Day is Like Sunday

1. Every Day is Like Sunday   (March 1991)

> *Armageddon – come Armageddon*
> *Come Armageddon, come.*
> *Every day is like Sunday.*
> *Every day is silent and grey.*
>   Morrissey: *Every day is like Sunday*

If you live in Dublin, own a car, and are at all interested in politics, I suggest that, some weekend soon, you leave down your newspaper, turn off *Saturday View*, and take a run down the country. Almost any direction will do, but for maximum effect you should travel west, in the direction of Galway, Westport or Ballina. As you leave Dublin, everything will appear as usual. You will notice nothing until you have passed through Kinnegad and begin to hit towns like Tyrellspass, Moate, Ballinasloe, Ballymahon, Loughrea, Lanesboro, Craughwell, Roscommon, Castlerea, Ballyhaunis, Balla, Ballaghaderreen, Charlestown.

In these places you will notice even less. It will take a few towns for the penny to drop. In one you will see a couple of old age pensioners huddled in a doorway, in another you may have to blow your horn at a couple of youngsters in danger of running onto the road in pursuit of a ball. But be assured there will be no traffic jams. You will see nobody between the ages of 18 and 25.

Initially, you may imagine that you have hit these places on a bad day – that Saturday, for some perverse reason, is Lanesboro's early closing day, or that some much-loved local personality in Moate has died in especially tragic circumstances. You may even get to imagining that you have somehow managed to sleep through Saturday, and make a mental note to see your doctor about those sleeping pills. But, as in town after town you are met with the same absence of life, it may begin to occur to you that something altogether different is amiss. It is. Welcome to The Land Where Every Day Is Like Sunday.

If you live in Dublin and don't own a car, you can still gain access to this world. Just inside the Abbey Street entrance to Eason's of O'Connell Street, Dublin, there is a section of shelving whereon is displayed the weekly provincial newspapers from all over the country. No matter where you come from, if you have any interest at all in the future of this country, I suggest you take a walk down there some Friday or Saturday and browse through the cover headlines on these newspapers.

Last Friday, I went down there myself, as I sometimes do, to buy one or other of the local papers from home, the *Roscommon Herald* or *Roscommon Champion*. I had already read, in that morning's national newspapers, that we Irish had a further reason to celebrate: we had just announced an inflation rate of 2.6 per cent which, we are assured, is among the lowest in Europe. This announcement had been greeted with the usual scattering of laudatory editorials and commentaries.

I cannot begin to tell you how proud I was feeling until I picked up a copy of the *Roscommon Herald*. The new inflation figures clearly came too late for its deadline, for its front page was preoccupied with somewhat more mundane matters. There were four main stories on that front page, three of which had a common theme: "Loughglynn meeting to highlight bus concern"; "Sligo/Dublin rail link under threat"; and "Castlerea reduced to village status with An Post 'crazy' proposals". These three articles from The Land Where Every Day Is Like Sunday are worth relating.

The first refers to the recent announcement of the abolition of the bus service from Galway to Ballaghaderreen, which leaves many people on the route, including the village of Loughglynn, without public transport. A spokesman for Bus Eireann was quoted in the *Herald* article as saying that his company had to operate "on commercial grounds". Services could be justified only if there was "a certain level of support" for them. The article mentioned claims by local people that the "rationalisation" was "another attempt by a semi-state company to close down rural Ireland".

The article about the threat to the Sligo/Dublin rail link arose out of statements by the Fine Gael TD Mr Ted Nealon, who alleged that Iarnród Eireann had recently abandoned a major track-renewal programme between Sligo and Carrick-on-Shannon – evidence, he said, that the company had targeted the Sligo line for closure. "There seems to be a concerted action of putting up the shutters on the north-west," Mr Nealon was quoted as saying.

The third report referred to a meeting held in Castlerea the previous weekend to protest at the downgrading of the local post office. Speakers at the meeting said that the decision, if implemented, would "turn the clock back", "reduce the town to village status" and make Castlerea "an industrial wilderness". The general secretary of the Communications Workers' Union, Mr David Begg, said that the downgrading was indeed a clear statement that the town was one of lesser importance and would result in industrial development being inhibited through the existence of a weaker infrastructure. But, he added, perhaps even more meaningfully than he imagines, "this is the age of people power".

The fourth report, headlined "Lynn's Lotto Luck", showed that An Post is not really such an uncaring organisation as people like to make out. It featured a Boyle woman who had won £347,584 in the National Lottery. "It's the first time", the *Herald* had it, "that 'Lotto Luck' has hit the town, or indeed the county. As the first Roscommon winner herself points out, it just goes to show that anyone can come up with those six winning numbers."

It is only a matter of time before people begin to make the necessary connections between these four articles: to begin to see that the kind of people who take away their essential services are the same kind of people who offer them the slimmest possibility of a lottery windfall as compensation for the death of their way of life.

There were over 700 people at the Castlerea meeting. This is the equivalent of 350,000 people attending a meeting in Dublin. Every weekend, in halls and reception rooms all over the Land Where Every Day Is Like Sunday, people gather in increasing numbers in an attempt to come to grips with what is happening to them. They do not meet to discuss the availability of condoms, the rate of inflation, the Brooke initiative, or the difference between social democracy and democratic socialism, but to find a way of preventing the further destruction of their way of life. In these gatherings there is the beginnings of a democratic revolution which has not yet penetrated to what we continue to regard as the mainstream political process.

I do not share the belief of rural Ireland that there is a conspiracy by Dublin to bring about its destruction, but I understand why a lot of people have come to feel this way.

The Dublin establishment, including the Government, the Opposition parties and the media, has become absorbed in a view of the country's economic condition which to most of its people is a fiction. The establishment congratulates itself on the latest inflation rates – proof, we are told, that the policy of fiscal rectitude is bearing fruit – but gives no thought to the cost of this abstract gain to the lives of the people who are unfortunate enough to populate this economy of ours.

Each percentage point of a decrease in the rate of inflation can be measured just as surely by a widening of the silent greyness which is enveloping rural Ireland in its cold embrace. We celebrate our "recovery" from our recent bout of economic frostbite, softening our focus to obliterate the loss of vital limbs and organs which have resulted from our choice of "cure".

I don't know what is going to happen to this country, but I know that there is not a vast array of choices as to the remedy. I think we can rule out the possibility of all of us coming up with the six numbers to bring us the "Lotto Luck" windfall which would ensure our survival. But I suspect – and hope – that people power will take a hand before it's too late.

If it does not, and if we continue to place ourselves at the mercy of the market forces which are destroying our towns and villages, then we are *all* destined to live in The Land Where Every Day Is Like Sunday. And if

Dublin stands idly by while market forces come for the Loughglynns, the Charlestowns and the Castlereas, who will be left to stand up for Dublin when the cold winds of market forces sweep in from Europe to take her as well?

> *Hide on the promenade,*
> *Etch a postcard*
> *'How I dearly wish I was not here'*
> *In the seaside town*
> *That they forgot to bomb.*
> *Come, come, come, nuclear bomb.*
> *Every day is like Sunday*
> *Every day is silent and grey.*

2. THE SMELL OF APPALACHIA

A response to a speech by the Governor of the Central Bank, Mr Maurice Doyle, which urged tighter controls on social welfare as a way of providing more incentives in the Irish economy.

(November 1993)

Just as I was leaving for work last Friday morning, I heard two women on the *Gay Byrne Show* going at one another hammer and tongs. One was married to an unemployed man, the other to a working man on a modest income. The wife of the working man was attacking the wife of the unemployed man. The other woman was giving as good as she got.

The discussion contained some familiar and wearying phrases about there being plenty of work if people wanted to do it, about unemployed people being too lazy to get up in the morning and so on.

Sitting back in his upholstered armchair in the Central Bank building in Dublin, Mr Maurice Doyle must have been feeling well pleased with himself. Over the past few years, I believed we had begun to think about subjects like the obsolescence of human labour in the modern workplace, the inexorable shift towards technological models of industry, the need for a re-evaluation of the way income is distributed in society, the shift in emphasis from productivity to creativity, and so on.

I didn't think I would ever again wake up to a debate which attempted to place responsibility for unemployment back on the backs of the unemployed.

The idea that dole should be paid only to those who are "genuinely without work, currently available for work and taking specific steps to find work" in an economy which is 300,000 jobs short of full employment belongs to the right-wing stupidity of ten years ago. The notion that an attack on social welfare "fraudsters" constitutes in any sense an "analysis" of what is wrong with the Irish economy is ludicrous.

It is not, however, either the insensitivity or the ignorance of Mr Doyle's remarks that should concern us. It is their simple-mindedness as a description of the Irish economy.

I sense a hint of desperation, of panic, at the heart of Mr Doyle's strange outburst of last week. I suspect that he has discovered something about the true state of the Irish economy which he imagines the rest of us are not aware of, and is beginning the process of off-loading the blame. Maybe he has stumbled upon the truth that any sensible observer has known for quite some time: that the Irish economy is in a terminal state of collapse.

But if Maurice Doyle imagines that our present situation can be addressed by tinkering with the various alleged "distortions" in the Irish economy, or by chasing social welfare fraudsters, he is way off beam.

In a previous infamous speech, Mr Doyle warned that the drive towards European union could result in Ireland becoming "the Appalachia of Europe". Like the stopped clock which is right twice a day, Mr Doyle was right on that occasion.

Perhaps Mr Doyle has caught a glimpse, through a chink in the blinds of the Central Bank building, of the abyss that now looms in front of us.

Walk into almost any town in the west of Ireland and take a deep breath. You will *inhale* the smell of the decomposition of the Irish economy. This is the smell of Appalachia. If you do not believe the evidence of your own lungs, look up the most recent census figures which show that every county and town in the west of Ireland suffered dramatic population losses in the five years to 1991.

We are losing our people at a frightening rate. Of course, in the fundamentally sound economy, the loss of population through emigration is not regarded with the alarm that it merits in the sentimental hearts of human beings.

This country is finished. A year or two ago, I might have added an "unless we do X or Y . . . " But the time for unlesses has run out. Our condition is terminal; it is just a matter of a few years. The fault for this does not lie with the unemployed, or with social welfare fraudsters, or with distortions in the marketplace, or with the world of recession, or with the absence of an enterprise culture.

The fault lies with the fundamental economic analysis which has been imposed on this State for the past 30-odd years. The fault lies with the preferred model of development, of industrialisation, urbanisation and

74

Eurocentrification, and with the market-driven ideological backbeat which gave it its impetus and reach.

And just look at the country that this ideological prognosis is supposed not merely to describe, but actually to supply with its driving force. Look at the countryside, the villages, the towns, the cities. Look at *Crimeline*, for heaven's sake, where last week we saw a young man walk into a petrol station, buy a gallon of petrol, spill it all over the attendant and set him alight.

We are the victims of a failed ideological experiment which turned our very nature on its head. Over the past twenty years, people have been sucked from the countryside to the larger towns, from the larger towns to the cities, and from everywhere to the cities or Europe and the world.

We have deluded ourselves with an analysis that this was simply a function of "the decline of rural society" (and a good thing too, declared the dominant ideology), but now we have to face the truth. What was happening was not happening to some vague entity called "rural Ireland", but to Ireland *full stop*.

Anyone who read Kathryn Hone's article about the decline of French villages in these pages last week will be able to make the obvious connections. The pattern, whether in France, Ireland or anywhere else, has been the same.

In the 1970s, people left the farms and villages to settle in small regional towns; in the 1980s, they moved to the cities. In the 1970s, it was the smaller Irish towns, like John Healy's Charlestown, that died out. In the 1980s, it was the larger towns, like the Tuams and the Boyles. In the 1990s, it will be the Sligos and the Galways. In the 2000s, it will be the Corks and Dublins.

Our condition is terminal and irreversible. It has nothing to do with rural-versus-urban, and everything to do with the failure to value what we are and what we might achieve on our own terms – with the craven following of other people's prescriptions to the point of repeating the mistakes they had already made.

The basic difficulty with coming at the situation from Maurice Doyle's perspective is that, although he may have spotted some blip on the screen in his economic traffic control tower, he cannot have any insight into the true nature of the problem.

Mr Doyle inhabits the world of the fundamentally sound economy, where the sense of reality is defined by GNP figures, inflation levels and interest rates. Such data have only the most tenuous connection with reality and it is loosening with every passing hour.

This is not in the least surprising to anybody with a grain of common sense. In the unlikely event of the young man who tried to burn that garage attendant to death being caught and imprisoned for his crime, he will end up contributing as much to GNP as a dozen workers on the average industrial wage. Strange, but true. The way GNP calculations are made, the cost of keeping someone locked up in prison is counted as a *productive* element in the economy.

Just think about that, and then ask yourself if you should be surprised that there is a widening chasm between the descriptions of our economic condition as provided by people like Maurice Doyle, and the reality of life as experienced in the homes and communities of this Republic.

The true state of our economy is to be observed not in the balance sheets and ledgers of the Central Bank but along the streets and roadways of Ireland. Our situation is not suddenly disimproved because Mr Doyle has noticed some blip on his radar.

We are dying of an ideological blight that has no cure.

The people who put that ideology in place and preserved it long after it had demonstrably failed were not the unemployed or the social welfare dependants, but the political and economic elite, including the governer of the Central Bank, which fuelled the ideological smokescreen and flooded the economy with European money so as to conceal the extent of their massive pretence.

3. THE ALLIES OF OUR OWN GRAVEDIGGERS
(April 1993)

To be absolutely modern means to be the ally of your own gravediggers.
Milan Kundera, *Immortality*

One way of describing what has been happening to Ireland in the past twenty years or so would be to say that the country has been going out of fashion. I do not mean that it has become unfashionable to be Irish, but that the realities of what it is like to live in Ireland and the aspects of Irish life which might ensure the health and stability of future life here have all been rendered unfashionable within the public imagination of the State. Although the word "fashion" itself conjures up notions of ephemerality and superficiality, I believe that the condition I speak of is a dangerous one and might even prove fatal.

The entity we have come to know as "rural Ireland" provides the most basic example. Even the most well-intentioned and sympathetic public responses to the situation of this entity can be observed to make the assumption that rural Ireland is, so to speak, a couple of bales short of a trailerload.

We have come to characterise rural Ireland as a "problem" area undergoing a "crisis" of some kind. The tone of concern with which such diagnoses are delivered suggests that something will have to be done by someone or other, if this place is not to disappear altogether.

At this point, we come upon a sort of ideological divide between those who say that we should attempt to prevent this happening and those who say "good riddance to rural Ireland and all who sail in her". These latter belong to what is sometimes referred to as the "modernising tendency" – those who wish to live in an Ireland where none of the things which they associate with rural Ireland will any longer exist.

"Rural Ireland" is a phrase that means whatever you want it to, depending on your perspective. Within the vocabulary of mainstream political debate, for example, "rural" has come to be used as a synonym for "conservative", "backward" and "reactionary". By means of an ideological dripfeed, the public mind is gradually being conditioned with the notion that this place called "rural Ireland" is *ipso facto* sub-modern.

Much political analysis takes the form of evaluating and assessing the extent to which Irish politics has "modernised", and invariably what is meant by this is that the bad habits associated with politics in rural Ireland have been shaken off, to a greater or lesser extent, as the process of modernisation has proceeded.

I find myself torn between two seemingly incompatible responses to such discussions. On the one hand, as someone who comes from a place designated as falling within the entity known as "rural Ireland", I have great difficulty recognising any such neatly definable entity at all. In the same moment, I question whether we should acknowledge the existence of such

78

an entity, largely on account of the negative connotations which have come to surround it.

There is a sense in which you might say that rural Ireland has no existence *other than* as a negative stereotype. I am fascinated by the tendency of members of the "modernising tendency" to refer exclusively to characteristics of rural Ireland which, if they existed, might indeed be regarded as negative, but which I am utterly unable to recognise.

In drawing pictures, as it were, of this place, they invariably refer to institutions such as the GAA, the Catholic Church and the Fianna Fáil party, mentions of which function as the broad strokes of their sketchings of this elusive place. Sometimes, too, they make mention of a writer, such as Charles Kickham, on whose works the inhabitants of rural Ireland are presumed to have based their personalities.

A man from Mars might be led to conclude that those of us who grew up in rural Ireland spent our formative years in a contorted state, on account of the congenital habits of nodding and winking we inherited from our parents.

In this connection, I would like to draw your attention to an excellent essay by Luke Gibbons, "Coming out of Hibernation", published in *Across the Frontiers: Ireland in the 1990s* (edited by Richard Kearney and published by Wolfhound Press), in which he argues that many of the negative images of rural Ireland derive not from any such place itself but from idealisations of country living emanating from the city.

The longing for community and for primitive simplicity, writes Gibbons, "are the product of an urban sensibility, and are cultural fictions imposed on the lives of those they purport to represent. In the United States, for example, it was not cowboys who sang the praises of the Old West but rather writers and intellectuals from the East, intent on establishing a mythology of the last frontier. By the same token, it was urban-based writers, intellectuals and political leaders who created romantic Ireland, and penetrated the myth that, the further west you go, the more you come into contact with the real Ireland."

This provides the only real insight I have come across into why, although I am alleged to come from rural Ireland, the description of this place which is consistently served up in the Irish media bears almost no resemblance whatever to the place I recognise as my home. Much of the negative stereotyping we are bombarded with is a neurotic response to a romantic stereotype which emanated previously from the same quarters. It is in this sense that I deny the existence of rural Ireland at all.

But, from an ever so slightly different perspective, I will advance the notion that the term "rural Ireland" should be abandoned on the grounds that it is a tautology. Ireland is overwhelmingly a rural society, not merely in its culture and structure, but in terms of its ability to maintain itself in economic terms. I suggest that, in as far as Irish society has shifted away from its rural configuration, this exercise has largely been counter-productive and very possibly foolhardy.

The most appalling social catastrophes of recent decades have resulted not from the collapse of rural society but from botched attempts at urbanisation. Not only have the modernisers failed to evoke an imaginative model of what a modern Ireland might be like; they have also failed to indicate how this "post-rural" society might provide for itself.

To put it another way – and to accept for a moment the logic of the modernisers – our attempts to progress have for the most part resulted in failure. There are two ways of responding to this: (1) to conclude that we are stuck for ever in the mire of rural backwardness; or (2) to argue that there is an altogether different way of seeing things.

By attempting this argument at all, of course, I have, within the logic of the modernisers, identified myself as a reactionary. What other kind of idiot could possibly advance the notion that things urban are not "four legs good," and things rural "two legs bad"?

This is what I mean when I say that Ireland has made itself unfashionable. We have literally allowed the fundamental nature of what we are to seem out-of-date to ourselves. In our attempt to become "modern", we have denied the very essence of our own ability to survive at all. We have, in Milan Kundera's words, become the allies of our own gravediggers.

This is not to say that Ireland, rural Ireland, or any other definition of Ireland, is actually, in any meaningful sense, out of date. Reality, by and large, is pretty indifferent to the wishes of ideologues and wishful thinkers. Outside the window of the room in which you or I now sit, reality continues about its business as though ignorant of the requirements of fashion.

In a thousand years from now, our descendants will still have to grow potatoes and fatten cattle in order to stay alive. In this sense, the activities associated with the entity we speak of as "rural Ireland" are timeless and universal and will survive for precisely as long as humankind itself.

What is less certain, however, is whether we, the Irish people, will in the immediate future be capable of seeing such activities as sufficiently modern and will as a consequence be in a position to play to our strengths with confidence and purpose.

Even though the extent of the failure of the modernising project is already becoming clear, it will take some time for us to admit our mistakes, undo the caricatures we have created of ourselves and move on to a sensible and sober evaluation of our state of health.

To begin with, I believe that the correct question to be addressed in relation to the perceived threat to rural Ireland is not "How are we to provide for those left behind by the process of modernisation?" but "Is the concept of modernisation we have been preoccupied with a good idea at all?"

4. CHAUVINISM AND CENTRALISATION

(February 1993)

Although I have covered what I believe to be a fairly wide and eclectic range of topics during my two years writing this column, I have found myself dragged, again and again, towards a couple of central themes, namely "Dublin domination" and "rural decline".

These are not necessarily the subjects that most interest me, but they are the subjects I get asked about when, occasionally, I participate in conferences and seminars. They are also the subjects on which I feel I have been least able to make myself understood. The more I deal with them, the more conscious I become of the fog of misunderstanding that has gathered between the argument I have been attempting to make and the conventional wisdom on such matters.

For example, I have long been aware that these subjects constitute not two themes, but one. They are, in my view, cause and effect, chicken and egg. This should be a simple enough idea to communicate, but somehow it gets lost in the welter of special pleadings and partisan responses that greets any attempt to deal with these issues as a single analysis.

If you make an argument perceived as sympathetic to "the country", you are assumed to be making an attack on Dublin, and vice versa. I also have a strong sense that, if you attempt to analyse such matters outside the limits of the conventional wisdom, you must use a language which has been developed to serve a logic that is both separate from and inimical to the one you are trying to articulate. As a result, everything you say on the subject is likely to be perceived within the dominant logic that you are seeking to question, and thus readily dismissed by those to whose views it is inconvenient.

There have, for example, been a number of recent attempts to "refute" the notion that Dublin has received preferential treatment at the expense of "rural Ireland". One such was made in a recent article in the *Sunday Business Post*, written by the newspaper's editor, Damien Kiberd. This subject has also been the theme of two recent columns in *The Irish Times* by Dr Garret FitzGerald, the latest of which appeared on Saturday.

Both gentlemen have made extremely cogent points about the economic decline of Dublin. Damien Kiberd, writing on 31 January, pointed out that in the 17 years to 1991, "only 23 per cent of the £2,360 million provided for industrial grants and supports went to Dublin, which accounted for 32 per cent of the workforce during that period." Dr Garret FitzGerald, in an article in this newspaper on 2 February, wrote along similar lines, arguing that, because of a "long-standing and deep-seated negativism towards the capital city", the magnitude of Dublin's current social and economic problems is not appreciated in the State at large.

I heartily concur with the thrust of both these articles, and with Dr FitzGerald's column on a similar theme last

Saturday. The trouble is, I get the distinct impression that both of them are responding to an argument that has never been seriously made, i.e. that Dublin has been disproportionately favoured in economic matters at the expense of the rest of the State.

It is as though, by advancing arguments which go to prove the opposite, they are attempting to "redress" the perception of Dublin domination that has undoubtedly gained great currency in recent years. Moreover, they are both to some extent indulging in a tendency normally associated with the other "side" of the argument, that of labelling "Dublin" and "the rest of the country" as separate and competing entities, rather than as interdependent part of a single society.

Let us get one thing straight, once and for all: the fact of Dublin domination of this society is irrefutable.

"The growth of Dublin", wrote Professor (now Senator) J. J. Lee in *Ireland 1922-1985: Politics and Society*, "is a distinctive feature of contemporary Irish social and democratic experience. Most other European capitals expanded in the 20th century. But none, except Athens, grew to Dublin's relative size. In 1926, Dublin city and county contained 17 per cent of the national population. In 1985, they contained about 35 per cent. Very few European metropolitan areas contain more than 20 per cent and that proportion has been generally stable for a generation or so, whereas Dublin's has been rising rapidly."

Where I think the argument made by Mr Kiberd and Dr FitzGerald is somewhat misplaced is that I am not sure that anyone has ever seriously suggested that Dublin domination has resulted in greater prosperity for Dublin itself. The point, I thought, was that Dublin domination was bad for *everyone*.

My own argument, for example, has always been that

excessive centralisation has resulted in a fundamental erosion of the State's ability to fend for itself, a process which would ultimately result in the destruction of the State by a series of economic seizures extending inwards from the west coast. Surely no one could have imagined that Dublin would be spared this calamity?

The figures presented by Mr Kiberd and Dr FitzGerald are unimpeachable, as far as they go. It is true, as Dr FitzGerald says, that Dublin's rate of outward migration in the 1980s was higher than average for the rest of the State. Given the excessive growth of the city's population prior to that period, this haemorrhaging at a time of sharp economic decline was both unsurprising and surprisingly slight.

Similarly, while Mr Kiberd is quite correct in noting that per capita industrial expenditure in Dublin during the 1970s and 1980s was lower than for the rest of the State, this statistic needs to be seen in the context of the already heavily distorted demographics of the country as a whole. Such spending could be seen as a misguided and futile attempt to reverse the prevailing drift to the capital.

But, no matter how you perceive these figures, none of this does anything to challenge the view that Ireland is an excessively centralised society.

One could quote other figures, to do with social welfare transfers or public service wages, which might serve to bolster one or other "side" of the argument, but they would all be equally beside the point. All of us in Ireland, whether we live in Dublin or elsewhere, should be on the same side in this argument.

It cannot be sufficiently emphasised that the decline of Dublin is occurring not *in spite of* the centralisation of economic and political power there, but precisely *because* of this. Centralisation seriously distorts whatever is the economic and social equivalent of the ecological balance, and it is logical that this will have consequences close to, as well as distant from, the epicentre of power.

Put another way, the underlying causes of the problems afflicting north Clondalkin in County Dublin are the same as those which result in the devastation of parts of the west and north-west.

The core of the matter is the question of a driving ideology. Over the past 30 years or so, Irish public policy, as well as the dominant discourse that fuelled it, has been driven by a view more or less indistinguishable from a liberal theory of industrialisation.

This analysis has assumed that Ireland would follow along similar lines to what were considered comparable societies in becoming more industrialised, more urbanised, and therefore more "modern". Although the consensus behind this analysis becomes increasingly shaky, it continues to be the dominant ideology of this society.

This theoretical view has had a most pernicious influence on our development over recent decades. Among its manifold consequences has been to insinuate into the national consciousness the notion that the so-called "traditional" model of society perceived as being left behind was, *ipso facto*, backward and sub-modern. Moreover, it has led us to follow blindly along an ideological and developmental path that was rapidly being evacuated by those societies to whose standards we have aspired.

We now find ourselves running out of steam, halfway between the disintegrating "traditional" society we have come to disparage and the dissolving mirage of the promised land. There is a profound connection between the situation in the neglected wastelands of north Clondalkin, where the vast majority of people is under forty, and that of towns in the West of Ireland, where hardly anyone is left between the ages of 20 and 40.

Where the influence of Dublin *has* been pernicious is in relation to the promulgation of this ideology. There is now a strong case to be made that the term "rural Ireland" is in fact a tautology – that there is no other way of seeing Ireland than as a rural society with towns and cities in it, and that any attempts to see it in another light have resulted in appalling social disasters.

The problem has been that these ideas, which were utterly unsuited to the country as a whole, *appeared* to make sense for a while within the ever-contracting location of power in the capital. These dubious ideas came to dominate disproportionately the running of a State apparatus that had itself come to dominate disproportionately the State as a whole.

The intellectual and cultural dominance of the capital, immensely reinforced by the national media, resulted in these ideas becoming unassailable within the society they were destroying. In the end, they are bound to destroy everything and everyone, even those who have advanced them with such certitude.

Over 25 years ago, the late John Healy warned that Dublin was becoming "a monstrously swollen head on a shrunken rural body, a gross cancer which feeds and devours its body." This was ridiculously interpreted as an attack on Dublin, which resulted in its warning going more or less unheeded. (Healy actually loved Dublin, having lived there for most of his life.) That phrase still provides a most powerful description of what has been happening to this society.

Think about it, because Healy chose his words and images with both sympathy and care. Forget the partisan arguments, the jaded notions about jackeens and culchies, which have no meaning now, if they ever had.

It is not a question of Us and Them, the head versus the body in a fight for survival. That would be a fight to the death. The head will not live long after the body has died, any more than the body can function without a head on its shoulders.

The answer, as I think everyone will agree, is in a system of local democracy that will be capable of distributing both power and creative ideas throughout this society. In other words, if we want to get ahead, we had better look again to our heart.

5. POSTCARD FROM THE MONOCHROME CITY

North Clondalkin in the 1992 General Election campaign
(November 1992)

Last Thursday afternoon, a meeting was held in the Rowlagh Community Centre in north Clondalkin to launch the report of a task force established to examine the problems of this, perhaps the most marginalised, area of Dublin. Among the speakers were Dr Tom Collins, chairman of the task force, John Bennett and Grace Wills, two local community workers, and a veritable galaxy of local politicians who had suddenly rediscovered in themselves a profound concern about urban decay. When the meeting began at 2.30 pm, there was one journalist present, i.e. myself.

At precisely 3.20 pm, 50 minutes into the meeting, the doors of the community hall burst open and in walked the leader of the Labour Party, Mr Dick Spring. In his wake appeared a gaggle of political aides and at least two dozen media people, including camera crews, reporters, "colour" writers and photographers. The invaders trouped noisily to occupy the few remaining seats. For the next half-hour, the event was appropriated by a media circus concerned only with capturing the "flavour" of the Labour leader's campaign. All around the hall, cameras clicked and flash-bulbs flickered. The banalities of politicians, which for the previous half-hour had been evaporating into thin air, were now being written down in notebooks and recorded on tape recorders. The invasion resulted in a couple of photographs in the following day's papers and a couple of token mentions of the event which would not otherwise have appeared, but the purpose and the content of the occasion were largely ignored. North Clondalkin was in the "news" because the leader of the Labour Party happened to have it on his schedule for the day.

This incident provides a succinct comment on the nature of the relationship between the communities of the desolated wastelands of modern Ireland and the official Ireland which they adjoin. Over the 20-odd years of the failed project of modernisation, the State has created a surfeit of such sprawling disaster areas as now exists in north Clondalkin, and in the end decided that the disaster was none of its business. Estates like Neilstown and Ronanstown have been stigmatised, scapegoated and damned with the responsibility for their own predicament.

Politicians throw their hands in the air and, at election time, touch briefly down to assure the natives of their unqualified support and concern. Newspaper editors despatch journalists to write cautionary tales of urban decay and violence under headlines which invariably incorporate words like "riot", "terror" and "no-go". Always there is the sense of a journey being made *out* to such places, from the "real" world of economic fundamentals and lifestyle supplements.

The modern Irish state effectively creates, as a by-product of its own incoherence, vast areas of institutionalised poverty and deprivation and then contrives to portray them as marginal aspects, somehow disconnected from itself. To add insult to injury, when in search of headlines or votes, it colonises anew the tragedy which, through the same appalling ignorance, it has earlier spawned, co-opting the language and analysis of those among the wronged people who have begun to fight back.

Thus, the people become more firmly locked into their situation and there is even less chance than ever of breaking through the analytical shell with the suggestion that the real world may be here, in north Clondalkin, and that "fundamental" Ireland's attempts to avert its gaze from this reality may be a dangerous self-deception.

North Clondalkin, and the other places like it in Dublin, Cork, Limerick, Waterford, Galway and elsewhere, represent the dirt under the carpet of the spick-and-span, fundamentally sound Ireland of 1992. Because it began as part of the modernising delusion and finished up as it did, it provides us with a perfect polaroid of our present condition. Built in the early to mid-1970s, places like this were intended as the flagship estates of the new urban, industrialised Ireland. They were conceived to a blueprint based on American B-movie notions of what modern life should be like, created for the notional contented, blue-collar generations whose boats would be lifted by the rising tides of the post-EC Ireland. Even today, in a bad light, it is possible to see the shadow of the fantasy lurking among the neat rows of houses and the sweeping green spaces. Here, it was intended, would reside the new working class of a thriving industrialised metropolis, with two cars in every driveway, a chicken in every oven and a hypermarket on every corner.

The dream was very soon interrupted by reality. Today, it stands as a monument to the folly of a half-educated, post-colonial country and the poverty of its official vision and leadership.

Of the 4,500 households which make up the north Clondalkin area, 60 per cent survive on social welfare. Ninety per cent of the population is under the age of 45. Many of the residents came here having been displaced from their natural, inner-city communities by what was regarded as "progress and development". With a total population of over 16,000, north Clondalkin has one pub, no banks, no cinema, no theatre and no restaurant. The "Plan for the Development of North Clondalkin", launched at last Thursday's meeting, compares the area to Wexford town, which has a similar level of population; Wexford has six banks, 10 restaurants, three hotels, one cinema and two theatres. The area has four primary and two post-primary schools, catering for over 4,000 children. Absenteeism and under-achievement are rife.

There is no industrial/manufacturing-type employment in the area and, because of the absence of the normal urban infrastructure, an almost total dearth of service employment. Because of the failure to complete the Fonthill road, intended to provide a main artery through the area by linking the Dublin-Galway and Dublin-Cork roads, the area suffers from isolation from its immediate hinterland and a consequent lack of attractiveness for industrial development. The only access which residents of north Clondalkin have to the village of Clondalkin, less than a mile away, is via a narrow, humped-back bridge. North Clondalkin, as Dr Tom Collins said in launching the report of his task force, is "seriously *uncoheded*".

The General Election is of limited interest to the people who live in the infamous estates of Neilstown, Ronanstown, Rowlagh, St Mark's and Quarryvale. They have a record of low turnouts – an average of about 40 per cent; less in last year's local government poll – and this election is unlikely to provide a break with tradition.

They view politicians now with something approaching detached derision. The only responses the inane pronouncements of their elected representatives elicited last Thursday were a couple of desultory "tut-tuts". To ask them what impact they think the election may have on the quality of their lives is to invite a pitying look. This is not all bad. They have stopped waiting for politicians and have begun to bypass them. The community has started its own fightback and earnestly wishes that, if politicians are unable to be of assistance, they at least stay out of its way. There is a growing interest in community action in the area, and local community workers say they now find it more expedient to deal directly with EC agencies than with national government. The important thing is to neutralise the local politicians who might inadvertently queer the pitch.

What they want, as expressed in the report of the task force, is that their area be designated a priority area for industrialisation, education, health and environmental initiatives. They want a policy of positive discrimination in favour of areas like theirs. More specifically, they want a start to be made on developing a town centre in north Clondalkin. They want the Fonthill road completed and the railway station at Clondalkin reopened. Most of all, they want their communities to be empowered in a manner which will enable them to take control of their own situations. Local government reform, they plead, is an essential element of their hoped-for recovery.

What they do *not* want are more political promises and lip-service, more official hand-wringing, more media scare-mongering about the "no-go" territories of north Clondalkin, or more "colour" articles by journalists who pay their children to be photographed behind the wheels of burnt-out cars. There is no "colour" to be found here, they stress; as the task force report puts it: "It is the archetypal monochrome, single-class, local authority suburban housing estate which has none of the advantages of urban living and all the disadvantages."

Meanwhile, life in the fundamentally sound Ireland continues to a different backbeat. Along the roadside on the way into the Rowlagh estate last week were dozens of Fianna Fáil posters with photographs of Albert Reynolds and the slogan "We can make it happen." As you move through the wasteland of north Clondalkin, the phrase rapidly acquires a malign irony. "It" happened here a long time ago.

The writing is on the wall. The problems of the desolated urban landscapes of modern Ireland are no longer problems of marginality, but symptoms of the core disintegration which now threatens us. As Tom Collins said on Thursday: "The experience of north Clondalkin indicates that one can no longer manage what one does not wish to change." As Dick Spring responded: "It now comes back to government."

6. STRANGULATION BY STEALTH   (August 1994)

After an extended lull, the last few weeks I've been getting more letters than ever about An Post. Most of them relate to what seems like a renewed threat of sub-post office closures in various parts of the country.

You may recall that, following the scrapping of An

Post's infamous 1991 viability plan, the issue of sub-offices disappeared from public view. There is every sign that the plan is now being implemented by stealth.

A letter on a related subject, from a woman in Kenmare, Co. Kerry, tells of how the mail-car contract which had been in her husband's family for almost 200 years has been taken away at three days' notice. Her son, who had been operating the contract for 25 years – the fourth generation of his family to drive the mail-car – was told recently that he was to be replaced by a part-timer. His father had operated the contract for 50 years, from the age of fifteen.

I find the letter both innocent and sad. This woman has written to me because she knows that I, too, drove a mail-car and that my father before me drove one for over 50 years. She thinks that such things still mean something in this country. She writes of how she once met Albert Reynolds when he was Minister for Post and Telegraphs. They had to ask him to intercede when they were looking for a small rise in the payment for their contract.

He told them, she writes, that they had something to be proud of. "Never let that go," he told them. Now it is gone and she thinks this should mean something. She thinks that if she can simply remind people of the history of her family's dedicated service it will all turn out to have been a big mistake.

I had to write to her to say that the country is not like that any more. I told her that it didn't matter that her son had done the job for 25 years. Nor does it matter that his father had done the job for 50 years. Nor that *his* father, or *his father's father* had done the job, or how well they had done it, or how selflessly, or how diligently, or how proud they had been.

The last 200 years do not matter any more. The next

200 years do not matter either. All that matters is today and that's the bottom line. That is the way the country is now, I explained as gently as I could.

I might just photostat this reply and send it also to the woman from Carracastle, Co. Mayo, who writes to tell me that her local sub-post office is to be closed following the death of the postmaster a short time ago. The man's daughter had been running the office since his death and she had been told that the contract was to be put up for tender. Then, out of the blue, came the news that the office was to be closed.

Last week it was closed. "Please, please help," the woman writes. The sub-post office in Carracastle, which I served myself when I drove the mail-car, has existed for 127 years. The woman from Carracastle seems to think that this might stand for something, that she can say it or write it and expect someone to react as though it meant something. She writes to me that it is odd, "with all the talk of rural development", that An Post should be allowed to close down post-offices in this way.

No, I say, it would only be odd if the talk about rural development was supposed to mean something. If, as I have always known, it is utterly without meaning, the closure of post offices makes perfect sense.

I have had letters, too, from residents of the Mallow area about the imminent downgrading of 17 post offices and the resulting redundancy of 22 postmen. They point out to me that this is the viability plan by the back door, and they argue that there is a domino effect in the closure of post offices leading to the disappearance of other services and a rise in emigration.

I know that what they say is true. No sooner was the viability plan issued in 1991 than An Post realised it had made a mistake – but a *tactical* mistake rather than a moral or social one.

In May 1992, a report by a company of consultants commissioned by the National Economic and Social Council advocated a series of "rationalisations" which were actually far more swingeing than those proposed in the original plan. The consultants recommended that An Post reduce its retail network of post offices to a size which would "adequately serve its market". This, it specified, would mean *more* than the 550 closures proposed under the viability plan.

The report also recommended that the company proceed with the introduction of roadside boxes, despite conceding that these constituted a reduction in the quality of the postal service to many customers. The justification for this, they suggested, was a saving of £6.7 million per annum.

The report estimated that these steps would mean the loss of 200 full-time and 290 part-time jobs for postmen and postwomen. These job-losses were "unavoidable", the NESC consultants decided. Roadside letter boxes, the report averred, are "essentially labour-saving devices and it is the reduction of the labour costs that are their major justification".

So there you have it. How can there be any meaning to 127 years of service, or 200 years of service, or even 1,000 years of service, in such a regime? The two concepts are utterly irreconcilable. And because the idea that the reduction of labour costs provides a "justification" for inconvenience, hardship and neglect is now the dominant idea of this society, all one can say to the woman from Kenmare, or the man from Mallow, or the woman from Carracastle, is that they or their lives do not matter any more.

Perhaps the relevant agencies and Government Departments could prepare a standard letter to be sent out to all those who write to complain: "Dear Sir or

Madam, You do not matter one whit, nor do the lives of your father or your father's father. Yours sincerely. . . "

Or perhaps the Taoiseach might consider requisitioning some time on RTE, as he did during the Maastricht campaign, to explain to the people of Kenmare, Carracastle, Mallow and other such places that they do not matter any more.

For my own part, although I am pleased that people think of writing to me, I have come to realise that there is no point in my writing about such matters. For a while, I foolishly thought there was, that those in power and influence merely required to be reminded of where they themselves came from to be spurred into action.

I now know that by doing so I have merely added to the perception of my own eccentricity and to the ridiculousness of the claim of the people of Kenmare, Mallow or Carracastle to live full and proper lives. I merely add cross-hatching to the caricature that I and these people have become. They are sub-modern anachronisms; I am a ridiculous crank full of half-arsed opinions.

The "truth" is that these people are living on borrowed time and should be grateful for the indulgence they have been shown up to now.

I have one last suggestion on the subject of what we are pleased to describe as "rural Ireland". Has anybody thought about using napalm? It would save *such* a lot of money.

7. It's All Wrong, Jack

In the last 1980s, Jim Connolly set out to find a way of helping unemployed families who wished to escape the helplessness of life in suburban wastelands to resettle in

rural Ireland. The result was Rural Resettlement Ireland.
(November 1993)

The more I listen to discussions about how to address
our present condition, the more I sense that such efforts
are doomed to fail. We have locked ourselves in. We
clamour around the door, attempting, by brute force, to
push it open. Nobody notices that the door has a notice
which says, in tiny lettering, "pull".

I have this fantasy that, one day, a tiny voice from the
back of the room will whisper the magic word "pull",
and in a brief lull in the clamour of pushing, we would
hear the word and try it, just to prove him wrong. And
the door would open and send us tumbling back in
alarm and surprise.

There are a few people, I sometimes fancy, here and
there in the throng, who might just be in the right place
to utter the magic word. These are people who, perhaps
lacking a stake in the way things are, have no reason to
think, or not to tell the truth about what they see.

One such is Jim Connolly, who lives near Loop Head
in County Clare. You may have come across him on the
Late Late Show or the *Gay Byrne Show*, talking about his
hugely successful rural resettlement project, which has
rehoused over 100 urban families in rural Ireland, mostly
in the west. Rural Resettlement Ireland (RRI) now has
almost 2,000 families on its waiting list.

I called on Jim Connolly recently at his home in
County Clare. I came away with a feeling that there is
still some little hope of a return to sanity in this State
while people like this gentle and reserved man are
thinking and whispering things that others have forgotten.

In the "modern" Ireland, Jim Connolly's activities are
treated at the level of lip-service as worthy and exotic. In
fact, Connolly has stumbled upon the central malfunction

of Irish society, and has presented us with the solution. He has identified the precise root of most of our social and economic problems and provided a working model to illustrate how we might reconstruct this disintegrating State of ours.

Jim Connolly has now prepared a document outlining how the philosophy and approach of RRI might be applied in a more general way to the Irish economy. His plan, entitled *A Policy for Rural Renewal*, is aimed at both policy-makers and the general public, "to get people to pause, take stock of our present situation, to reflect on where we as a nation have come from during the last few centuries, and whether future generations will have reason to be grateful to us for the way we manage this free country which we so recently inherited."

The problem is that, while nobody doubts the reality of rural decline, there is little sense that it is other than inevitable, and even, one suspects, a notion that it is an unavoidable by-product of "progress". The statistics, however frightening, are insufficient of themselves.

The leaks from the forthcoming report of the western bishops suggest that the West will lose about 20 per cent of its population within twenty years. This, though deeply shocking, only hints at the dimensions of the decline, which will not occur gradually, but rather as the demographic equivalent of the Cliffs of Moher. Those leaving will amount to virtually the entire coming generation.

Jim Connolly, one notices, does not quote statistics. Instead, he'll talk about a recent drive through Mayo, or a walk down his own road, and how he *felt* the decay all around him. He does not need surveys or task-forces to tell him what is under his nose.

"I'm very concerned that the official mind has written

off rural Ireland," he says. "In the absence of any visible policy for rural renewal, I, for one, have no choice but to believe that the doomsday scenario of huge areas of our beautiful countryside becoming wastelands without people will inevitably come to pass – much of it in the foreseeable future."

His most urgent call is for a national policy of rural renewal. This is necessary, he says, not just for the sake of rural communities, but for the survival of the State as a whole. "To treat the problems facing rural communities as something totally separate and divorced from the rest of Irish life would be a fundamental error," he writes. The disintegration of the fabric of our cities, blighted by crime, drugs and unemployment, is a direct consequence of the disintegration of the countryside.

Connolly's analysis identifies a fundamental process in which a sense of value has been lost through the cracks in our system of economic and monetary exchange. The reason life is becoming worse and worse for a greater number of people, while so much of our real resources remain untapped, is a consequence of our failure to value adequately what we have and find a means of sharing it.

"Money has ceased to be an accurate means of value," he says. "The real wealth of Ireland includes such things as space, environment, peace, access to culture, natural beauty – and a million other things. Such things have always been available to those with money and yet have not been included in the equation defined by the dominant economic order."

To give someone the chance to live in a fresh, scenic part of rural Ireland is to hand them an *economic resource*. As a result of the drift to the cities, the moderately well-off citizen must spend large sums of money to obtain a level of benefit in a city environment which is available for next to nothing 50 or 60 miles down the country. The result has been a double-edged distortion, with rural decline at one end and urban overcrowding, pollution and crime at the other.

Because the evidence or rural decline has been so visible, we have thought of it as being irrefutable. The dominant ideology not merely institutionalised this thinking, but managed to imbue it with virtue. Jim Connolly states the case simply: "We must change our views about country living. In my opinion, after some minor adjustments in lifestyles and perhaps some development in their sense of values, virtually *anybody* can live a better life there."

He does not suggest that trends in farming patterns can be dramatically altered. This is not the issue. The mistake has been in thinking that the decline of particular forms of farming should be allowed to mean the end of rural living. This thinking has placed both country and city under threat.

He accepts that there are many aspects of the problem, such as the European dimension, that we cannot fight. "Those policies are outside our control. But it's essential that some counter-balancing measures be taken."

In an 11-page document, which he is sending to the Government this week, Jim Connolly outlines both his analysis of our present situation and his ideas about addressing it. He calls for a policy of rural renewal, so as to arrest the present decline and focus energies towards reversing it. His specific suggestions range from the reintroduction of grants to upgrade housing, to a return to the concept of essential services – such as transport, post and medical care – being a basic right no matter where you live.

He is not suggesting that these ideas represent a

complete or an original plan for rural renewal. In most instances, what Jim Connolly says is obvious. But it is the clarity of the connections he makes and his conviction deriving from personal experience of the issue that give his contribution such weight.

This is not merely about rural renewal, he says, although that is where we must begin. What is needed is a fundamental overturning of our present philosophy so as to put the needs of the people back at the top of the agenda. "My personal concern isn't for the grass, or the lonely roads, or even the lonely houses. My personal concern is for the people who might live there and the fact that they could have better lives.

"The philosophy whereby our country functions at the moment is the philosophy of 'I'm all right, Jack.' It goes throughout families, throughout communities, throughout society. This is deadly and inhumane. To my mind, *sharing* is the only philosophy that counts.

"We're going to have to start with our children and say, to their surprise, 'You're a human being. We are fellow members of a human race.' The changes needed in our philosophy towards life are so basic that it's only with extreme difficulty that we can address our problem as a society."

Acknowledging that such a shift in values remains a long-term ideal, Jim Connolly comes back to what is practical now. "I see this beautiful countryside around here and not a soul in it. We can share this, in a practical way, with not just hundreds, but thousands, and maybe tens of thousands of families, to everybody's benefit."

Seeing that RRI has rehoused over 100 families, and has nearly 2,000 more on its waiting list, imagine what might be achieved, he says, by a major Government-backed programme of renewal.

VI

THE DISMAL SCIENCE

1. THE GREAT THREE-CARD TRICK

A response to yet more business "scandals".

(May 1993)

I once lost £40 to a three-card-trick man. On the final day of the last Lisdoonvarna music festival in 1983, I was walking among the stalls at the perimeter of the concert site when I happened on a crowd grouped around a man shuffling three cards around a small table. I had never seen a three-card-trick man before, although I had been warned enough to know better than to have any truck with them.

The man's hands moved like a pair of windscreen wiper blades in a downpour, sliding the three cards around the table, occasionally turning one of them face-upwards, as all the while he kept up a seamless babble of talk, inviting the onlookers to try their luck and see how easy it was to get rich. I watched for a while and observed a number of people coming forward to bet on the cards. Sometimes they won, sometimes they lost.

When they lost, they would shake their heads in bafflement and annoyance; when they won, they would stuff the wad of notes they had received into their pockets and say goodbye to the man behind the table, whose turn it now was to shake his head and go "tut-tut" to himself. I think I must have been well aware that they were almost certainly accomplices of the man behind the table, but, if I was, I succeeded in pushing this knowledge to the back of my mind.

From the edge of the crowd, I was able to pick out the queen every time. It looked easy to me. In my pocket I had £40, a week's pay. Within two minutes I had lost the lot and was stumbling through the crowd in a daze of shame, disappointment and self-hatred.

If it is possible to speak of the feelings of a whole people, I would say that, collectively, we must feel a little like that right now. For we live in a world where the three-card-trick man has become a god. We do not call them three-card-trick men, but "entrepreneurs" and "risk-takers".

Once upon a time, business must have been conducted for the purpose of making the world function, enabling human beings to eat and clothe themselves and generally improving the standard of living in many ways. Money was the medium by which all this could be achieved; it functioned as a kind of lubricant, facilitating the free exchange of labour, goods and services. It was an added incentive, additional to the satisfaction gleaned from doing a job well and paying one's own way with the sweat of one's brow.

If you are in doubt that this was ever the case, take a walk around any of the great cities of Europe, say Prague or Berlin, and ask yourself if such architectural excellence could have been achieved on the basis of the profit motive alone.

What has happened is that money has been transformed from lubricant to fuel. Once one's money was as good as the amount of skills, labour or genius it could buy. It was mere paper or alloy, a token of exchange. The real currency was work.

But in the modern economy, where skills and labour have been devalued to the point, in many instances, of obsolescence, the token has become the reality. The slogan "money isn't everything" has become both a cliché and a lie. In fact, nothing matters *except* money, because nothing else is quite so able to retain value.

In such a world it should not come as a surprise that many men of business have come to deal *only* in money. Why bother employing people to work, or in any way contributing to the creation of a better world when you are able to get rich faster and so much more safely? Why should you care about the state of the world when, by dealing in mere tokens, you can cut down on the overheads and make that extra margin that allows you to shut yourself away, behind high walls and tinted glass, from the ugliness of the world that modern business is creating? Why go to the trouble of establishing a reputation for the quality of your work when you can make a hundred times more as a three-card-trick man?

In the world of three-card-tick men, there are rules but no morals. Profit has finally become disengaged from notions of value, or work, or goods, or services. There is only money. It moves around the table of the world's money markets at speeds which have little relation to anything that occurs in the world of industry or work.

The people who operate the tables do not contribute in any way to the improvement of life on the planet. Yet their rewards are far greater than the rewards of those who do. They have cut out of the transaction equation all the troublesome activity that used to intervene between the initiation of economic activity and the arrival of handsome dividends. And all the while there is the accompanying babble of incomprehensible talk about incentives, acquisitions, bull markets and buy-outs.

The three-card-trick man of modern business does not conduct his enterprise surreptitiously from the back of a Hiace van, but in the full glory of the modern media's obsession with profit-making. He wears a sharp suit, drives a sleek dark car and is written about in the business pages of respectable newspapers. The bigger the profit he is able to command for the least possible effort or benefit, the more newsworthy and revered is the entrepreneur.

The editors of our newspapers would doubtless be insulted if you suggested that they write profiles of some of the three-card-trick men who operate around the fairs and festivals of Ireland. But, while the modern operator may be playing for bigger stakes, he inhabits the same moral universe as my friend in Lisdoonvarna.

Just as that three-card-trick man was able to relieve me of a week's hard-earned income in seconds, those who understand the world of three-card-trick business are able to make vast profits without ever raising a sweat. Those of us who remain in the real world can only watch in fascination as the entrepreneur buys a building for, say, £6 million and sells it within weeks for, say, £9 million, without ever having to pay out – or perhaps even *possess* – the £6 million in the first place. In one deal, he has made more than a skilled craftsman, a doctor or a teacher could earn in a lifetime of work.

We read the details of revealed transactions and attempt in vain to discern in them any semblance of the reality of the lives we ourselves lead. We try in vain to unscramble the codes by which such transactions are governed, and when we fail, we put it down to a deficiency in our own knowledge of the mysterious world of business.

Even when the same newspapers, which have

previously lionised the "risk-takers", suddenly inform us about some "scandal" that has been uncovered in the world of business, we have difficulty in comprehending precisely what it is that makes this transaction "unethical" or "immoral" when all the others have been passed as perfectly correct. "I have done nothing illegal," the entrepreneur protests and, however much his actions may stink to high heaven, he is almost always right about this. The world of modern business has become a parallel universe, with its own language, practices and morality, retaining few points of contact with the real world.

If morals were absolute, many's the household name would be languishing behind bars. Much of what is acceptable in what is now called "business" would in the real world be indistinguishable from theft. People who get rich by shuffling pieces of paper around do not do so in the detached neutral manner which their internalised concepts of morality might suggest. They get rich by stealing from those who have no choice but to remain in the real world, and whose lives are dictated by the economic order created by the three-card-tricksters.

Far from adding to the quality of life in the real world, many of our modern "entrepreneurs" are in the business of plundering and dismantling that world for their own short-term gain. The entire culture of modern business is structured to facilitate this purpose.

There is a marvellous article in the 1 May issue of the Catholic weekly, *The Tablet*, in which Professor Donald Nicholl makes a strong case for a re-examination of the morality of usury, or interest-taking, which he argues is at the root of much of the poverty and injustice in the modern world. Most of what is perfectly acceptable in the world of stocks and shares, he points out, would in the street be regarded as stealing. That is not to say that everyone working in the City is wicked or selfish, "but that the system they are working, and in which almost all of us are caught, is inherently immoral."

Morality has become a confused concept. What we think of as morals are more often simply arrangements of convenience dictated by the technical necessities and ruling ethos of society. This is why modern business can seem mysterious to those on the outside, because it operates by a different set of "moral" values. It may surprise you to learn that, up until the Reformation, usury was considered immoral by the Catholic Church.

The idea now seems absurd, but only because we have been conditioned by the amoral culture of modern commerce. According to Professor Nicholl, only the Muslim religion continues to regard the taking of interest as immoral. Perhaps if the Catholic bishops have a little time off in the coming months from brooding about the private practices of homosexuals, they might address themselves to the possibility of restoring this rather more vital element of the moral code.

2. Pay What you Like

Thoughts on yet another tax amnesty
(June 1993)

I'd never have taken Albert Reynolds for an economic radical, but there you are. Last week, when he justified the proposed amnesty for tax evaders on the grounds that there would be no financial loss involved for the State, and that, moreover, the State had "everything to gain", he was saying, whether he meant to or not, that there is actually no moral basis to the collection of taxes. The notion of rendering unto Caesar the things that are

Caesar's is now apparently *passé*.

What the proposed amnesty means is that those who have made rational choices to evade their taxes by removing their excess cash from the jurisdiction are retrospectively to be given the seal of approval by the State. It is scarcely possible to do this without giving credence and recognition to their reasons for evading tax in the first place. Most of them, I am sure, will offer in their defence the complaint that taxes in this State are inordinately high. Therefore, implicit in the proposed amnesty is an acceptance of the complaint that taxes, at least those levied on people with large amounts of money, are too high, and that those citizens who seek to evade them on this basis are justified in so doing.

To put it another way, what the amnesty does is reduce the matter of the payment of taxes from the status of moral obligation to one of optional gesture. It is no longer a question of "Pay what you owe", or even of "Pay what you can", but of "Pay what you like, if that's all right by you".

This is a commendably radical initiative by the Government, and one which will be welcomed by all of us who have in the past been in receipt of official demands for outstanding taxes – these usually, for even the most modest dues, being accompanied by threats to break down our front doors and take away our furniture. Have no fear the next time you receive a letter from the Collector General advising you that, failing immediate payment of the outstanding amount, he will be obliged to "enforce recovery with costs either through the Sheriff or through the institution of court proceedings, or by specifying the item(s) in a notice of attachment under Section 73 of the Finance Act 1988." In the culture of the Government's proposed tax amnesty, you will be able to respond to such demands as follows:

"Dear Sir, I am in receipt of your recent letter and have noted its contents. However, following due deliberation, I have decided that I will not be paying any tax this year after all, but will be opening a Swiss bank account instead. I hope this does not inconvenience you too much. Why not get in touch again next year and we'll see how the land lies? I trust the wife and family are keeping well. Yours, etc."

There are, of course, even more far-reaching possibilities arising out of this laudably radical initiative. Now that we have begun to transcend that primitive inhibition about each citizen being obliged to contribute according to his or her means to the upkeep of the State, there is no knowing how we might begin to alter the economic perspectives which have governed us.

One of the central messages of the proposed amnesty is that payment of tax is a functional rather than a moral imperative. If the citizen declines to pay what he owes, then – rather than being subjected to legal threats or sanctions – he will simply be requested – politely – to pay whatever he likes. There is no reason why, once accepted, this approach should not be extended into other areas of our economic management. (Nor is there any reason why the logic of the amnesty should not also be used to alleviate the pressure on the prison system. In future, impoverished citizens caught, for example, stealing a pound of sausages could be enabled to avoid the customary ten years' imprisonment by returning one or two of the sausages to their rightful owner. The possibilities, as you can see, are limitless.)

Take, for example, the question of foreign debt. The last time I checked, this State's foreign debt was still running well into the double figures of billions of pounds. For a long time, it has been common knowledge that practically every penny of income tax collected in this State has been going towards the servicing of this debt. More to the point, it is likely that this situation will continue into the foreseeable future, causing further paralysis to the already strangulated Irish economy. Once or twice, reckless people like myself have attempted to suggest that we put an end to this rather unpromising situation by announcing to the international bankers that we had decided to cease payments on the national debt. The letter from the Taoiseach to the presidents of all relevant banks might go something like:

"A chara, We're a bit fed-up with this crack of paying so much interest and getting nowhere. You may not be aware, but since the foundation of the Irish State, we have been able to support only about half of those people born in this country. This situation is having a number of profound and unforeseen negative consequences, and we would like to resolve it if at all possible. Accordingly, we have decided to, let us say, *postpone* further repayments on our national debt until further notice. Instead, we intend to embark on a radical programme of national reconstruction, building hospitals, schools, railways and other socially useful infrastructure, and providing work and prospects for the hordes of young people our rather antediluvian attitudes to birth control have lumbered us with. I'll be in touch as soon as the situation improves. I hope this does not inconvenience you too much. Regards to the wife and family. Yours, etc."

In the past, these suggestions have met with open hostility from the political and economic establishment. Such actions, they fumed, would result in Ireland becoming an "international pariah", by which they largely mean that Irish politicians would be unable to borrow any more money internationally. Pausing momentarily for a brief dry smile at the implications of this apocalyptic circumstance, let us move on to the other traditional objection: reneging on our financial liabilities would be *immoral*. (This, usually, from people who could close down a couple of hospitals before sitting down to a hearty breakfast, but let us not get into any more tedious deliberations upon the meaning of morality.)

Thankfully, such primitive scruples are now behind us. The Government's proposal for an amnesty for tax evaders shows clearly that the official view of this State now is that there is no moral obligation to pay tax. And since interest is simply a tax on debt, there is no longer any moral imperative with regard to repayments on foreign debt.

As to the question of Ireland becoming an "international pariah" – *get real!* Again, in the proposed amnesty, we observe that what happens to those who refuse to pay what is considered their due is that, far from being cast into outer darkness, they are offered incentives to bring their hot money in from the cold. Rather than breaking down their doors and taking away their furniture, we trot out the fatted calf (minus a nominal 15 per cent to take the bare look off things) and plead with them to return to the bosom of the economic family. Why should be expect any different treatment from the international banking sector when we get our affairs sorted out in a few years' time? What's sauce for the citizen is sauce for the State.

What the begrudging critics of the amnesty initiative have clearly missed is that this proposal is merely the first step in a complete reconstruction of the State's approach to economic management. Clearly, this amnesty contains a signal of a new, morally integrated and holistic approach to matters of financial debt.

And when you begin to think about the amnesty proposal in this integrated manner, it acquires an almost poetic symmetry. Think about it. If the logic of the amnesty is carried through into areas like the repayment of Government debt, one of the likely consequences would be that the foreign assets of Irish citizens would be liable to seizure by distressed and anguished international bankers. This threat would practically guarantee the total success of the amnesty, with every single one of the defaulters likely to opt for the 15 per cent tax at home, rather than risk losing everything to the disgruntled international financial community.

In this way, the Government would ensure that every single penny of the estimated £2 billion of Irish money now said to languish in foreign bank accounts would be immediately repatriated. This, combined with the £2 billion annual saving in interest repayments, would render insignificant any loss of cohesion or structural funding that might arise from our refusal to play ball with our "partners" any more. In a few years, should things improve sufficiently for us to consider rejoining the international community, Mr Reynolds should have no trouble in convincing all concerned that they would have "nothing to lose and everything to gain" from allowing us back on our own terms. And you thought that this man lacked vision?

3. NEGATIVE ASSETS

The "downsizing" of Aer Lingus

(June 1993)

Don't hold your breath, but one of these days we might cop on to ourselves a little and stop to listen to what we are saying about rationalisation, redundancy and unemployment.

Take the following comments of the Taoiseach, Mr Reynolds, last week, in relation to the Aer Lingus plan:

"Jobs will have to go, unfortunately, but we should hope that the discussions between management and unions will keep that at the lowest possible number. What is important is that we have to ensure that the company survives in the first instance.

"There is a gap in costs that has to be bridged between management and unions to restore the company's viability. That's the Government's objective and we are determined to see that, first of all, the company is in a state of commercial viability, and secondly that the national airline is maintained."

He added: "I can assure you that the Government are fully determined to take the decisions that are necessary."

The result of the Government's "determination" will be hundreds of people, if not the full 1,500 initially mentioned, trotting down to the dole office.

This, of course, is not one of the Government's "objectives", but it might as well be. It is the only thing guaranteed to come out of the rationalisation process.

The promised subsequent "viability" of the airline is a matter of crossing fingers and hoping that if you shoot enough horses, you'll have that much more grass. The likelihood is that, having brought the pistol into use on one occasion, more of the same will be required at a later date.

We should listen to ourselves. What we are saying is that the 1,500 people facing the dole do not matter, or at least matter less than other considerations, such as the "viability" of the airline. The job-losses are "unfortunate", but so it goes.

OK. So, how many potential job losses would need to arise before the balance would tilt in the other direction? If it were suggested that the viability of the airline required the shedding of, say, 10,000 of the 12,683 people employed by Aer Lingus, would this be regarded as too high a price for viability or not?

I suspect that it would not and, in saying so, I'm not suggesting that there would be any lack of hand-wringing by politicians mindful of their seats if that situation arose. Rather, I am stating that, in this society, the viability of commercial enterprise is now considered more important than *any* number of jobs.

It would, of course, be argued that the maintenance of jobs depends, first of all, on the viability of business and that it is pointless talking about the question of maintenance separately from that of viability, just as it is pointless talking about the right to life of the child separately from that of the mother (not that that ever stopped us talking).

But what I am asking is: what does viability mean? What is the purpose of commercial viability? Why is it important at all, when the working lives of human beings are apparently expendable?

In the case of Aer Lingus, for instance, why is it so important to ensure the company remains viable? "To safeguard the remaining employment" will be the response of the politician or the executive. It is noticeable, however, that neither is prepared to be specific about where the line is to be drawn, so I'd be pretty confident in ruling out employment-security as the reason for all this concern about viability.

To take it from another angle, let us look at the function that Aer Lingus performs. It flies people and goods to and from various destinations around the globe. Who are these people and why are they so important?

Clearly, the Government and the management of Aer Lingus have already decided that such people, and their need to be flown hither and thither, represent a much more important consideration than the need of 1,500 people to have a job and all that goes with that.

Why is this so? To keep Aer Lingus viable and to ensure that the national airline is maintained is clearly not simply a question of pride or national sentiment. There is an assumption in, for example, the Taoiseach's remarks that the airline will continue to be of some *use*. But to whom will it be useful? Certainly not to the 1,500 people currently threatened with redundancy.

Bear with me. The question arises: are the people who fly *in* aircraft constructed of some different material or substance, which places them in a different category to those who simply fly these planes and hand out duty-free catalogues? This is one possible conclusion arising out of official concern for the paying passenger, at the expense of the wage-earning worker.

To put it another way: why is it that Government and business show a concern for people and their needs in some situations and not in others? The answer, of course, is that *they don't*; they only pretend to.

The purpose of the present rationalisation is not to ensure the viability of Aer Lingus in order to safeguard the remaining employment. The purpose of rationalisation is rationalisation itself. Its only function is to maximise profits, not to improve the life of a single human being.

In the modern economy, there is little tolerance of human beings. The only guises in which we are welcomed are as consumers or units of production. Modern commercial "realities" require that those who subscribe to them adopt a form of logic which is essentially treacherous of their own species.

As the chairman of Gulf & Western, Mr Martin S.

Davis, put it, loyalty to workers or communities, even to nations, is no longer relevant to business, with all such allegiances being "viewed as expendable under the new rules. You cannot be emotionally bound to any particular asset."

Human beings are now, in commercial terms, negative assets. The interaction of the profit motive, automation and the growth imperative has created a treadmill on which human beings are accepted in the workplace on sufferance only, for the shortest possible period.

In the language of modern economics, the biggest "problem" is the existence of human beings and their peculiar needs, like food, shelter and heat. The possibility that, at some earlier point in human evolution, the concepts of business and economic activity were propounded with a view to improving the lot of mankind has about it a sense of fairytale unreality.

Last week, we heard much discussion of the "age profile" of the Aer Lingus workforce, in the course of which regret was expressed at the fact that so many of the staff were young and, therefore, had potentially long working lives ahead of them. We have reached the point where youth and the appetite and ability to work for a living are regarded as *obstacles* to economic progress. The attitude of modern business is increasingly that the ideal worker is a redundant worker.

This negative view of humanity is replicated in the approach to social policy, for when the human unit of production is rendered obsolete by the economic process, he is cast at the mercy of the State which regards him with similar hostility. The logic of this new order is leading us to a proverbial Last Day of economic activity, when only one man in the entire world will remain in employment. The fact that such an eventuality might seriously erode the value of the rest of humanity in their capacity as consumers appears to escape the attention of the enthusiasts of this new order.

And the curious thing is that the new order is being maintained not by some alien species antipathetic to human beings, but actually by men and women who, to the naked eye at least, have all the appearance of being human themselves. The man whose job it is to find and justify redundancies in his company has no difficulty in performing that role. Like the Taoiseach, he regards it as unfortunate but necessary.

If, as I have observed happening in one company recently, he performs his job so efficiently that he has left his employers with no further need for his services, he will be as aggrieved as any human being in a similar situation. But this very human sense of hurt is something he will be capable of experiencing only as a consequence of being a redundant and obsolete personnel manager, of becoming, if you like, a human being once again; as an employee, he cannot allow such considerations to impinge on his work.

The logic of modern business requires a profound dislocation between his humanity and his function in the workplace. He is, for all practical purposes, two different people.

And that goes for all of us. When we hear about the latest purge or workers in this or that company, we shake our heads and regret that economic imperatives and the greater good have made necessary the pain being experienced by our fellow humans. We appear incapable of asking the obvious questions. Like, who gains anyway, and where is all the pain leading us? It is unfortunate, we tell one another, but there is "no gain without pain".

We speak glibly about the need to "bit the bullet", but are rather less blasé if or when the bullet is pointed at our own heads. We acquiesce numbly in a game of Russian roulette which proceeds according to rules that we feel we have no right to question or even understand.

4. BREADHEADS (July 1993)

Breadhead: *A disparaging slang expression for someone who is interested only in money and getting rich, a capitalist. It was common in the hippie era of the 1960s and 1970s, when such an attitude was much frowned on, and is still in use.*

Brewer's Dictionary of
20th-Century Phrase & Fable

It all comes down, in the end, to bread. Or perhaps you have forgotten that the Johnston Mooney and O'Brien building in Ballsbridge, Dublin, about which so much has been heard again in recent days, used to be a bakery. This would not be surprising, for if this fact is mentioned at all in the acreage of commentary about the "fallout" of the Glackin report, it is purely as an aside, as though as an added, gratuitous crumb of information.

It is, on the contrary, the only "fact" of this whole business that really matters. Four and a half years ago, on Good Friday 1989, the Johnston Mooney and O'Brien plant at Ballsbridge closed it doors, adding 485 people to the dole queue. The bakery had made bread and cakes for the people of Dublin for over 150 years, employing a range of skilled and semi-skilled workers. The longest-serving workers got redundancy cheques for up to £13,000, while others left with a few hundred pounds.

Then the breadheads moved in. The Ballsbridge building was firstly sold by the liquidator for £4.4 million. Following a process which, despite wall-to-wall media coverage, remains a mystery to most of us, the building ended up the property of Telecom Eireann, which paid out a sum of £9.4 million for it a year later, in May 1990.

How does a building come to gain £5 million – an added 113 per cent, roughly – in a year? The experts, financiers and consultants would have us believe that the added value of the site has something to do with the expectation of planning permission, but this is merely a superficial aspect of the reality. Even in the world of high finance and capital acquisition, there has to be a fairly sound underlying reason for such a sudden manifestation of added value.

There is a very simple and fundamental reason why this building should suddenly and magically increase in value: because nobody works in it any more. In the modern economy, buildings appear to acquire value in inverse proportion to their level of occupancy, or usefulness, to human beings. Hospitals, schools, factories, airports, all these are economically problematic for as long as they are inhabited and used by large numbers of people. As soon as they are depopulated, however, they accumulate value at an incredible rate.

Workers are a nuisance to business. They tend to be autonomous and unpredictable. They demand wage-packets at the end of the week. They come down with influenza and occasionally need to stop working in order to eat. Luckily, as technology has developed, modern business is required less and less to depend on these unreliable creatures. Within a very short time, I shouldn't wonder, we will have dispensed entirely with the need for human involvement in economic activity. When I say "we", I mean, of course, "they".

The process which ended with the Johnston Mooney and O'Brien site being sold to Telecom Eireann did not begin when the building was vacated by the bakers; it had its roots in a much wider and more profound process which has to do with the role of human beings in the future life of the planet. This is the *real* process underlying the phenomenon we insist on describing as "unemployment" – the gradual removal of human beings from economic activity. Modern business operates to a system which is the economic equivalent of the neutron bomb, destroying human "collateral" but leaving buildings and other infrastructure intact. If you had tried to sell the Ballsbridge bakery with the human workers still inside it, it is far more likely that its market value would have been reduced than doubled.

Remember, too, how the eventual purchasing company, Telecom Eireann, came to be sufficiently "in funds" to splash out on the Ballsbridge building. If you recall, while this scandal was first breaking, two years ago, we had to sit through several re-runs of a television interview with the then chairman of Telecom, Mr Michael Smurfit, in which he boasted about how he had "slimmed-down" the company's workforce from 22,000 to 14,000, and suggested that he might be able to reduce it even further. Politicians and economic commentators paid tribute to the "management skills" which "turned the company around", and in the next sentence pondered upon the intractable mystery of unemployment.

In the three years or so since Telecom purchased the Ballsbridge site, the 8,000 people whom Michael Smurfit "rationalised" out of economic existence have cost the Irish taxpayer, at a conservative estimate, £250 million, which rather puts in perspective the amounts involved in the current controversy. Even the forgotten bakery workers have cost the Irish taxpayer a sum in excess of three times the profit made on the building in which they worked.

But this is not even the point. Whenever we discuss

the continuing "scandals", we translate them into a code which allows us to be outraged while altogether missing the point. "It is always the taxpayer who foots the bill," we whinge. But it isn't, actually. Just as the "scandal" of the Ballsbridge site is but a minor distraction, the £80 million per annum tab which the taxpayer picks up as a consequence of Mr Smurfit's extraordinary entrepreneurial skills is merely an approximate token of the real cost of the rationalisation process for which he is responsible.

The taxpayer "foots" but a nominal sum. It is always the poor, the unemployed, the workless, the excluded, who foot the real bill. Those of us lucky enough to have taxes to pay are, for the moment, protected from the consequences of the process of obsolescence which we implicitly support, or at best choose to ignore. Only when the process threatens our own slice of the cake do we begin to get agitated.

And given that we appear, as a species, to be entirely indifferent to our own imminent economic extinction, it is somewhat remarkable how we continue to be able to work up such fury about what are, in the final analysis, merely the most trivial of its symptoms. The "scandalous" aspects of the Ballsbridge site deal which have preoccupied us again in recent days betray their relative irrelevance in their complexity. The meaning of a true scandal would be obvious immediately to an eight-year-old child – so the opaque quality of the alleged wrongdoing in this case leads one inexorably to the conclusion that the true scandal lies other than in the wheeling and dealing which took place to maximise the return of the various investors.

The true scandal lies in the fact that we have allowed a situation to develop in which buildings designed for work and human activity are more valuable when they are empty, when the human beings and their shouts and jokes and laughs and whistles are no more, when the things they made, the cakes and loaves and bracks, are more profitably produced without human intervention and the workers are dispatched to the economic scrapheap as the world contracts to exclude them.

This is the principal – perhaps the *only* – lesson of the Telecom site scandal. What it illustrates is that we have foresworn the notion of honest work and human activity in favour of idolatry of money and the ideology of the marketplace. Not only do we no longer respect the working man and woman; we venerate their very antithesis. Bakers, millers, confectioners, van-drivers, all of whom gave loyal service to their fellow Irishmen and women, are placed on the scrapheap to make way for the stock-jobber, whose role in life is shuffling money about with no benefit to anybody except himself and his paymasters. We are, moreover, too stupid to see that the process we have unleashed will accept no instructions to spare even its proponents and short-term beneficiaries.

Had we not allowed such a system to evolve, and failed utterly to address the reality of what the system is doing to us, it would not be possible for the breadheads to move in and break the world of human work up for scrap. That is what is happening, and it is the only thing we need to perceive amid the complexity of the Telecom affair. Pursuing one or other of the protagonists will be an exercise in scapegoating, nothing more. The questions raised by the Ballsbridge deal are fundamental questions about human beings and bread and butter. When we have an inquiry or an investigation to examine *these* questions, then and only then will the true scandal become visible.

5. The Value of Feelings   (August 1993)

The impulse of modern business is to remove itself as far as possible from any form of dependence on human

123

beings. And as humans become superfluous, it is likely that the favoured models of economic thinking will continue to create exclusion. What is emerging is a sort of economic short-circuit which excludes that which economics was developed to serve – the interests of mankind as a living species.

Everything that is important to us – our health, happiness, the right to live good lives in harmony with our fellows and the planet – is rapidly being removed from the economic equations that govern the world.

In the words of J. M. Keynes – almost uniquely, an economist *and a thinker* – economics is, when correctly practised, a *moral* science. Moreover, its morality and its potential for efficiency are not independent or separate aspects, but part of a common apparatus for perceiving truth. Economics deals, said Keynes, with introspection and values, but also with "motives, expectations, psychological uncertainties".

The economist had constantly to be on guard against treating the subject matter of economics as homogeneous or fixed. "It is as though the fall of the apple to the ground depended on the apple's motives, on whether it is worthwhile falling to the ground, and whether the ground wanted the apple to fall, and on mistaken calculations on the part of the apple as to how far it was from the centre of the earth."

Keynes was talking about the possibility of an economics to mirror the human condition. But even if this remains a fantasy, the challenge which economics must surely confront is to find ways of quantifying the human and moral elements of transactions which are rendered invisible by conventional economic calculus. Modern economics appears incapable of informing proper moral choices, or indeed making anything but the most simplistic calculations about cost and value. Economics is the sanctified telling of lies.

Environmental damage, for example, is something that economics appears incapable of accounting. Take an example of two identical objects on a shelf in a shop in Galway. One has been made from locally produced materials by a local craftsman and is on sale for £5. The other has been imported from Korea and is priced at £4.50. The logic of market economics tells the shopper that the Korean object is the better value.

But how much of the "bargain" appeal of the Korean-made object results from the fact that its costs are not properly evaluated? What about the environmental cost of the motorways and trucks which transported the object along various parts of its journey? What about the human cost of the exploitative nature of the labour market in the originating country? The exclusion of such factors from the price of the finished product means, in effect, a form of subsidy which makes nonsense of the notion of a "free" market.

Economics, being in the service of utilitarianism, regards human costs as little above irrelevant. But what is to be the fate of the Galway craftsman who is unable to sell his wares because a Korean brand, as a result of distorted costings, can undersell him? Should the welfare payments on which he is obliged to live as a result of being unable to sell his wares not also have a place in the transaction? What about the possibility that his sons, through lack of opportunity, will take to drugs or crime? Does this not *also* have a cost, which must be accounted for before the purchaser can, on the basis of the two price-tags, dismiss the Galway-made object in favour of the Korean one?

The most important element of economic survival in the future will be the capacity of states, societies and communities to instil concepts of loyalty into their own people. This will not be a romantic or chauvinistic loyalty, but a loyalty to the truth in the face of the reality that the game has been rigged. This loyalty will lead the shopper to buy the locally made object, even though it is identical to the cheaper foreign-made one, not because of insularity or sentiment, but because common sense says there is more to the equation than meets the eye.

There is nothing chauvinistic about this. The consumer is also, perhaps, a taxpayer and a potential victim of crime. The same loyalty/common sense would lead the person confronted with two similar objects in a Korean shop to buy the Korean-made object, because that will keep the Korean craftsman in work and his sons out of jail.

What is required is a new and more complex model of economic accounting which can identify and factor-in all the conceivable costs of any transaction, at least in a notional way, and make this intelligence available to the consumer at the point of sale. Thus, goods or service on sale in the open market should be either priced to reflect the total amount of their costs under a broad range of headings, or at least be obliged to reveal fully the extent to which their prices are distorted for whatever reason.

A possible system might follow along the lines of the current requirements for the detailing of ingredients, nutritional and environmental aspects, which are now commonplace labelling practice. In the same way as the label on a jar of horseradish sauce informs the purchaser that it contains malt vinegar, sugar, vegetable oil, salt, skimmed milk powder, etc., and has 19g of carbohydrates per 100g of sauce, why not a similar system for imparting information about the environmental and human factors relevant to the purchaser?

Thus, the benefits of keeping employment in a locality by purchasing a locally made product could be quantified on a label under the heading Local Employment Factor. This calculation could include elements like the reduced social welfare bill and crime figures in the region resulting from the maintenance of employment.

Similarly, the Environment Factor would be based on a quantification of the reduction in environmental damage resulting from transportation, because the product is made nearby. And so on. Every possible aspect of work and human living – from occupational stress to the benefits to local self-confidence – could be estimated and incorporated in some notional way.

The labels on imported products would contain similar data, except that this would be more likely to reflect in a negative manner factors resulting from distance, ecological wear-and-tear, inferior production methods, poor wages or working conditions, and so on. Thus, even if the prices of similar products were different, the customer would be able to make a full and proper decision based on the actual, rather than the market-regulated, costs.

Such a holistic economic calculus would help restore the equilibrium of local economies everywhere by protecting them from the gadfly global market. An airplane ticket for a flight by a domestic airline, for example, might include a calculation of the benefits to the national economy of having over 12,000 people employed in secure employment who might otherwise, through unemployment, be a major drain on the financial resources of the intending passenger in his role as a taxpayer.

This information might make one pause for thought before opting for the loss-leading "special offer" from the competing multinational airline with no responsibility or loyalty towards the domestic economy.

Or, if an investment prospectus was obliged to

include calculations of all the likely implications of a particular investment for the economy in which the potential investor was resident, the option of offshore deals might appear considerably less appropriate or attractive.

John Maynard Keynes, who, as he put it himself, was "brought up to respect free trade not only as an economic doctrine which a rational and instructed person could not doubt, but almost as part of the moral law", come eventually to the view that financial dealings which did not include a view of their impact on the community of the investor were not merely ill-advised, but actually *wrong*.

"There may be some financial calculation," he wrote in 1933, "which shows it to be advantageous that my savings should be invested in whatever quarter of the hospitable globe shows the greatest marginal efficiency of capital or the highest rate of interest. But experience is accumulating that remoteness between ownership and operation is an evil."

By this he meant that the investor should take account of aspects other than profit-margin and security, not for sentimental reasons, but out of responsibility to the larger laws of economic reality.

In short, what is needed is a re-evaluation of *value* and its relationship to the concept of *values*. Values arise not out of some abstract moral system, but from the technical necessities of survival and social efficiency. Values have been largely bypassed by modern economics in pursuit of short-term return, which is then confused with *value*. What is needed is a reorientation of economics to take account of human needs, now and in the future in a world without end.

The 19th-century British economist David Ricardo wrote of the role of "feelings" in economic thinking.

Certain "feelings", he believed, induced "most men" to be satisfied with "a low rate of profits in their own country, rather than seek a more advantageous employment for their wealth in foreign countries". *Feelings*, in this sense, of course, is a synonym for "responsibility", for consciousness about the complex web of consequences of every financial or economic decision. We will know we are back on track when we hear a modern economist speaking of "feelings" without a curl of the lip.

6. WHERE THE MONEY COMES FROM   (August 1993)

On this page on 19 August, Mr Brian Patterson, chief operating officer of Waterford Crystal, wrote that my views on economics are "not just wrong but dangerously misleading" because I fail to make what he described as a "connection with reality" by not answering the question "where does the money come from?"

Mr Patterson cited two examples. It is interesting that, in respect of one – the 1991 sub-post offices issue – he defined the question I have not addressed as "who pays?", but in respect of the Aer Lingus issue he defines it as "where does the money come from?" It does not appear to have occurred to him that "who pays?" and "where does the money come from?" are two different questions.

The first I have attempted to answer many times. The people who pay are always, *always* the poor, the unemployed, the old, the sick and those not yet born. The rest of us may *think* we are paying, may gripe about increased taxes and so on, but *actual* payment is made not in pieces of paper but in cold, pain, hunger and misery. Money may be used to *represent* some forms of payment, as a token of certain recognised transactions, but – largely because of the limitations of modern economics – it is a crude and inexact medium at best.

The second question, "where does the money come from?" is a familiar catchcry of Irish economists wishing to conceal the nature of their own role. It is largely a technical question, not, as Mr Patterson would have us believe, one of the absolute supply of resources. It is about choices between options.

Take the sub-post offices issue. Mr Patterson writes that my defence of these post offices is "from a social perspective a good argument". This implies that the word "social" has an application outside the realm of economics, to do perhaps with compassion or philanthropy. Elsewhere, he refers to what, with just a hint of irony, he terms my "humanitarianism". The subtext is: in an ideal world, it would be nice to be able to maintain all these post offices, because after all, we are all in favour of old people and communities, but we must face "reality".

My argument for post offices is an economic one. The politicians, under advice from bad economists, close down a post office on the basis that the across-the-counter transactions do not pay for the operation of the service, and immediately a range of interdependent elements in the local economy begins to collapse. The post office has been drawing people in to do business in the local shops and pubs, but now they travel to the nearest town, perhaps 15 miles away. Dozens of cars are now whizzing daily in and out of town, 15 miles away, resulting in the loss of man-hours, wear and tear to road infrastructure and permanent damage to the environment. The postman no longer goes to every door but drops the mail in a box at the head of the road.

These are some obvious changes which result from

the closure. My point is not that they are lamentable consequences of modern methods, but that they are phenomena with economic consequences which economists ignore.

What about the increased risk to elderly citizens as a result of the postman having been declared unviable? Does this not have an economic cost? What about the environmental costs? What about the bigger picture arising out of the decline of services across an already depopulated region?

First the post offices, then the shops and pubs, then the schools, and soon everything and everyone is gone. Does this not have "economic" consequences, for example in the loss of a tourism resource to the overall economy? Why are economists not required to take account of these factors?

This is what I meant when I wrote that the modern practice of economics is the "sanctified telling of lies". When an economist proposing the closure of a post office is able to show that he has taken steps to account for all the possible economic consequences of that measure, *then* perhaps the question of "viability" may arise. But at that point, might it not be asked whether a seemingly "unviable" operation should be maintained with a view to reinvigorating the local economy?

Economists may be familiar with this concept; it is called "investment". If and when these questions have been fully explored, and it has been shown beyond reasonable dispute that the service in question has no prospect of becoming "viable", the question of "social perspective" may arise. *Then*, my alleged humanitarianism may become relevant.

But even then, are we to assume that "social" benefits accruing from "unviable" activity are without an economic basis? This is a larger issue, raising fundamental questions about the role of economics. I would argue that the *only* role for economics is in social organisation, that otherwise the law of the jungle is a sufficient mechanism of itself. To talk of "social" arguments separately from economics is therefore misleading.

The question "where does the money come from?" is not as decisive a question as economists would have you believe. It is *always* a matter of choices and preferences. In their disingenuous way, economists attempt to suggest that the availability of money in an economy is analogous to the way income is available to the average worker. This too is misleading.

Money for governments running their national economies is not a finite resource but rather a lubricant with which to tap the real wealth of human beings and the earth. It functions like blood inside the human body, carrying benefits to the various limbs and organs of the economy. Tying a bandage tightly around an arm or a leg does not result in a "saving" of blood, but in the atrophy of the limb and an increased vulnerability to disease.

The average citizen, in managing a personal or household budget, does not have power to expand the money supply or increase taxes, but he *can* move spending from one area to another. Governments have infinitely more power and control. The point is that economists work on the basis of choices, usually based on considerations that are either political, ideological or the expression of a vested interest, a reality concealed behind crude costings and untruths. Their favoured options are frequently adverse to the weakest sections of society.

When economists suggest that there is "no money" for something, what they mean is that they do not believe that the investment in question is as worthwhile as some other form of spending. If this merely involved the expression of an opinion, there would be no great problem, but economists have a great deal of influence on government policy and it is therefore a matter of grave concern when they justify their recommendations on the basis of inadequate calculations as to true value.

"Enterprises which are not viable will either collapse or have to be subsidised by taxes on the money or wealth generated by someone else," Mr Patterson asserts. This is rather obvious, but what it leaves out is a recognition of the pervasiveness of subsidies in the modern economy. Almost everything is subsidised in one way or another, whether it is private housing or farming or industry. The *real* question is why economists always seem to recommend some forms of subsidy and not others.

Economists shake their heads and say that we can no longer afford a hospital or railway line, but blandly talk about investment in, for example, the chemical industry, as though this were the most necessary and sensible thing in the world. In neither case do they attempt to go beyond the most obvious accounting procedures in justifying their opinions.

In effect, they are acting not as economists, but as *accountants*. It is surely not the economist's job to tell us what we can or cannot afford, but to find ways of achieving what is beneficial.

We are told that it is necessary to destroy 1,500 jobs in order to make Aer Lingus "viable". I say this is a bad economic choice. Assume, for the sake of round figures, that each of those workers is earning £15,000 a year. Of this, some £6,000 reverts to the government in income tax and other levies. The net cost of each of those jobs is therefore £9,000. If someone is made unemployed, the State will have to pay them in social welfare and other supports a sum roughly equal to the net cost of keeping them in work.

The so-called "saving" achieved within Aer Lingus will

have created an equivalent degree of real costs externally. And this is not even to begin accounting for the myriad of indirect costs associated with the decline of morale among the redundant workers, the decline in quality of the product offered by the airline and the innumerable ripples throughout the economy. Thus, a decision made in the interests of economic "viability" creates a movement of invisible consequences *which are themselves of an economic nature*.

So, when Mr Patterson asks me "Where does the money come from?" I answer in two ways. First I ask *him* where he thinks the money will come from to pay for the increased policing and other costs incurred in a society disintegrating because of the abolition of work and the absence of the cohesion provided by public services. Then I give him the answer, which is that the wherewithal for services essential for a good life is already *there*, but has been rendered invisible by bad economics.

Sub-post offices "pay" for themselves, many times over, in the level of cohesion they contribute to the communities – and therefore to the economies – of countless Irish villages. Without that cohesion, there would be no communities, no Ireland, and therefore no economy worth talking about. Humanitarianism doesn't come into it.

7. THE STRUGGLE AGAINST PLACELESSNESS

(August 1993)

For most of the present century, we have conducted a debate on the basis of the spurious dichotomies between public and private, capital and labour. The economic questions facing the human race as we enter the 21st century will not be to do with ideology but with people and place. The real issue, it must increasingly be apparent, is between the global and the local, between the external and internal, between big and small.

Nor is this a matter of chauvinism or isolationism, as many of the soon-to-be-redundant orthodox voices would have us believe. When I make an argument on behalf of, for example, the West of Ireland, I am not simply being "loyal" to a particular place; I am pleading for *everyplace*, using the west of Ireland as both parable and example. I am expressing the need that now exists for each human being to realise a loyalty to a place he or she can call home.

Simple-minded ideologues will always attempt to respond to such arguments by converting them into jingoistic battles between one place and another. One town's gain is another town's loss; one region's wealth is another's poverty. This is usually either stupidity or dishonesty, and frequently both. The real battle is between everyplace and noplace, between those who believe in the idea of home and those who believe only in the idea of money. The great British economist John Maynard Keynes was in the habit of defining the driving force of capitalism as a vice, which he called "love of money". Capitalism has come to believe inordinately in that element of its own propaganda which held that, because we have failed to develop an equally efficient but more worthy motivator of human activity, the profit motive is virtuous of itself.

Moreover, because the main impulse of political leadership is to expand its power both upwards and outwards, there has been an unhappy coincidence between the aspirations of politics and the vested interest of big business. The moral imperative with which we might have put a rein on both politics and business has been almost entirely eroded as politics came to be

135

exclusively concerned with the development of stable global finance systems to enable the maximum freedom of economic movement between states and nations. We are fast moving to a situation where there will be at most two or three competing units in the world economy, rendering national boundaries and local cultural integrities increasingly in the face of transnational and planetary forces.

To further this process we have, over the past couple of decades, been subjected to a relentless campaign of "softening-up", designed to release our holds on concepts of nationhood, community and home. "You can't buck the market," they tell us. "There's no such thing as society." Emigration is a legitimate economic instrument. "We're all Europeans now."

What they mean is that we're all *consumers* now. The loyalty that is required of us a "Europeans" is not to a culture or a history or a society, but to a consumer superstate in which a citizen's worth is measured in purchasing power. Within this economic superstate, the only philosophy or vision on offer is the law of the naked market. Competition is the chief mediator of right and wrong, weakness and strength. Economies of scale have superseded considerations of local benefit, and specialisation has led many once largely self-reliant countries and communities to put all their eggs in one basket. Big is bountiful. The market and its intrinsic even-handedness is a matter of almost religious faith.

Such uncritical adoration of the free market in a world of topographical and climatic diversity, and populated by unreliable humans, is, it must be obvious, utter folly. The ideologues of the free market talk as though the Earth were flat and smooth and inhabited by stainless steel robots without the need to cry or laugh or sing. In such a world, the breezes of the free market might well blow gently and evenly over all the world, bestowing benefits on every robot in more or less equal measure, with the range of possible inequity being statistically calculable according to a mathematical formula. In the real world, which as we know is characterised by varying landscapes, ungeometrically shaped mountain formations and unpredictable features like oceans, rivers, forests and suchlike – and inhabited by people of all conceivable shapes, sizes and temperaments – the free market works better as an idea than a reality.

It is virtually inescapable that the enforcement of this free-market fantasy in an even-handed fashion, on the variegated world of people with short legs and long legs, differing strengths and talents, loud voices and soft, some with post-colonial trauma and others with post-imperial hubris, should result in the perpetuation of inequality and the supremacy of the strong. Market forces, when applied to a world of entrenched differences, result in the convergence of wealth in places of maximum opportunity, as surely as gravity draws water to the lowest points on the land. To assume the neutrality of such forces is to behave as though the world were a swimming pool with a flat bottom.

Among the consequences of the unambiguous veneration of the global market is a serious distortion of the relationships between people and place. The notion that "we are all Europeans now" requires someone living in Leitrim, or Clondalkin, or Dublin's inner-city to, economically speaking, perceive his own neighbours in precisely the same way as he regards a notional citizen of Bonn or Strasbourg. The globalism of the free market disallows concept of loyalty to nation, culture, locality, community or home. Only the price-tag is allowed to matter.

If an individual community – be it family, town or city

– wishes to survive, it must strive towards operating conditions comparable to those of entirely different societies on the other side of the globe. As the vice-chairman of Goodyear has so succinctly put it: "Until we get real wage levels down much closer to those of the Brazils and the Koreas, we cannot pass along productivity gains to wages and still be competitive." The logic is simple: if you cannot make free-market economics work in the real world, you make the real world more and more homogeneous until the reality fits the theory. Any manifestation of difference, be it geographical, environmental, cultural, psychological or developmental, becomes a negative asset in this drive towards efficiency and productivity, because some less precious and "parochially minded" community will always be got to undercut and make do.

We are all of us, even the economists, human beings, with a human need for home and community. All of us have a vested interest in the restoration to economics of a sense of place. The alternatives are not between Korea and Leitrim, or between Dublin and Bonn, but between a *place* and a *non-place*, between *place* and *placelessness*. The real conflict is between the reality of human life and work and the abstract and arbitrary rule of the free market. In choosing the "parochial" option, the shopper is striking a blow for the survival of a particular place and human community, as opposed to striking for the supremacy of free market forces which have no loyalty to place or person. The true choice is between love of neighbour and love of money.

The advocates of the free market, of course, are quick to interrupt such argument with shouts of "protectionist!" and so on. There is, however, quite respectable opinion to be found on this subject. J. M. Keynes, hardly a raving communist, and certainly no bleeding heart, wrote: "I

138

sympathise with those who would minimise, rather than maximise, economic entanglement among nations. Ideas, knowledge, science, hospitality, travel – these are things which should of their nature be international. But let goods be homespun whenever it is reasonably and conveniently possible and, above all, let finance be primarily national."

What is at issue is the fundamental principle of democracy itself. For in a global economy, inhabited by consumers rather than people, the human being is doubly disenfranchised. He is disenfranchised firstly by virtue of the denial of the integrity of his humanity as existing without need of further justification. Only the human being who is also a fully participating *consumer* is a full citizen. But he is disenfranchised also by the failure of the marketplace to value his contribution as a human being – his work, skills, talent, genius – and his right to remain in a place he calls home.

What this attacks is the very *independence* of the human person. This failure to value the individual's contribution and place nurtures profound dangers for the democratic process, because a citizen without rights cannot reasonably be expected to exercise responsibility. The current disrespect for person and place will lead inexorably towards the alienation of everyone and the consequent inhospitableness of everyplace.

8. BOOM FOR WHOM? (April 1994)

I heard an economist on the radio last week suggesting that we were within a whisker of full employment. He was very plausible. In terms of the way he sees the world, he is undoubtedly correct. His analysis was that, if you subtract from the 300,000 jobless total the number of people who are long-term unemployed (long-term unemployment, he explained, is a "different problem"), and take into account the normal employment turnover and the need for a pool of people to supply the jobs market, and blah-blah-blah, then if we can create a few thousand more jobs per annum "we will effectively have full employment".

I don't know if he was using mirrors, but nobody seems to have expressed the slightest incredulity at his analysis. So why should I? The truth is whatever you want it to be.

The subject under discussion was the impending era of boom and bloom, as predicted by the recent Economic and Social Research Institute (ESRI) report. The economist's response might, in a certain light, pass for a reasonable encapsulation of the generality of public responses to that report. When I say "public responses", I do not, of course, mean the responses of *the public*. The public is a completely different matter. What I mean is the "range" of responses in the public discourse which emerged in the media.

That "range" was almost surprisingly narrow, even for this society. There was the odd note of slight caution, the occasional grave warning about not counting chickens, the token nod in the direction of the "less fortunate". But by and large the ESRI report was greeted without scepticism. We were invited to forget the realities and feel the "feel-good factor".

It is tempting to enter at this juncture a slight note of begrudgery. But this, of course, would be churlish, pointless and perhaps a little absurd. One might be tempted, for instance, to go back through the record of previous ESRI reports, the observe the way in which practically every single report of the past five years advanced similarly optimistic predictions. It would be a waste of time. Given the logic and statistical context in which they are based, the ESRI predictions are absolutely irrefutable.

And it would be niggardly and small-minded to note that, in its report of August 1989, the ESRI predicted that growth rates of up to 6 per cent in the coming years would result in a net drop of 36,000 in unemployment by 1994. The official unemployment figure at that time was 230,000. I could lamely suggest that, instead of the 1994 figure of 194,000 unemployed which the 1989 ESRI prediction might appear to have anticipated, we are now rumoured to have something in the region of 300,000 people out of work. But, of course, I am unable to make any such obvious calculation, because I don't know whether that prediction was intended to exclude the long-term unemployed, the normal turnover of workless persons, those people over a certain age or of a particular height, girth or eye-colour. Clearly, any conclusion I might come to about this is open to contradiction by those who make up the rules by which the "reality" of this economy is measured. I literally don't know what I'm talking about.

Up to a point, all this doesn't matter in the least. ESRI reports are ESRI reports, the public discourse is the public discourse, and reality is its usual unco-operative self. On the other hand, there is a certain element of cause and effect. ESRI reports are not like the astrological predictions in the more popular papers, which you can read for a laugh and then forget all about. ESRI reports are taken seriously by those charged with running the economy. When the ESRI calls for reductions in borrowing, decreases in public spending, or less funding for agriculture, such advice is likely to have an impact on the way the economy is organised.

A number of questions arise from this. Firstly, on

whose behalf is the institute's influence brought to bear on the public debate about economics? Secondly, what is the actual effect of the kind of forecasts and advice which the ESRI provides? On the first question I would say that the influence of the ESRI is overwhelmingly applied to the interests of the status quo. While the institute occasionally engages in mild criticism of government policy, the broad thrust of its contributions has been to support conservative policies and to urge caution at every turn. While the institute does occasionally produce reports dealing with poverty, that subject is invariably treated separately from its main business of commenting upon economic trends. There is very little evidence of any integrated thinking which might attempt to perceive the Irish economy in a broadly social or human context.

The answer to the second question flows directly from the answers to the first. The thrust of ESRI reports in recent years has been to buttress the national complacency in the face of the crisis which this society faces. Anyone with even a superficial knowledge of the realities of this economy will be aware that the present perception of buoyancy is due in large measure to the inflow of European funding and the expansion of the non-indigenous sectors of Irish industry. These periodic interventions, which blithely throw around growth figures with little or no basis in the reality of this society's capacity to sustain itself, contribute in large measure to the perpetuation of self-delusion. The trend can be seen in the kind of comment which follows such reports, like that of the economist mentioned above.

What is striking is the way the selective information provided subtly begins to suggest the possibility of a society somewhat smaller than before. The "real" economy contracts to embrace the good news. Boom and bloom, they tell us. *For whom?* we ask. The answer is implicit: *for people like us.*

Increased emigration due to an improvement in international conditions is again one of the factors on which we will depend for a rise in the living standards of some of those who remain. Meanwhile, we are being encouraged, it seems, to discount also many of those "less fortunate" who remain. Fuelled by the optimistic predictions, *people like us* seek to make the delusion even more invigorating. Inconvenient unemployment figures begin to be rationalised out of existence, so "normality" can acquire an even more positive complexion. All of a sudden, we find that the "long-term unemployed" are not a problem anymore, because they are less than full citizens, "a different problem". What is the definition of "long-term"? Twenty years out of work? No. After just one year out of work, you become "a different problem", by implication one with a less pressing need of a solution.

It must become obvious that, with such statistical flexibility at our disposal, there is no longer any reason to be pessimistic about *anything*. The ideology of complacency allows us to simply narrow the goal posts whenever the fundamentals seem inconvenient.

Thus, we observe the absolute folly of arguing with our economist friend. By his analysis, it is theoretically possible to have "full employment" in an economy in which not a single person is working. If you *want* to "feel good", you can. Only the lowest form of begrudger would find fault with your optimism.

9. THE CAVALRY SIGHTED   (September 1993)

Perhaps the most disturbing aspect of Irish social and

economic failure has been its tendency to perpetuate itself. What Professor Joe Lee has called the "thought deficit" at the heart of Irish public affairs has created wave upon wave of emigration, which in turn has reduced even further our ability to think our way out of the maze.

In my view, this haemorrhaging of thought is a more serious consequence of emigration that the much talked-about loss of "entrepreneurial spirit"; indeed, the obsession with the entrepreneurial spirit may itself be seen as a symptom of the deficit of thought.

This is partly the explanation for the current abysmal state of Irish economic thinking. Unfortunately, there are few statistics available relating to the rate of emigration among young economists, but the fact remains that no younger generation of economic thinkers has emerged to challenge the Methuselahs who have dominated the public stage for the past two decades.

There may be just the faintest hope that this is about to change. Last week, at the annual social policy conference of the Conference of Major Religious Superiors in Dublin, I listened to a talk by two Irish economists who appear to have defied the prohibition on thinking which governs their profession in this country.

Eamon O'Shea and Brendan Kennelly, two young economists from University College, Galway, presented a paper entitled "Poverty, Values and Public Policy", which causes me to pause a moment before pulling the chain on Irish economic thinking. (And yes, I am aware that the notion of a "young" economist appears anachronistic of itself, but I promise you that their average age is almost certainly on the tender side of forty).

Judging from the *Irish Times* letters page, there is an impression abroad that I am unsympathetic to economists. In point of fact, I am unsympathetic only to *bad* economists; the problem has been that in Ireland we see very little of the other kind.

Most of the leading Irish economists – those who staff the economics departments of Irish universities, whom we see on *Prime Time* and who advise politicians on policy – have been unable to escape from a particular moment in recent economic history. To say that they are all of a neo-classical bent is only partly to describe the situation.

It may have struck you that most of them are about the same age – mid-40s to mid-50s. Most can be traced to what has been called the Doheny and Nesbitt School – a mischievous designation, perhaps, but one which gives a hint of their shared beliefs.

Almost all our currently most influential economists were educated in the Keynes era but finished their training in the white heat of the 1970s' reaction to his interventionist ideas. Most of them appear to have acquired a pathological aversion to Mr Keynes and his philosophy and to have high-tailed it in what they perceived to be the opposite ideological direction.

As a result, virtually all of them have subscribed to the same ideas – mainly those of right-wing, market-fixated economists like Friedman and Hayek. Their dogged adherence to such views is partly explained by their formative experience of 1970s' Irish deficit budgeting, for which they have posthumously and somewhat implausibly placed much of the blame on Mr Keynes.

For more than a decade, their simplistic prognoses were entertained in public discussions as the only plausible antidote to past madness. As Proinsias Breathnach, of St Patrick's College, Maynooth, observed at a recent conference at Queen's University, Belfast, Irish economists have been preoccupied with cost minimisation and have shown "little grasp of the broad social structures which constrain and shape the behaviour of individual economic actors."

For a long time, the public has been sold the myth that no alternative form of thinking existed or was possible. The Doheny and Nesbitt stream had seeped into every crevice of public thought, with its mantras being parroted by every two-bit entrepreneur and commentator whose opinions were solicited.

Newspaper leader-writers and radio and television anchorpersons appeared to see their role as policing the implementation of these narrow doctrines in every area of Irish life. "Where is the money going to come from?" they chorused, until we relinquished all right to ask any other questions.

But now, I tell you friends, I have seen the first of the cavalry come over the hill. "This paper", write Eamon O'Shea and Brendan Kennelly in the first paragraph of their presentation to the CMRS, "is written by two economists who profess, publicly at any rate, to follow a discipline that, for the most part, ignores values." Not a bad admission for a start.

The paper goes on: "Neo-classical economics, by concentrating mainly on individualism and efficiency, often ignores the implication of its theories for poverty and the distribution of income." This, I hear you think, sounds like the basis of another pious aspiration, but it is nothing of the kind.

Using an analysis of recent Irish debates about poverty as an illustration, O'Shea and Kennelly address the fundamental question of the relationship between equity and efficiency in a modern economy. Conventional economic thinking has perceived the pursuit of equity as inimical to efficiency. Concepts like "solidarity" and "justice" have been seen by traditional economists as optional extras to be addressed only when the economy was functioning "properly".

As O'Shea and Kennelly point out, neo-classical thinking has entirely disregarded the role of community values. If I understand them correctly, they are saying that utilitarianism is not merely "unfair", but that it leads to incorrect evaluations. To say, then, that economists have discounted community values is not merely a comment on the preferences of those economists, but also on their inability to perceive and quantify the multiplicity of benefits which accrue as intrinsic aspects of transactions at levels beyond the exercise of rational individualism.

In other words, in an economy comprising human beings engaged in a multitude of complex inter-relationships, equity and social justice are not questions of altruism, but are a prerequisite for *efficiency*.

The implementation of just social policies is therefore not something to be pursued in the wake of successful development, but is a *sine qua non* for such development. Compassion is beside the point, and yet becomes it, willy-nilly. Words like "morality" and "ethics" require to be seen for what they are – concepts relating to competent organisation rather than simply abstract theologising.

The "coincidence" between what is "right" and what is most efficient, of course, is anything but accidental: "the common good" is at once a technical and a moral proposition. "If individuals recognise certain social relationships are part of their own self-identity," write O'Shea and Kennelly, "then acting for others is not a constraint or a pre-determined abstract imperative but a way of pursuing one's own good."

And as they also point out, what we most urgently require is a common language to express our mutual solidarity, a language "that will allow us to communicate with each other about the needs that make us human".

147

Over the past decade, many such needs, as well as the intricate web of consequences they unleashed, seeped from under the conventional analyses and as a result went unquantified.

The outcome has been a disjunction between descriptions of reality and the reality itself, a growing chasm between the "fundamentally sound" Ireland and the place which such rhetoric purported to describe.

Elsewhere in recent times, there have been signs of the stirring of change, a growing recognition that the market no longer works in the way conventional economies would have us believe. In this connection, I could mention the unrelenting good sense of John Kenneth Galbraith, or recommend a new book, *The Market Experience*, by the British economist Robert E. Lane (Cambridge University Press).

As in so many things, we might reasonably have expected to need to wait ten years for such new ideas to percolate into the Irish mind. Thinking such as is present in the O'Shea/Kennelly paper suggests the faintest hope that we may be able to cheat fate at least this once in a while.

Every politician, priest, newspaper pundit and public servant should take a day off work to read their paper, which is published in the CMRS booklet, *New Frontiers for New Citizenship*. RTE producers, on reading it, might even be prevailed upon to alter their long-standing approach to economic issues, and, in doing so, give members of the McDowell family a much-needed rest.

10. UP THE BEGRUDGERS   (May 1991)

For some time now I have been meaning to undertake a defence of what is perhaps the most maligned species in

Irish society: the begrudger. In the light of comments by the psychiatrist Dr Anthony Clare, at the recent Irish Management Institute conference in Killarney, I now feel that this is something that cannot continue to remain on the long finger.

"Fatalism, pessimism, begrudgery and subservience," Dr Clare told the assembled businessmen, agog for clues as to how they might extract a few more drops of sweat from the brows of their workers, "the list of negative attributes pinned opposite the Irish character is truly formidable."

I have the height of respect for Dr Clare. He is a fine psychiatrist and a brilliant broadcaster. If, as is sometimes hinted, he were to run for public office, I would have no difficulty in voting for him. But, really, is this the sort of thing he should be saying in front of mere businessmen?

There was a time when it was quite acceptable to be sceptical of businessmen, but nowadays this is regarded as something of a sin. The pendulum has now swung completely in the other direction, and there is a widespread belief that successful businessmen are, by definition, more intelligent than the rest of mankind, that they are "leaders of men".

This belief has been promulgated mainly by members of the business community themselves, though with some help from that extraordinary branch of my own profession, business journalism. Even I myself have been taken in by this propaganda – so much so that on one occasion in my early days in journalism I volunteered to do a series of in-depth interview/profiles on leading Irish businessmen for a newspaper which I perceived to be below average in its coverage of the heroic deeds of the business community.

I pointed out to the editor that none of the business coverage in his newspaper conveyed anything of the sheer breadth of genius which clearly populated the boardrooms of the land. "Have you ever actually met any of these guys?" he asked. "No," I replied. "Well, take my word for it," he told me, "they are among the most stupid people on God's earth."

Successful businessmen, he declared, were by definition vain, narrow-minded, egotistical, uncultured and totally lacking in any social vision. In fact, he averred, such characteristics were not only compatible with a highly successful business career, but seemed, in fact, to be downright essential.

I found this hard to believe. In fact, to be honest, I immediately had the editor down as a begrudger. I went ahead and attempted a couple of interviews anyway, interviewing some household names among the entrepreneurial classes. Both the individuals in question turned out to be, as the editor had assured me, "among the top ten bores in the world". A fortnight later I walked back into his office and apologised for having doubted his opinion.

It is for this reason that I now question Dr Anthony Clare's wisdom in talking about the hugely complex subject of begrudgery in such literal-minded company. Perhaps Dr Clare surmised that this is the kind of stuff that businessmen like to hear, in which case he is undoubtedly correct. Such ideas are music to the tone-deaf ears of a breed which appears to have an almost pathological need to believe that the rest of us are out to topple its pile. From the mouth of a doctor as – quite rightly – respected as Dr Clare, such notions are the stuff of their auto-erotic dreams.

It is time, I think, to reclaim the concept of begrudgery for its rightful custodians: the begrudgers themselves.

There is certainly a strain in the Irish personality which will forever begrudge others their good fortunes and advancements, but I do not believe that this is necessarily a trait which we should disparage, and particularly not in the company of businessmen. Professor J. J. Lee, in his excellent volume *Ireland 1912-1985: Politics and Society*, credits us Irish with coining the word "begrudger" as a means of self-deception, but he also notes, in the course of a fine mini-essay on the subject, that the documentary evidence of the effects of begrudgery on our behaviour is pretty thin on the ground.

It is interesting to note that Professor Lee found himself the somewhat bemused key-note speaker at the same conference as Dr Clare addressed. I wonder if it wasn't that two-page analysis of begrudgery (in a book of 750 pages) which merited Professor Lee his invitation.

In his book, to be sure, Professor Lee hits the begrudgers a couple of well-aimed slaps over their skulking, dandruffed heads. He notes that it was a tradition of Irish society that "immense amounts of time were devoted to spiting the other fellow". But he also observes that "the begrudger mentality did arrive fairly rationally from a mercantilist concept of the size of the status cake", and that since the size of that cake was more or less fixed, "one man's gain did tend to be another man's loss".

These are the kind of subtleties which the professor's audience in Killarney could afford to allow to drift over its head, in the sure knowledge that it would escape also the net of the trade press in its pursuit of that most succulent of headlines: "We are a Nation of Begrudgers!"

Over the past few years, I've noticed, members of the Irish business community have begun to take refuge in the concept of begrudgery in much the same way as we Catholics have been brought up to believe in the devil. Even the merest hint of a criticism of their motives, methods or manoeuvrings, immediately invites the taunt of "begrudger" – regardless of the motivation of the criticism. This is a handy way of discouraging all scrutiny of their activities and of defusing all dissent.

To listen to a particular brand of entrepreneur, one would think that the only thing standing between the Irish people and boundless wealth and happiness was this unfortunate tendency to "begrudge" those who get up at the first burr of the alarm clock. Those who do not wholeheartedly endorse the entrepreneur's breathtaking path to glory, his savoir faire, intelligence and wit, his hale and uninhibited enjoyment of the fruits of his endeavours, his boundless munificence towards his employees, his ability to get up early in the morning, are portrayed as malevolent and small-minded, carping sneeringly out of the sides of their mouths about the success of their betters.

I suggest that, on the contrary, our undoubted talent for the well-turned jeer is practically the only thing standing between us and the utter depravity of an unfettered capitalist "culture". If you require an insight into what is involved in this truly appalling vista, I suggest you spend a couple of hours one weekend perusing the gossip columns of the Sunday newspapers, most of which concern themselves with the wit, wisdom and wherewithals of the entrepreneurial classes. But don't attempt it on a full stomach.

Most of what passes for socio-economic discourse in this country has to do with the tension between the individual's right to make a profit and that of the majority to continue to eat. Or, to put it another way, with the extent to which a brake should be put on the activities of the entrepreneurial classes in the interest of the common good. Given the levels of inequality which already exist in this society, it seems to me that, in this context, the Irish tendency towards begrudgery, far from being disparaged, should be elevated to the status of a fundamental and inalienable human right. Anyone for a referendum?

VII

THE ABSURD WORKPLACE

1. BEYOND LIP-SERVICE (March 1991)

Has it ever struck you as strange that the people who speak on behalf of "The Unemployed" are, by definition, not themselves unemployed? This is dangerous territory, mined with platitudes and kneejerk responses, but it is one in which a little reality need to be reasserted.

Unemployment and its social effect is now a feature of the turn of every month. In the newspapers and on the broadcast media, the announcement of still more "alarming" unemployment figures is followed hard by a succession of politicians and professional spokespeople engaging in extended bouts of hand-wringing about the "tragedy" of the "jobless".

Everything – and I mean *everything* – written or stated in the Irish media about unemployment comes from one of just two perspectives, with the result that any attempt to create new models of discussion is subjected to wholesale – and probably wilful – misunderstanding.

The first, and most common, is the orthodox left-wing perspective: that unemployment is the result of an inherent weakness of the capitalist system. The second, the right-wing position, is largely confined to the doublespeak of the business columns; this holds that unemployment is a function of inefficiency in the marketplace, brought about by the imposition of "impurities" such as social welfare, wage agreements and the right to withdraw labour, which distort and confuse the all-knowing, infallible market mechanism.

The most remarkable thing to be said about both these positions is how similar they are in essence. Both of them implicitly take for granted the notion that unemployment is intrinsically a Bad Thing, and assume that it is a reversible by-product of imperfections or inadequacies in the present way of doing things.

It seems to me that both these responses – far from being opposing, counter-balancing viewpoints – represent mutually supportive ends of the same problem. In a sense, the pinstripe-suited entrepreneur on the business programme and the be-sweatered social worker on the News are on the same side, though for completely different reasons.

Both help to sustain the fiction that unemployment is eradicable, and serve in their different ways to make unemployed people feel bad.

The businessman has an obvious and transparent interest in promoting a consciousness of unemployment as an unattractive and somewhat shameful state. The ethos of modern business leans more and more towards the elimination of work, the "success" rate of the executive being measured in his ability to shed jobs. This, however, is clouded in the culture of hand-wringing, and doublespeak about "rationalisation" and "natural wastage".

Although the modern entrepreneur spends most of his time thinking up ways to abolish work, he must spend the remainder contributing to the culture of lip-service about the unpalatable nature of unemployment.

He does this, not because he is a nice guy, but

because his ability to create profits depends on the concept of unemployment as deterrent. He needs people to live in fear of the dole queue so that they will continue to work for him for less money and under less favourable conditions than they might if the dole queue did not exist.

Thus, it can perhaps safely be concluded that, despite his platitudes about the desirability of a climate in which unemployment can be eradicated, the businessman is not on the side of the person who is out of work.

But what of the professional spokesman, usually a cleric or a social worker, who speaks to the world on behalf of the unemployed? At the turn of every month, and sometimes in between, they parade across our TV screens, telling us how awful it is that more and more people are being thrown on the scrapheap of our economic life.

It goes without saying that these are invariably people who act and speak from the best of motives; they are, one doesn't doubt, sympathetic to the situation of the person who is out of work. But what if this very sympathy represented, in itself, part of the "problem" that unemployment is perceived to be?

Such people, you may have noticed, appear always surrounded by both the imagery and actuality of employment. Almost invariably they are interviewed in busy offices or book-lined studies, perhaps with a fax machine or word-processor in the background.

Like the businessman, they speak as though high levels of unemployment were an aberration. They talk about the indignity of worklessness, the despair of the unemployed and the stigma of unemployment. In order to alleviate these things, they say, we need to create more jobs. Never, ever, do they suggest that we address the despair, indignity and stigma as phenomena in themselves.

It strikes me that if such people did not exist, the businessman would have to invent them, for who else would inculcate the fear of unemployment into the minds of the people who work for him.

This, as I say, is tricky terrain. This concept of unemployment has become gummed up with notions of "compassion" and social "concern". Almost all discussion of the subject is dragged towards platitude and sanctimoniousness by the very emotiveness of the climate which infuses it.

While the unemployed remain a minority, it seems, we will continue to see the issue in "humanitarian" terms: something to be the occasion of "sympathy" and "concern". We edge the workless towards the margins of the social scullery and salve our consciences by throwing them bigger and better crumbs from the main table.

But what if unemployment were to become a majority, rather than a minority issue? Let us assume for a minute that unemployment is more than a temporary patch of economic inclemency, that it is a permanent fixture on the social agenda, that far from being correctable, it will continue to grow and grow, that if all the businessmen in all the world have their eventual wicked way, we will – all of us, including even many of the wicked businessmen – be "rationalised" out of employment.

Would we then, I wonder, continue to buy both the doublespeak of the businessman and the sympathetic lip-service of the social worker? Would we sit in our metaphorical sculleries watching the News, ever vigilant for signs of an upturn in the economy? Would we continue to sanctify the idea of work and torture ourselves with our failure to achieve it? Would we feel stigmatised as a people, as a race? I think not.

I imagine we would begin to rethink our whole

attitude to work, to employment, to the way in which the generation of wealth is connected to the distribution of resources among people.

The businessman, for instance, might be called upon to divvy-up some more of his profits among the people he had "wasted" – whether naturally or otherwise. The social worker who continued to bemoan the high incidence of mental illness among the unemployed might be asked whether he thought if he himself, in the context of this process, was the chicken or the egg.

As the grip of technology takes a firmer hold, this is the direction in which we will find ourselves moving. The question we should ask ourselves is: at what point do we, as a society, begin to see unemployment as a common, rather than as a marginal, condition? At what point should we begin to eradicate the notion of unemployment-as-problem, and see it perhaps as a common opportunity? Should we wait until half, or three-quarters of the "workforce" is unemployed, or should we begin somewhat earlier, even while it remains for most of us a peripheral issue?

Should we not, in fact, already have begun? Should not the unemployed in this society, far from being marginalised, perceived as "problem" and "failure", be seen as existing on the very front line of the social and economic destiny of the human race? Even if this generation, and the next and the next, manages to avoid the full impact of technology, this is something with which the human race must cope – and within the foreseeable future.

There are innumerable problems in this society at the moment related to the inefficiency of the mechanisms by which we run our collective affairs. The place is falling apart for want of a little elbow grease, while at the same time over 200,000 people languish in a sort of inactivity limbo which is as much a philosophical as a social creation.

It should not be beyond our wit to bring there two problems together in a creative way. But we need, first of all, to begin dismantling the apparatus by which incentives were generated within the old, antiquated system of doing things.

This includes dismantling the work ethic, on which the capitalist system has depended. To do this we need to destigmatise unemployment, and make worklessness – to begin with – a respectable status in this society. Having done that, we need then to create a whole new system of incentives in order to promote activity and growth in areas where the market mechanism has palpably failed.

But before we do any of that, we need to get used to the fundamental changes in language and perception which it will entail. We need to kill the fiction of unemployment-as-malfunction, and see it as a natural, even *welcome*, by-product of the advances in technology. We need to stop the hand-wringing about unemployment, and put our grey matter to work.

It may not, as Dear Frankie might have said, be our problem today. But it will be some day.

2. THE ABSURD WORKPLACE (January 1994)

Let us say that you want, for example, to have a wall built in your front garden. For the sake of argument, say you have £100 to spend on building the wall. Obviously, you would prefer to have the work done as quickly as possible. The work could, of course, be done by one person, but it would be more efficient to employ two.

Suppose, also, that there are two men on your road

who are equally capable of carrying out the job. No, let us decide, in the interests of equality and peace, that there is one man and one woman on your road, both of whom are in the business of wall-building, and who are, as it happens, free to carry out the work in question.

Okay. Now ask a five-year-old child, if you have one to hand: what is the best way to go about the business of having the wall built? Unless the child is irredeemably backward, he or she will immediately tell you that the best thing to do is to employ both the man and the woman to build the wall together.

The man can mix the concrete and collect the material from the hardware shop, while the woman gets on with laying the bricks in the appropriate order and pattern. Or *vice versa*. When the wall has been finished to your satisfaction, you pay the man and woman £50 each.

What happens after that is their own business. They may decide to go to the pub and have a drink, a chat and a sing-song. Undoubtedly they will have much to say to one another about the business of wall-building, and perhaps other matters as well. Who knows, they may even become romantically involved with one another, get married and set up their own construction company. The five-year-old could not, of course, reasonably be expected to foresee such eventualities, but it is nevertheless one of the many possible scenarios which flow directly from his or her very sensible suggestion.

But say that, instead of pursuing the matter in the manner suggested by the child, you decide to go about the matter as follows. You employ not two but one of the eligible and qualified people. You decide to pay the full £100 to that person for doing all the work – for travelling up and down to the hardware shop, mixing the concrete, laying the bricks and sweeping up afterwards. This will be more efficient, you decide, even though the work, needless to say, will take at least twice as long.

In fact, because it is all more awkward with just one person, it will probably take far longer. As the person you have employed gets on with the job, the other qualified person stands outside the fence looking on and making desultory conversation with his – or indeed her – working colleague.

Already, our five-year-old, listening to your proposal, is beginning to wonder about your state of mind. But worse is to come.

Having paid over the £100 to the tradesperson on completion of the job, you then propose that this person give you back £50. This, you will explain, is to give to the other person, whom you decided not to employ, and who has been standing outside the fence looking on while the work was in progress, so as to compensate him or her for your failure to provide work for two people.

Remember that this individual was more than willing to assist with the work, but you decided against this. It was more efficient to keep this person idle. You propose to pay this person half the allocated £100, regardless.

And for the sake of developing this scenario a little further, suppose that the person who has completed the work does not beat you to a pulp, dismantle the still unset wall and encase you alive in a brick tomb, but instead meekly hands over the said £50. And suppose you then hand this money to the person outside the fence.

What do you think will happen next? Is it likely that these two people will repair to a public house for a few pints, a chinwag and a sing-song? I think not. Is there the slightest hope of a romantic entanglement? I don't imagine so. Already, they are mortal enemies.

161

One resents the fact that the other has been given the opportunity to engage in meaningful work, to display skills and industry and earn a living by sweat, toil and human ingenuity. The other resents the fact that his colleague has been able to earn as much money as himself by doing nothing at all, by looking over the fence as he works, and in fact distracting him from that work by her very presence.

At this point in the exposition of your industrial philosophy, the five-year-old makes an excuse and disappears to call an ambulance, leaving you to puzzle over why it is that you can't seem to get anyone to do any work for you any more, why your house and garden are going to rack and ruin for the want of a lick of paint or a shovelful of dung, and why everyone, including both those you have employed and those you have failed to employ, seems to resent your every effort.

This, in only very slightly simplified form, is a description of the manner in which work is organised in this society. The modern workplace has become the location of a series of absurdities which defies common sense and would cause a cat from Mars to laugh his way rapidly back to the space-ship.

Because of the fundamental nature of these absurdities, there is almost no point in attempting to address any of the problems arising from them. They defy any attempt at rational analysis and are only added to by any efforts to regulate them.

In fact, because every attempt to intervene is by way of adding a further absurdity or set of absurdities to those which already exist, the situation becomes more and more farcical as we, trapped on the inside of the absurdity, consider things to be getting more serious.

Practically every single aspect of what we perceive as the problems relating to employment, income-distribution and economic well-being derive fundamentally from the absurd nature of the organisation of work in this and other western societies. When we talk, then, about unemployment, we are not contemplating some natural phenomenon but the inevitable outcome of the way we organise our society.

Unemployment is not something that happens to us; it is something we do to ourselves, or at least to one another. Similarly, when we complain about excessive taxation, we are not talking about something immutable and fixed, but of the outcome of a particular way of organising our society.

Both unemployment and taxation are out of control, but not only in the sense that they will increase incrementally for as long as we leave in place the absurdities which create them. We can, of course, tinker around the edges of both matters, fudging the live register here or there, or replacing one form of taxation with another.

But we cannot deal with the problem itself within the present absurd models of organisation. The same, of course, applies to the other, less direct, consequences of what we call unemployment – crime, drug abuse, alcoholism, urban blight, family breakdown, human despair. All of them are the consequence not of the inevitability of poverty and inequality, but of a particular model of society, which we choose to perpetuate.

In the next couple of weeks, in advance of the 1994 Budget, there will be much of the usual talk about the need to create growth so as to provide jobs, about the state of the economic fundamentals, about the "climate" for job-creation, about the science of pump-priming, about taxation policy and the competing interests of various sectors wishing to have the present system adjusted on their behalf.

As we watch and listen to the daily parade of stockbroker economists, we should remember that the system they are talking about is not fixed, is not a bequest from God or nature, but simply *one way* of organising our affairs. The questions we should be asking ourselves are the ones that any sensible five-year-old would ask: why does it have to be like this? Who decides that this is the right way of doing things? Why does nobody seem to see how crazy it all is?

3. LIVING WITH THE MACHINE   (March 1992)

If one is writing on a typewriter, as I am now, it is almost essential to know in advance what it is, vaguely, one wants to say. Very often, before beginning, one will have worked out what the first sentence is going to be, and sometimes even the second as well.

If one makes a mistake, other than a straightforward misspelling or a minor syntactical impairment, one can either live with it or begin all over again. And so, one of the things that you quickly learn about writing is that only a small part of it consists in making impressions on a blank page: much more important is the thinking which one is able to do in advance, the accumulation of various thoughts and ideas, and the achievement of a certain pitch of concentration, the better to convey these in reasonably comprehensive sentences.

It is not new to suggest that new technology is changing all that. Let us for a moment leave aside the question of better or worse, and agree that word processors and computers make the act of writing *different*.

I have had a word processor of my own for over a year now. The reason I am writing this on a typewriter is part symbolism and partly because I am writing it in Roscommon. And since, as you may have read elsewhere, *The Irish Times* is currently converting to new technology, this column may be one of the last of its kind.

I would not be the first to suggest that the computer/ word processor has radically altered the function of writing. At the very least, the word processor has shifted the emphasis from the *preparation* to the *act of writing* itself.

No longer is it necessary to know in advance what it is you want to say; you simply spew out via your typing fingers all the information you may have on the subject in question, add everything you can think of, mix in what you *think* you think about it, and then leisurely press various buttons to shift the paragraphs about until they begin to assemble themselves into an orderly argument.

After that you simply jab around at the keyboard until you have converted this raw material into smooth-yet-provocative journalese, before instructing the electronic printer to play out the finished manuscript in flawless type which covers all your tracks.

Whether this is good or bad is a big argument, involving a broad range of feelings and opinions. At one end there is a school of thought which holds that the word processor has rendered writing *easier*, and therefore made it *better*. One writer of my acquaintance speaks of his personal computer as though it were a musical instrument: it mediates, he claims, with the least possible delay or interference, between his muse and the blank page, the words pouring out like music, via the keyboard. And, while at the back of one's mind wondering how yer man Shakespeare ever managed to write so many plays with a quill, it is possible to see his point.

Now I'm no Luddite, but as Inspector Columbo might say, something bothers me. It has from time to time occurred to me that, whereas for people of my generation and older, the computer/word processor is certainly a useful tool in polishing up writing skills which already exist to a greater or lesser extent, for those who grow up with this technology the tool and the skill will be inseparably fused.

What I mean is that, once a single generation has been raised communicating through computers, mankind's ability to so communicate must thereafter depend to a large degree on the availability, capacity and convenience of the technology. The skills, intellectual powers and creativity which heretofore were intrinsic to the human being, will henceforth be possible only through the good graces of the computer. We will have enshrined part of ourselves in the technology and will have access to it only through the keyboard.

Stuff and nonsense, you say? Well, maybe writing skills do not provide the best example: words, after all, will always be words, and they *have* managed to survive previous threats from the steel nib and felt-tip pen. But, consider the impact of new technology on the role of the draughtsman.

In his book, *Architect or Bee?*, the Tuam-born technologist Mike Cooley advanced the very plausible notion that the skill of draughtsmanship is just one of the myriad human functions under threat from the computer.

In the past, he points out, the draughtsman was the centre of design activity: "He could design a component, draw it, stress it out, specify the material for it and the lubrication required." Nowadays, not only have these functions been separated by technology, but each one of them has individually been imprisoned in the machine.

"What the draughtsman now does", writes Cooley, "is

work on the digitiser and input the material through a graticule or teletype. An exact reading is set of the length of each line, the tolerance and other details. The design comes out as a tape which is expanded in the computer, after which it operates some piece of equipment such as a jig-borer or a continuous path-milling machine. After that, the equipment itself will do the inspecting."

In the past, he argues, a skilled tradesman had a tacit understanding of such disciplines as mathematics and mechanics. However, "more and more, that knowledge has been abstracted away from the labour process and has been rarefied into mathematical functions." Knowledge, which previously made up a man's trade, livelihood and meaning, is now trapped inside machines, where only a privileged few have access to it, and then only on a highly dedicated, specialised and need-to-know basis.

Cooley is certainly not a Luddite. He is, as I say, a technologist, as well as a trade unionist and industrial philosopher. Any of the usual kneejerk arguments suggesting that the thrust of his argument is such as to wish to impede "progress" simply will not wash.

"Quite apart from the destruction of the creativity the worker used in doing the job," he argues, "what must be of concern to all of us is where the next generation of skills is coming from. Skills which will need to be embodied in further levels of machines. The feel for the physical world about us is being lost due to the intervention of computerised equipment, and work is becoming an abstraction from the real world. In my view, profound problems face us in the coming years due to this process."

The effect of technology, as Cooley illustrates, is multi-layered. In the first instance, of course, it destroys work, and also dehumanises what work remains. The general thrust of these processes is to reinforce the power of elites over the majority, and of systems over the individual.

Cooley believes that a society's technology is an integral part of its politics, and that the computer is therefore a means of asserting economic and political control, in particular by multinational corporations. His argument is not an anti-technological one, but rather a call for different forms of, and uses for, technology in the workplace.

But he makes a further point which seems to me to be of particular relevance to quality newspapers. It seems to be obvious, given the conditions in the marketplace, that for a newspaper group to set its cap against new technology would be an act of madness requiring the certification of everyone from the editor down to the humblest copy boy.

But newspapers do not exist in a social vacuum any more than an economic one. Cooley paints a most intriguing picture of what a post-technological society might be like; he writes of the "proletarianisation" of society, firstly at the blue-collar, and later at the white-collar, level. Society is first of all conditioned to accept a permanent pool of unemployed persons, and this deterrent is used to squeeze more and more out of the dehumanised "machine appendages" still in work.

This has profound implications for work and for people, but equally so for society, for democracy and for the prospects of a continuing free and democratic press.

The press is more than an adjunct to democracy: it *is* democracy, or at least it should be. The press and democracy are as chicken and egg: the most democratic societies have the best newspapers, and any dilution of one is a reduction of both.

A considerable factor to be contemplated is the extent to which the exclusion of large numbers of people from

168

the active interest in society provided by work is creating a *different model* of society, in which democracy, and by extension a democratic press, is increasingly under threat.

Practically every news story in your newspaper this morning is about work or the absence of work, or is – ominously – once removed from the world of work, as in, for example, reports from the criminal courts. Newspapers, even those produced on new technology, refer to a *world of work* as much as to the world at large. This is particularly true of the "quality" press, and it is arguable that the further newspapers move away from this definition, the less entitled they are to be called newspapers. It is almost impossible to imagine a world without work, except to say that it would also, in all probability, be a world without newspapers.

It is therefore equally impossible to escape the conclusion that, whatever the short-term advantages of the new technology in terms of the commercial interests of the newspaper industry, it behoves those who favour the notion of a free and democratic press – including journalists who collect bonuses for operating the technology – to be acutely alert to the various implications of the arrival of the computer in the workplace.

And even if this involves the apparent hypocrisy of opinion columns and editorials opposing new technology, which themselves have been written with the aid of such devices, then so be it. There are worse things in this world than apparent hypocrisy.

4. MAKING THE WORKLESS COUNT   (September 1992)

I want to propose what I believe might provide the means for a solution to what we describe as the "problem" of unemployment. It is simply this: that we

169

give unemployed people, their spouses and eligible dependants two votes apiece in all government and local elections.

I first made this suggestion at the annual social policy conference sponsored by the Conference of Major Religious Superiors (CMRS) in Dublin last week. The theme of the conference, as you may recall from media reports, was "Power, Participation and Exclusion". These issues were addressed by several excellent speakers in their every aspect – from the logistics, viability and efficacy of voluntary activity, through the philosophical and sociological perspectives, to the possibility of alternative, more benign, systems of social organisation. I had been invited to read the four papers which were being delivered at the conference, listen to the day's proceedings, and give a 15-minute reaction to what I heard.

Thinking about the theme, I had the same kind of feeling I get from writing this column: that the apparent complexity of these issues is purely a function of our failure to see them in the proper perspective.

Writing here about a range of subjects in the past couple of years: rural decline, powerlessness, elitism, unemployment, the European "project", etc., etc., I am aware of constantly revisiting a core theme. It seems that all the drifts in modern society are moving inexorably towards a single point.

The concentration of power in ever more remote and distant power blocs seems to parallel an increasing alienation of the individual human being and the decline of forms of activity in which the individual human being retains control. The same process is spawning the horrific acceleration in unemployment, which in turn boosts crime statistics and the destruction of humanity as a result of drug abuse, etc.

What we are really dealing with is the extent to which

our society, far from revolving in an orbit of our dictation, is careering off at a tangent, out of control.

One of the speakers at the CMRS conference referred to the way we perpetuate the illusion that full employment is attainable, even as the evidence points overwhelmingly in the opposite direction, and to how both the "problem" and the response are couched in terms which characterise them as "minor and temporary malfunctions".

It seems to me that whereas we tend to see our society as broadly healthy, albeit with a few rough edges, the reality is the opposite: we have a fundamentally flawed society with an ever-contracting and self-deluding centre. Nothing captures this delusion better than the current mantra among economic commentators: "the fundamentals of our economy are sound".

We in the still-healthy centre of the economy are in the grip of what will prove a fatal hubris. In our arrogance, we continue to see the contracting "centre" as the core of the society, whereas in reality, the society is reshaping itself even as we sleep. We regard the "excluded" – the unemployed, the poor, the voiceless – as victims, as "underprivileged", as "casualties". Even the language we have evolved to talk about this subject lets us down, preventing us from seeing what is happening.

The issue of marginalisation, or exclusion, goes beyond concepts such as justice, compassion or equality, however worthy these concepts may be. Unemployment is not simply a question of lack of equal opportunity, or of a top-heavy social welfare system. These are no mere "problems"; they represent a fundamental crisis which threatens to unscramble the fabric of Western civilisation. Is it not time we began to see the "marginalised" not as unfortunates who are, for whatever reason, unable to share in the spoils of modernity and progress, but as a

171

warning to all of us that the process of modernity, without supervision, regulation and correction, will not be accountable either to all or any of us?

This realisation would flip all our perceptions over on their heads.

Instead of seeing the unemployed as the unfortunate victims of a temporary malfunction, we would see them as the shape of things to come. Instead of occupying the fringes of our society, they move to centre stage, providing a convex mirror image of all our futures, of the possibilities of success or failure for our society.

Their concerns would immediately become those of the society as a whole. Were this to happen, we would not merely be able to embrace those at present excluded, but be able to see clearly the way to build a model of society which, as technology advances even further and faster, would not cause the kind of marginalisation we now experience.

Sooner or later, we must move towards this kind of model, or the negative alternative we are willy-nilly creating at the "margins" will assert its right, on its own terms, to be the dominant element of society, and a very different kind of sea change will occur.

Father Sean Healy and Sister Brigid Reynolds, in their paper, referred to John Kenneth Galbraith's book *The Culture of Contentment*, which I have mentioned in this column before. Galbraith's theory is that by voting strictly for their own short-term interests, the contented sections of modern Western societies have locked their democracies into a situation whereby the excluded or their concerns have no political expression. The contented, he points out, are opposed to any public policy which is geared to the long-term, preferring short-term action which protects their immediate well-being.

Issues such as employment, public education,

homelessness, drug addiction and poverty are largely excluded from the political agenda, since they affect most immediately those who can be relied upon not to exercise the democratic franchise in a manner threatening to the contented majority.

The agenda of the contented is kept at the forefront of national consciousness by the media (run and operated by members of the contented class), and by high-profile economists who provide a constant flow of quasi-scientific rationalisation for the selfishness of the contented.

The contented class in every Western society is at present clinging to a merely temporary plateau on the spiral downwards towards self-destruction. For this reason, even the contented, if they were capable of looking even into the medium-term future, must soon realise that their own continued survival depends upon a dismantling of the culture of contentment.

How can this be done? Not by minor adjustments or tinkering with the present system. The necessary correction can be achieved only by radical means, by turning our society inside out, by moving the margins of our society into the centre, by engaging ourselves with the concerns of the excluded, not out of sympathy, but out of common sense. We could do this by giving unemployed people a double franchise.

Such a move would, I believe, have the following effects. It would signal to the unemployed that they are, after all, included in society. It would give them a sense of increased political muscle, which would help to redress the drift towards disillusionment and apathy among them.

It would make it more worthwhile for them to organise politically, and give an increased possibility of tangible achievement. It would go some way towards redressing in democratic terms the extent to which they have been denied economically, and would bring immediate pressure on the power points and on policy-making to address this denial.

It would ensure that, in the course of the normal democratic process, the issues which impinge on the people at present excluded would be pushed to the centre of the political agenda. Politicians, far from being protected by the workings of the culture of contentment, would have to take account of the votes of the unemployed as representing something close to half the electorate.

This would be good, individually and collectively, for those at present unemployed. But equally, it would be good for the society as a whole, in which unemployment is an indiscriminate cancer which might any day now strike down any one of us, and which threatens to paralyse all economic activity unless it is addressed.

In a very real sense, the unemployed person exercising his or her double franchise would be voting for each one of us who might at some future time find ourselves in that situation. They would be voting for generations as yet unconceived, who will almost certainly have to live in a very different world, in terms of work, income distribution and related issues.

What I am suggesting would provide an antidote to the present culture of contentment, replacing it with a culture of reconstruction. We would effectively be moving ahead of ourselves, pre-empting the worst consequences of the present drift, by placing a corrective mechanism in place in advance.

For the overall good of this society, the unemployed in this society, far from being marginalised, perceived as "problem" and "failure", need to be seen as existing on the very front line of the social and economic destiny of the human race. Even if this generation, and the next and the next, manages to avoid the full impact of automation and obsolescence, these are things with which the human race must eventually grapple if civilisation is not to self-destruct.

If we are serious when we talk about unemployment as an "unprecedented crisis", then we must be prepared to adopt unprecedented measures to arrest its advance.

VIII

WHAT GOOD IS GOD?

1. SEARCHING FOR A COMMON CONSCIENCE
(from *The Furrow*, May 1993)

A couple of years ago, I came across an interview in the Carmelite magazine, *Carmel*, with the former Taoiseach, Dr Garret FitzGerald, in which he made a passing remark which, it seems to me, captures the essence of the dilemma facing both the Irish Catholic Church and Irish society in general. "It is funny," he said, "but for a country which professes to be Christian, we seem reluctant to speak about Christianity to justify our actions."

One could go further and remark that discussion of issues in a Christian context is now almost entirely confined to the pages of publications such as the one to which Dr FitzGerald was speaking. Christianity has been confined to a ghetto of its own design and construction. Christianity, as a way of seeing the world, has somehow become marginalised and reduced to a peripheral, additional or optional aspect of life in modern Ireland. The notion of a Christian morality has become detached from the central mechanism of Irish society. Among the many consequences of this is the fact that questions of faith, spirituality and God have been forced underground.

There are other, perhaps more serious and immediate, consequences.

Part of the reason, as Dr FitzGerald argued in a more recent article in *The Irish Times*, has to do with the abuse of the concept of morality itself. "The institutional Church", he wrote in his Saturday column last autumn, "lost virtually all moral credibility with the great majority of people – inside as well as outside the Catholic Church – by its insistence on elevating the issue of the possible impact of contraception on sexual *mores* to the level of an absolute that must take precedence over all other considerations." The moral vacuum which resulted, wrote Dr FitzGerald, "is not being filled by any alternative force. Issues of fundamental importance to our society are consequently going largely by default because they are almost never seriously addressed in any forum."

This is undoubtedly part of the explanation. Most thinking Catholics have long been aware of their Church being increasingly on the defensive in this society. In as far as there has been a Church input into the dominant debate, it has come to be perceived as a reactionary voice. Over a period of years, the Church has been edged into a rapidly diminishing territory, comprising what have become known in this society as "moral" issues, i.e. sexual and related matters.

"In Latin America," I was told recently by an Irish Catholic who had just returned home from that part of the world, "the Catholic Church has huge credibility; in Ireland the Church lacks *all* credibility. The Church here has no sense of the word 'moral' – it has almost become a dirty word. Any association with the Irish Church creates impressions that aren't terribly favourable, so you create obstacles before you begin. If you used the term 'Christian concerns', people thought you were against divorce, which would be the furthest thing from my mind. The Church here needs to refind the meaning of morality, and that is a painful thing."

It is undoubtedly true that, by narrowing the definition of "morality" to embrace only sex, the Church and the hierarchy effectively yielded authority in all other areas. They also, of course, yielded authority in matters of sexuality, because the high standards they prescribed, being unattainable for most people, were privately ignored. This created a generation of what were disparagingly described as "*à la carte* Catholics" – people who became disconnected from their Church because they were unable to conform to all its rules. Moreover, the hold the Church maintained over politicians ensured that no secular leader would dare to challenge its version of morality within the territory it had mapped out for itself.

The notion of an Irish politician, for example, invoking the concept of Christian morality is now, as Dr FitzGerald noted, almost absurd. The word "morality", therefore, if used other than in its sexual context, could mean whatever the speaker wanted it to. In Irish politics, for example, it became a convenient weapon for beating political opponents. The result was a moral fragmentation, whereby morality, where its validity was asserted at all, was reduced to a set of internalised codes by which various "games" were conducted in public life.

But there is an even more immediate, though related, reason why Christianity has become marginalised in the public life of modern Ireland: that most of those who claim to deliver its message have surrendered its claim to transcend all other "codes". Listening to many Irish priests and bishops today, one could be forgiven for concluding that they had unconsciously decided that Christianity was old-fashioned and out-of-date. They talk about many of the ways, developments and technologies of the modern world as though these were beyond the ken of Christianity. One gets the sense that the Church is standing helplessly by as the world takes a shape which it feels itself incapable of influencing.

The notion of a common concept of morality in public life has been eroded and replaced by a number of other, smaller systems or codes, which now govern the workings of individual areas of life. Each of these has its own internalised logic, impervious to any wider set of ethics or rules. The most obvious example is economics, which is now the most pervasive system of regulation for much of what happens in our lives. The logic of this self-contained system, as well as its immediate consequences, branches out into other systems for ordering our affairs, like, for example, social policy. By donning an "economic" hat, a public figure can automatically absolve himself or herself from the necessity to bear witness not merely to Christian values but to almost any ethical or moral considerations at all; the issue becomes that of his or her definition of "good" or "greater good", rather than of right or wrong. This, of course, means that the thought process of the society is determined by considerations which are likely to be subjective, individualistic and self-interested, rather than detached and absolute.

It seems to me that the major failure of the Church has been its refusal to challenge any of these internalised systems of logic, except in the narrowest and most timid of ways. The Church's competence is "human and ethical rather than economic", the hierarchy tells us, implying that economics is not subject to the jurisdiction of human and ethical considerations.

What the Church, at an official level, appears to be saying is that it actually accepts the legitimacy of each of these self-contained areas, and acquiesces in their refusal to be subject to a common or higher form of morality.

Instead of providing a sustained critique on issues of public importance from a Christian perspective, it seems to me that (with some notable exceptions) the Church and its personnel have contented themselves with calling for a measure of restraint in the application of systems of amoral and unchristian thinking in modern life. The hierarchy calls for a measure of "social justice" in the running of economic affairs, seemingly oblivious of the fact that, if economic affairs were pursued along lines of Christian morality to begin with, no such corrections would be necessary. It is as though we have come to accept that the only mechanisms capable of generating economic activity must of necessity be inimical to Christian values, but that such values can retrospectively be added-on so as to ameliorate the most undesirable consequences of these mechanisms. Given the way that many of the self-enclosed systems are themselves disintegrating, this bland acceptance of their integrity is profoundly dangerous in a society which should be attempting a fundamental re-evaluation of the logics which govern it. That such a re-evaluation might be delayed because of the reticence of the Church would be appalling.

There are numerous examples that one could choose to illustrate the point I make. I will take just one which, to my mind, captures the essence of the difficulty which the Church has effectively placed herself in. Unemployment is, by common consent, the most pressing social problem facing this society and the Church's response to the problem might be said to indicate its general state of health in the country. Although the recently published Pastoral *Work is the Key* has received favourable mention from official quarters, it is doubtful, in my view, if it will have the slightest effect on either unemployment or official thinking about it. The reason is that the Pastoral does nothing to challenge existing official thinking on the subject of work or employment, but once again accepts the imposed logics which relate to this subject. One is forced to wonder if the praise which has been heaped on this document by the establishment is not indeed an expression of the relief and gratitude in official circles that it does nothing to rock their boats.

In *Work is the Key* the bishops are no doubt seriously concerned about unemployment but there is no searching analysis of the problem. For example, the document appears to accept, despite overwhelming evidence to the contrary, the notion that unemployment is eradicable. "High unemployment is not something to be lived with," the bishops inform us. "It ought to be banished from our island." Dismissing issues like the role of technology and automation in the modern workplace, the bishops lament the "growing fatalism about the supposed inevitability of high unemployment", and then go on to address the question within the tired framework provided by the question of how to create more jobs.

The Pastoral talks of the necessity of transforming the taxation system, the urgency of building a climate of enterprise, the possibility of extending the agenda of the social partners to include the unemployed, and so on. All of it we have heard before, from people who made no claims of being motivated by moral considerations.

What is dangerous is that the Pastoral dismisses out of hand the whole range of radical and alternative analyses that have been advanced by people with a great deal of knowledge and experience of the issue. The role of technology in the growth of unemployment, for example, is dismissed with the assertion that "other small open economies have much more advanced technology than Ireland and yet much lower unemployment rates". Is that really all there is to it? If so, why did the Bishop of

Cork and Ross, Dr Michael Murphy, recently feel moved to criticise An Post for introducing technology at the expense of jobs? Why was the very cogent argument he made on that occasion not incorporated into the Pastoral? Surely a document purporting to provide a Christian analysis of a growing worldwide problem should have taken on board some of the thought about obsolescence and the nature of the post-industrial societies now being engaged in throughout the western world?

The bishops' Pastoral may be a "responsible" approach from the point of view of the conventional economic analysis, but it is unclear what defines it as a *Christian* response. There are ways of looking at the current levels of unemployment other than through the prism of conventional economic wisdom. "Vast as the scale of the problem is," write the bishops in a bland assertion which is typical of the document, "we are aware that the Church is present in boardroom and dole queue. Everywhere, baptised and confirmed men and women, filled with the gifts of the Holy Spirit and believing the message of the gospel, are present and are anxious to find ways of witnessing to the dignity of human work and of practising the virtue of solidarity."

If this were true, there would be no such thing as unemployment or poverty. The reality is that the fixed system which governs our economic life, and which the bishops themselves refuse to question, grants no space to either the Holy Spirit or the gospels. The entrepreneurial spirit, which the bishops and others are so anxious to foster, is not unduly affected by either baptism or confirmation, but is driven by the motive to make the biggest possible profit for the smallest possible outlay. If, to begin with, you accept the legitimacy of this objective, you are on shaky ground when you blithely call for "responsibility", "solidarity" and "social justice", none of which has the slightest role to play in the making of profit.

"Social justice" must surely be the stock in which an economy run to Christian principles is cooked, not a discretionary sauce to be added afterwards.

"Fostering business enterprise need not lead to greater selfishness and inequalities of wealth," the bishops argue, but without elaborating on how these undesirable side-effects of the present system are to be avoided. At what point does the concept of Christian responsibility come into play in a free market economy? How is the balance between conflicting interests to be achieved? What do the bishops have to say to the businessman who, his Christianity notwithstanding, declares that his only responsibility is to his shareholders and the bottom line?

Curiously, while laying considerable stress on the Christian responsibility of business people, the Pastoral plays down the role of the State and the EC. To look to Brussels for the answer is yet another example of "fatalism". As a result of European integration, the bishops acknowledge, "national banks and governments will be less and less able to boost job-creation by cuts in interest rates or new tax incentives, so more and more will depend on the efficiency of companies and on the quality of their investment and business decisions." What about questioning the purpose or logic of a process of integration that has this effect? Would this be outside of the bishops' competence? Why?

Clearly the bishops are of the view that there is a "crisis" in the area of conventional employment, and yet they accept unquestioningly the assumption that job-creation is the only solution. Any other approach is dismissed as "fatalism", which enables the Pastoral to skirt around the fundamental questions of income distribution and the reorganisation of society to allow for a broader concept of human development. The Pastoral contains a range of suggestions about how the Irish unemployment rate might be reduced, but the question of what is to be done, if and when these suggestions have also proved inadequate, is shirked.

Work is the Key is intellectually inadequate as well as politically circumspect. It makes mention of the "dreariness" and "sense of rejection" associated with unemployment, but makes no attempt to analyse whether these are the consequence of unemployment per se, or simply the result of *having no money*. How sure can we be that the negative feelings that unemployed people undoubtedly suffer are the consequence of worklessness rather than of poverty? Why do the bishops not concern themselves with the "dreariness" of the lives of the idle rich?

"We see no convincing argument or evidence that there is any sound alternative if we are to respect the vocation to work and the human dignity of people who are unemployed," say the bishops. How hard have they looked? What research have they done? Have they, for example, studied the work of the Conference of Major Religious Superiors on this subject? If so, what aspects of it do they regard as unconvincing? They make no mention whatever of it.

Is this the fullest extent of the Christian response to unemployment? Is the Church happy to merely admonish the tide? Does it not have a responsibility, in the face of the proven uselessness of this approach, to look elsewhere for the answer? Is there, in fact, *any* other way of seeing the role of work within the frame provided by Christianity? Yes, it appears there is. "In the western world," this bishops state later on, "it is economic activity which increasingly gives purpose to individuals and to

184

society. This is an absurd inversion of what makes for full human living." Unfortunately, the Pastoral as a whole runs counter to this grand assertion. The entire packaging of the issue is in the manner of the favoured approach by business and government. The central assumption is that the "problem" of unemployment can be dealt with only in an incremental manner by creating more work, and by persuading the economic system to operate in a more "humane" manner.

All this logic belongs to a concept of society which has long since revealed itself as a mirage. In the relatively functional models of the past, it was possible to believe that full employment was at least theoretically attainable. But recent economic history has shown us that even where growth and expansion occur, this is likely to translate into *less* employment rather than *more*. There must be a point at which we begin to question the fundamental structures by which we organise our affairs.

In the old model, the businessman had an obvious and transparent interest in promoting a consciousness of unemployment as an unattractive and somewhat shameful state. His ability to engage workers at sufficiently low rates of pay to create profits depended to a large extent on the concept of unemployment as deterrent. He needed people to live in fear of the dole queue so that they would continue to work for him for less money and under less favourable conditions than they might if the dole queue did not exist. The ethos of modern business leans more and more towards the elimination of work, the "success" rate of the executive being measured in his ability to shed jobs. Meanwhile, the older "deterrent-driven" system is kept in place, just in case. Although the modern entrepreneur spends most of his time thinking up ways to abolish work, the society at an official level continues to stigmatise the status of worklessness, largely because the public imagination has not yet been allowed to see the full picture.

The definition of unemployment as a "crisis", while suggesting sympathy and compassion, serves to bolster the outdated notion of the deterrent and simultaneously perpetuates the misery and marginalisation of those who are unable to find work in a society which celebrates employment in inverse proportion to its availability. The bishops' Pastoral perpetuates this approach. That it derives from a benign instinct does little to mitigate the charge, since its very sympathy could be regarded as contributing to the perception that to be without work is to be a second-class citizen.

Like the businessman and the politician, the bishops speak as though high levels of unemployment were an aberration. They talk about the indignity of worklessness, the despair of the unemployed and the stigma of unemployment. In order to alleviate these things, they say, we need to create more jobs. Never do they suggest that we address the despair, indignity and stigma as phenomena in themselves. Never do they deal with the question of the Christian response in a world without conventional employment. If people like the bishops did not exist, the businessman would have to invent them, for who else would inculcate the fear of unemployment into the minds of his notional pool of prospective employees?

The problem with the bishops' Pastoral is that it is essentially a political document. It does not question the conventional wisdoms but asks that they be pursued with greater vigour and more humanity. The result is that the bishops have been seen by other branches of the establishment to make a "responsible" contribution. They have signalled that they intend to extend the scope of their moral vigilance beyond the bedroom door, and so have met one of the most persistent liberal criticisms head-on. This might be seen as beneficial in the wake of recent controversies and sensations. But in what way could their Pastoral be seen as a uniquely Christian contribution? Does it overturn the tables of the moneychangers? I think not. Do Christians not still have a responsibility to ask the eccentric questions? I hope so.

This is not to suggest that the motives of the bishops are in any way questionable. Neither is it to say that the Church is lacking in the kind of approach that I believe is required. Many individual priests and nuns, as well as bodies like the Conference of Major Religious Superiors, show that, if anything, the depth of radical thought on social and economic issues is greater in the Church than in any other area of Irish life. I have chosen this one example because it illustrates the extent to which the Church has in its official voice relinquished its role of articulating the common conscience of Irish society. What appears to be missing is the willingness at a leadership level to provide an analysis which would be likely to upset many of the established applecarts of Irish society.

A way of describing what has happened to the Catholic Church in Ireland would be to say that, under attack for its inflexibility on question of sexual *mores*, it has backed off from confrontation with other branches of the establishment in matters pertaining to points beyond the bedroom door. In the morally fragmented society that Ireland has become, the Church has adopted the morality of the dominant social grouping, i.e. those who continue to do well, and therefore hold the reins, in the disintegrating economy of the Republic. In other words, it has acquiesced in what the American economist John Kenneth Galbraith has called the "culture of contentment".

There are two main levels at which one might become concerned about this. The first is with regard to the consequences for the Church's own position and authority. Judging from the amount of concern expressed by Church sources about the threat of "secularisation", this is regarded with the utmost seriousness. I do not doubt that such concern is justified.

It might, however, be possible to take a neutral view of the survival of the Church's position and authority, if for example these had come to exist simply for their own sake. In other words, if the authority of the Church is to be used solely to secure the Church's position in a crumbling society, then the question of its survival becomes rather less critical.

But the second, and in my view more important, level at which we should be concerned about the present trend is with regard to the survival of a common conscience in Irish society. The kind of Christianity we have been inculcated with is not something that makes us *better*, a kind of optional-extra "goodness", complementing some presumed basic level of human goodness with which we are born. Our ability to be "good" at all, as a way of living in the world, is of a particular character which is composed of values which we recognise as "Christian". This "goodness" must be the transmission system of our existence as good citizens and human beings, not the handbrake or the communication cord to be applied in emergencies. The entire fabric of the morality which makes any kind of social life possible is inextricably bound up in our minds, and in our collective mind, with the principles of Christianity. This applies whether or not we continue to believe in God. Likewise, whether we continue to belong to it or not, the Church has had a central role in the formation of our consciences, and of the conscience of Irish society, to the extent that this continues to exist.

The Catholic Church, if it wishes to survive at all in

Irish society, has a responsibility to reclaim and restore our sense of common conscience. Without a conscience that is alive and conscious of the changing world, there will be no Christianity, and ultimately no society. The survival of such a common conscience *has* to be the reason why Christianity matters, not the other way around. God, I am sure, would be the first to agree that he is not an end in himself. That is why those who speak the Christian message must constantly interrogate their own stewardship of that message. The Catholic Church must call on its adherents to create a society where justice and equality are inbuilt aspects, not merely to ask the contented sections to be more concerned on behalf of those for whom the society does not work at all.

2. The Church and Street Cred (May 1992)

I'm no great fan, and no great foe, of the bishops. To coin a phrase, they have neither impressed nor oppressed me. But, watching them line up last week to each add his brushful of paste to the effort to paper over the cracks of the Bishop Casey affair, it was impossible not to feel sorry for them, if only because they were so far out of their depth.

In a world where the confessional State has shifted location from the shadows of the chapel alcove to the glare of the television lights, the bishops are yesterday's men. The sacrament of public confession, as celebrated on the Oprah Winfrey Show, leaves the traditional version for dead. In a time when the soundbite has eaten its way through to the soul of the world, members of the Irish Hierarchy going belatedly on television to stammer about the need for "humility" are no match for Annie Murphy, standing behind a forest of microphones declaiming, "We have all gone through pain."

The bishops, of course, have made their bed, and now they must wriggle upon it. Most thinking Catholics have long been aware of their Church being increasingly on the defensive in this society. In as far as there has been a Church input into the dominant debate, it has come to be perceived as a reactionary voice, and its contributions, when they occurred, have been characterised more by divisiveness than divinity.

Over a period of years, the Church has been edged into a rapidly diminishing territory, comprising what have become known in this society as "moral" – or, even more ludicrously, "social" – issues, i.e. sex and related topics. Among the many consequences of this is the fact that questions of faith and God have been forced underground.

As a result, even before the revelations of the past fortnight, the Church had already lost "credibility" in the "street" sense. To speak about your Christianity or Catholicism in public could only mean that you were against divorce/abortion/contraception/homosexuality, so those who were not obsessed by such matters tended not to bear witness to Church, faith or God. The fact that the Church now appears to have lost "credibility" in the other sense also is by far the lesser of the two losses.

By narrowing the definition of "morality" to embrace only sex, the bishops effectively yielded their authority in all other areas. Worse than that, because of the hold they maintained over politicians, they ensured that no secular leader would dare to challenge *their* version of morality. The notion of an Irish politician, for example, invoking concepts of morality is almost a ludicrous one. As a result, there are whole areas of Irish public life in which the writ of "morality" does not run at all (a factor which, incidentally, has left the Irish public without moral leadership for the past two weeks).

What has stepped into this vacuum is a form of à la carte "morality", no less "fundamental" in intensity, but lacking in any basis other than immediate self-interest. I speak, of course, of what we in Ireland have come to know as "liberalism". And if the dialectic of modern Ireland is the battle between liberals and the Catholic Church, then the past fortnight has been one of its most crucial rallies. The liberals, of course, have won this round. In the nature of things, this will probably please you greatly or not at all.

It doesn't please me, not because I am on the side of the bishops (I am not), but because I dislike the "liberals" even more. If there is any immediate prospect worse than rule by the Catholic Hierarchy, it is the tyranny of what have been deliciously dubbed "the liberal ayatollahs". A measure of this prospect could be gleaned by reading through some of the condemnatory newspaper commentaries which followed the Bishop Casey revelations, the most interesting aspect of which was the similarity of tone and content with the utterances of some of our more reactionary Catholic bishops.

Many commentators, for example, in dealing with Bishop Casey's past indiscretions, freely employed the word "sin", with little or no sense of irony. Some pronounced him guilty of the "sin" of exploitation of women. This charge gives a measure of the arbitrariness of the à la carte "morality" of the liberal ayatollahs. Their first commandment is "Thou shalt not exploit women". This means: *men* shalt not exploit women. There is no rule about women exploiting other women, nor about men exploiting men, and most definitely none about *women* exploiting *men*. Morality means just what liberals will have it mean. It is possible to glimpse, then, the random, reactionary nature of liberal justice in the probable Ireland of the future.

But is this the only option on offer? Perhaps not. Certainly, the bishops have for the moment been put into rather unseemly retreat. But they will rally once again, possibly after throwing Eamonn Casey to the wolves.

As ye sow, so shall ye reap. The Irish Church has been its own worst enemy. In enforcing its narrow view of morality, it forged both the liberal agenda and the liberal reactionaries. Having created an Ireland in which morality stopped at the threshold of the bedroom, it naturally finds itself rather badly placed when one of its eminences has been caught on the wrong side of the door.

The huge irony is that Bishop Casey, practically alone among the Irish bishops, offered the hope of developing an alternative Christian morality in this country. For all his faults, he is a man who in working for the excluded – whether in the Third World or the West of Ireland – acknowledged a morality more meaningful than that of either his present calumniators or indeed many of his fellow bishops. Although he remained, as we say, "conservative on social issues", Bishop Casey was unique among the Irish hierarchy in that he bore witness to the fact that the centre of gravity of the Catholic Church has over the past decade shifted away from the conservatism of Europe to the radical vision of Central and Latin America.

The most obvious symptom of this has been the dramatic decline in vocations within the European church, with many of the major orders reporting a drop-off of some 90 per cent over a couple of generations. Most of the new membership of missionary orders now come from what used to be known as the "foreign missions". This fact, and the associated growth of the radical Christian leftist ethos known as liberation theology, has resulted in a growing chasm of understanding between the established church in Europe and a missionary church which is now at the point of commencing the re-evangelisation of its erstwhile European homeland.

The people most disenchanted with the Church in Ireland were not the liberals, but the missionaries who came back here from the real world. Believing themselves to belong to a Church whose role was to create a context in which a radical view of politics, social justice and economics could exist side by side with a clear acknowledgement of Christianity, many of them were deeply frustrated by the attitudes of Irish Church leaders. The paradox is that, although such people wished to be merely reformers in the context of the Church, they were revolutionaries in terms of the external world. For this reason, they were even more despised by the liberals than by the bishops.

The Church they represented was ahead of Irish society in relation to external issues like famine, poverty and debt but they were also deeply conscious of the relevance of such thinking to modern Ireland. Eamonn Casey was their lifeline to an Irish Church obsessed with sex.

And this is the challenge, and the potential tragedy, of the Bishop Casey affair. It will either release this captive Church of Reality or imprison it even more. At the moment, the bishops are shaky on their feet, but they will regain their balance in time. The people, faced with a choice between the intolerance of the bishops and the intolerance of the liberals, will choose the bishops for the time being.

A sacrificial offering will be made of the scalp of Eamonn Casey, who will thereafter fulfil the same function for the episcopate as Seán Doherty was designated for by Charles Haughey. The shaky moral edifice of the Catholic Church in Ireland will creak along to the next crisis. And in the Oprah Winfrey world, the crises will come ever thicker and ever faster, until one day will be declared the final victory for the liberal ayatollahs.

There is another way, the way represented by a growing number of radical priests and nuns who have retained an integrated vision of morality in spite of both liberals and bishops. Theirs is the true voice of the Christian Church. They know what they want and what needs to be done. It is a question of seizing the moment. Either the revolutionary Church will snatch the moral high ground from under the bishops or it will stand idly by as we are delivered into the rule of the à la carte morality of the liberal ayatollahs.

IX

EUROBULL AND EURO-BULLIES

1. TELLING ROADS FROM ROUTES   (September 1993)

I'm not quite sure why, but whenever I hear one or other of our glorious band of politicians talking about "drawing down" this or that "tranche" of EC funding I am immediately visited by the image of the inside of a draper's shop in the town where I grew up. This particular shop was equipped with one of those overhead devices for dispatching money quickly from one part of the premises to another – like a miniature version of a cable-car system on a ski slope. As children, we spent many fascinated hours watching the little containers full of notes and coins zipping back and forth above our heads in what appeared to be a wholly patternless and indiscriminate fashion.

Maybe it is just that phrase "draw down," constantly in use in connection with structural funds, which brings to mind the image of a shop assistant pulling down a container when it stopped above her counter, screwing off the lid, pushing the money and receipt inside, replacing the lid and then pulling a cord to send the whole shoot whizzing across to the office in the corner. But I rather think it is something else that causes the mention of structural funds to bring this incongruous image to mind.

The overhead cash apparatus was, of course, a labour-saving device designed, funnily enough, to cut down overheads. While to our childish eyes it had the appearance of existing for the convenience of the shop assistants, it was – obviously – there to help maximise the profits of the shopkeeper. The assistants were merely appearing to obtain a benefit from the contraption. The real benefits, however, were being accrued out of sight behind the office door, where the takings were being counted and retained. The entire focus of the technology was not the shop, not the assistants, not the customers, but the office; that was where all the wires led. Without this rather basic insight, the childish observer could not conclude other than that this machine was some kind of high-class retailing toy which helped to pass the time in an enjoyable fashion for the assistants as they went about the work that had been made so much easier by the benevolence of their employer.

I think the reason I connect this image with the concept of structural funding is that it provides a precise symbol of the role of such funding in Ireland today. This may be because the concept of structural funds has come to be virtually synonymous with roads, which represent the most visible element of EC-sponsored development in this State.

Over one-third of all funding received by this State under the European Regional Development Fund in the 1989-1993 period, and three-quarters of the total allocation to transport infrastructure, was allocated to road-building. This rather helps put in perspective the possibility of a shortfall in the promised £8.6 billion under the 1993-1999 programme; essentially what we are about is so many fewer miles of tar.

Because we in Ireland have come to believe in the fiction of the free lunch, we tend to believe our politicians' implied suggestion that EC bounty comes without a price-tag. The roads and motorways which in recent years have cut swathes through our countryside are, therefore, part of our reward for being "good Europeans". Roads, we are told, are part of the infrastructure which will help us to "catch up" or, as the jargon has it, "provide equalisation between periphery and core".

To the naked eye, a road gives the impression of conferring benefits equally in both directions. In fact, like the overhead cash-transporting contraption in the drapery store, a road is actually part of an apparatus which draws benefits overwhelmingly in *one* direction.

Each individual road must be seen not as a separate infrastructure but as part of a network which is actually *of* the core, extending outwards towards the periphery, rather than as something that belongs to the periphery and extends inwards to the core. A modern road is an instrument of economic colonisation. To talk of roads allowing us to "catch up" on the core is like saying that the overhead cash-dispenser enabled the shop assistant to catch up on the draper.

In the modern global economy, roads are not what they used to be. The massive motorways and roads we see being constructed all around Ireland may bear the same appellation and basic description as those which once connected our towns and villages, but they are actually a different concept entirely. Perhaps it is time to make a distinction.

Roads and routes, wrote Milan Kundera in his novel *Immortality*, are "two different conceptions of beauty" and should not be confused. "A *route* differs from a *road* not only because it is solely intended for vehicles, but also because it is merely a line that connects one point with another. A route has no meaning in itself; its meaning derives entirely from the two points that it connects."

"A road", on the other hand, he wrote, "is a tribute to space. Every stretch of road has meaning in itself and invites us to stop."

"A route is the triumphant devaluation of space, which thanks to it has been reduced to a mere obstacle to human movement and a waste of time."

Such a linguistic distinction is vital in the prevailing economic conditions. The modern proliferation of roads – or, as Kundera puts it, of *routes* – and their identification with development, tells us something quite interesting about ourselves. What we see being built all around are no longer "roads" in the sense we had come to understand that word, but lines of demarcation, the borders of economic apartheid.

In the modern world, the most acute division is between those with too much time and those with no time at all. Structural unemployment has increasingly divided the resource of human time in two directions. In one direction, human beings need to find more and more ways of saving time. Everything is a barrier between them and getting and getting as quickly as possible to where they want to go. For them "time is money". For the rest of humanity, however, the equation moves in the other direction. *Their* time has been devalued to the point of negligibility. They must find ways of stretching their lives to fill almost endless realms of time. *They* have "time to kill".

The modern road, or route, is a symbol of the division between these two emerging classes of humanity. One class is pushed to the margins of society, as though by the all-pervasive road developments, sentenced to a lifetime of killing time, their communities torn asunder to make way for the cars and trucks of those for whom time is money.

The modern road is a symbol of what we have become. "Before roads and paths disappeared from the landscape," wrote Kundera, "they had disappeared from the human soul: man stopped wanting to walk on his feet and to enjoy it. What's more, he no longer saw his own life as a road, but as a route: a line that led from one point to another, from the rank of captain to the rank of general, from the role of wife to the role of widow. Time became a mere obstacle to life, an obstacle that had to be overcome by ever greater speed."

The way we spend the money that is "given" to us serves to exacerbate rather than ameliorate the damage which our skewed economic system has wrought. Not only do structural funds not make things better; they actually have the opposite effect.

Incidentally, the draper's shop I mentioned, the overhead cash-machine notwithstanding, has long since closed its doors, the victim of market forces and free global competition. In its place are two premises. One is a library, for those with "time to kill". The other is a bank, for those who count their time in pounds and pence. Hope and despair live next door to one another.

2. EURO NEWSPEAK   (December 1991)

At one point during my brief but interesting career as a current affairs magazine editor, I was sternly upbraided by my publisher for not carrying enough articles about the EC. "This is a very important subject," he assured me. "We must devote a great deal of space to it." On his insistence, I immediately commissioned a number of journalists to write about the EC and related issues. The next issue of the magazine duly carried about ten pages of explanation of the complex machinations of the European Commission, the Council of Ministers and the role of the MEP.

Shortly after publication, I ran into the publisher on the stairs. "I read that stuff about the EC," he began. As he said this, I noticed that a faraway look had come into his eye. He gazed into the middle distance and paused a while. "Ah Jezes! Ah Jezes! Ah Jezes" he lamented. "It's desperate stuff. Ah Jezes! I know I said to do it – but Jezes, life is too short."

Over the past month, listening to the many discussions about the Maastricht Summit, I have many times found myself ruminating on the brevity of life. Something at the back of my brain tells me that it is wrong to feel as I do; but, honest to God, I can't help myself. I know it is a very important subject, but I am only flesh and blood. When I contemplate the acres of space devoted to the summit by the newspapers, I catch a glimpse, for the first time in my life, of what it might be like to die of boredom.

People or places which come into contact with the EC immediately begin to turn grey. Take Luxembourg. For most of my teenage years, Luxembourg meant only Radio Luxembourg, Fab 208, pop music and the happy voices of men like Tony Prince and Kid Jensen. Today, the Luxembourg in my mind's eye is a grey metropolis peopled by mandarins who speak in a language that defies translation, about things which, though I know they are "important", I somehow cannot bring myself to think about.

Those who have read George Orwell's novel *Nineteen Eighty-four* will recall that in the fictional totalitarian state of Oceania, the official language was Newspeak, which had been devised to meet the ideological needs of Ingsoc, or English Socialism. The purpose of Newspeak was "not only to provide a medium of expression for the world-view and mental habits proper to the devotees of Ingsoc, but to make all other modes of thought impossible."

Newspeak, wrote Orwell, "was founded on the English language as we now know it, though many Newspeak sentences, even when not containing newly created words, would be barely intelligible to an English-speaker of our own day." The purpose of the language was "not to extend but to *diminish* the range of thought, and this purpose was indirectly assisted by cutting the choice of words down to a minimum."

I think about these things as I scan the acres and acres of opaque type in my newspapers on the subject of the Maastricht Summit. There is something strange and troubling about much of the language which is used to "explain" the EC. Not only do words not appear to retain their normal, everyday meanings (as far as I can tell, for example, simple words like "defence" and "security" seem to mean something entirely different in the EC than they do in real life) but also lose their capacity to enable objective discussion.

In a recent *Irish Times* article about the EC by the ex-commissioner, Peter Sutherland, for example, I came across the word "intergovernmentalism". To the best of my knowledge, this word does not appear in any dictionary, and does not appear to have any etymological basis at all. It therefore means whatever the user wishes it to mean. On first examination, it appears to possess the neutral meaning – which, in an EC context, one might assume to be related to contacts between governments.

However, it is clear from the use of the word by Mr Sutherland that the word denotes something on which he is anything but neutral. "Intergovernmentalism," he wrote, "by which is meant the conduct of international affairs by direct negotiations between sovereign states, was seen to be historically ineffective in maintaining peace and stability."

A paragraph later this ostensibly innocuous term has become heavily loaded: "if unanimity is required to establish policies, then this is essentially intergovernmental." It is clear that, for the "newthinkers" of Europe, the notion of "intergovernmentalism" cannot be discussed in neutral terms. It has become a Euro thoughtcrime.

This is just one example of a phenomenon which may explain the confusion felt by many people about EC matters, and also, perhaps, why certain politicians have been able, in the course of a few years, to adopt diametrically opposite positions on Europe, without seeming to be contradicting themselves. In the EC Newspeak, anything is possible, because there is a word for everything and a truth about nothing.

Six years ago, to give one small example, the present Taoiseach, in a Dáil Eireann debate on the Dooge Report, said the following: "The reality of the situation in which we find ourselves twelve years after becoming members of the EEC should remove from us any temptation to indulge in illusions. There is no case to be made for sacrificing our vital interests solely for the sake of being regarded as 'good Europeans'." Mr Haughey then went on to outline the effects of EC membership on the Irish economy: "When we joined the Community twelve years ago our unemployment rate was 65,000. Today it is around 225,000."

And later: "There is much talk from time to time about tendencies towards a two-tier Community, and the fear is expressed that we might be relegated to the second tier. But we have a two-tier Community now, and we are deluding ourselves if we think otherwise." Mr

Haughey concluded: "The Taoiseach . . . must not let his patent desire to be well thought of in the right circles lead him into damaging our national interests."

At that time, Mr Haughey, as you will have noted, displayed tendencies towards several forms of thoughtcrime. From time to time in a lengthy speech, it might have crossed an observer's mind that he might even be a closet intergovernmentalist. He even, at one point, quoted George Orwell: "All members are equal but some are more equal than others."

But, as all right-thinking Europeans will have noted, there was little evidence of such heresy in Mr Haughey's address to the Dáil on the Government motion on the Maastricht Summit a couple of weeks ago. Displaying a remarkable flair for the Euro Newspeak, the Taoiseach made it clear that, one or two reservations apart, he is now as convinced a Euro Newthinker as the next man.

The fact is that the language and logic of the EC are now so advanced that negative comment from within is now almost an impossibility. If we wish to discuss the EC, we must do so in the language which it has developed for its own protection. This language does not contain the possibility of fundamental criticism of the Community, nor of the logic of total integration.

As a result, for Ireland or any other country, there are only two logical positions with regard to the EC: to be totally absorbed or completely detached. The possibility of our arriving at a halfway house is a figment of intergovernmental crimethinking which will soon be totally eliminated. The idea that Mr Haughey has changed his position is merely the result of heretical thinking, undoubtedly the product of a conspiracy by intergovernmentalists.

3. The Sell-Out (December 1991)

And so, friends, we find ourselves at the very precipice overlooking 1992, the year that is to terminal boredom what 1990 was to Irish football.

As I've pointed out before, the boredom factor associated with matters to do with the European Community (stop yawning there at the back!) is not an accident. On the contrary, I suspect it is a cleverly contrived device to waylay attempts at detailed scrutiny by the European public of the undoing of several centuries of hard-won freedom and independence.

As such, if we are to believe recent poll findings, it is uniquely successful. Last week a poll in the *Irish Independent* indicated that 60 per cent of Irish people favour a federal Europe (whatever that is).

As someone who has been opposed to Ireland's membership of the EC right from the days when we knew it as the cuddly old "Common Market", I've got to admit that it's beginning to look as if I'm on the losing side of the argument.

Well, perhaps not the argument, exactly, unless you wish to glorify thus the greed-driven babble of cant and propaganda which we've endured for the past two decades on the subject of "Europe". It should hardly come as a surprise that, in the ensuing bored confusion, the champions of "European idealism" are about to carry off the prize.

For someone born, as I was, in the 1950s, and reared through the heady days of '60s nationalistic celebration, it is a quite surreal experience to be sitting here, what seems like just a few years later, being expected to clap and cheer as we sell what is left of our independence down the river.

Even more extraordinary is that many of the politicians

who are now advocating the sell-out were the most vocal in their adherence to what, in perhaps my naivety, I am unable to see as being other than a diametrically contradictory perspective to the current wave of Euro-consciousness.

At least in the communist countries of the Eastern bloc, reversals in public policy were almost invariably accompanied by personnel changes on the reviewing stand; but we, the unfortunate Irish public, have had to get our brains around the notion of the same set of politicians mouthing passionate platitudes about the flag, fatherland and faith of our fathers from atop the mountains to the heroes of our fight for national independence, and then dismounting to catch a plane for some unpronounceable place in the heart of the continent to sign us up to a new coloniser.

At this point, if they are still with me, the champions of the New Europe will have begun to smile smugly to themselves. For they have seen – have they not? – the tail of my green shirt. And we all know what that means!

Boredom and confusion have nurtured woolly thinking. One of the principal weapons in the armoury of the Euro-lobby in its attempts at coaxing us into a new era of economic and political enslavement has been the manipulation of the quite understandable fears and reservations of the Irish public on the subject of anything remotely mistakable for nationalism.

The argument is rarely openly articulated, but its unspoken logic is as follows: nationalism equals provoism, which is two-legs-bad; ergo its antithesis, which is Euro-consciousness, is four-legs-good. (There have even been those cynical enough to suggest that in the New Europe there will be no partition and no Provos.)

That such an overwhelming push for union with

Europe should have followed hard upon the renewed outbreak of hostilities in the North is completely understandable. We Irish have a lot of hang-ups to shoulder around, and the ride to European unity has allowed us to spread the weight about a bit.

There is no doubt that our mutual involvement in Europe has been good for the relationship between Ireland and Britain; we have been able to dissociate from the violently expressed xenophobia of our modern-day freedom fighters by rallying cheerfully to the European flag.

The trouble is that the process of European union is one without an end or a beginning; it simply goes on and on, hugging us ever closer to its own inexorable logic.

In the context of the EC, we have two options: being Irish or being what is disingenuously termed "European". There is possibly no final state, for example, which would involve us in being half-Irish and half-"European".

The reason this is so is that the EC, for all its name-changes, is driven by a single force: economic power. The EC is about making Europe safe for the major economies; Ireland is there as ballast, and will be the first to go overboard when the going gets rough.

In the confusion of language and definitions, we have lost our ability to think clearly. The Euro-lobby – by which I mean those leading us by the nose towards a United States of Europe – would have us believe that the issue is between jingoism and what they term the "European ideal".

We are already Europeans, they aver, part of a common culture going back several centuries.

They are correct, of course, but this has nothing whatever to do with the European Community. To be anti-EC is not to be anti-Europe. It is easy to become confused by media coverage which presents the issue of European union in terms of the role of Irish writing in European literature, or the Europeanisation of Irish rock music as evident in the rhythms of "Achtung Baby".

The EC is about economics and power – not culture, literature or rock 'n' roll. James Joyce was a European writer, but he was not an EC writer; there is a crucial difference.

Anyone who has ever tried to wade through an EC document on cohesion or subsidiarity will be conscious of the ludicrous aspects of the EC claiming to be part of any kind of literary heritage.

There is one question to which none of the Euro-bullies has yet been able to give me a satisfactory answer: *Why?* Why is it so important that we move towards greater unity with Europe? Why is a United States of Europe such a desirable end?

Of course, they will utterly reject any suggestions that what they are about is the creation of a superpower. And anxious though we may be to take them at their word, it is difficult to find in their rationalisations even the beginnings of an argument worthy of their obvious passion for their stated objective.

Most of them, when asked the w-question, offer variations along the lines of, "Everyone else is in, so we have to be too", or "Sure aren't we better off in than we would be out?" or "Well, we're already too far down the road to turn back."

Apart from the nonsensical proposition that European unity will serve to prevent another world war, I am not aware of any other arguments in favour of the integration of the nations of Europe in a single political unit.

And since all these arguments are transparently facile and self-contained, it is fair to conclude that we must look elsewhere for the impetus which carries us forward towards what may well be our doom as a self-determining people.

Clues can be gleaned by listening to the way Euro-bullies speak of the "European ideal". It soon becomes clear that very few of them have any commitment whatever to the common cultural heritage of Europe; their only commitment is to their own careers. They speak of a united Europe as a concept which is pleasing to them because of the symmetry it offers in terms of their own lives, a cosy end to a cosy career.

It has been noted in Britain that the drive towards European unity there derives almost exclusively from the generation which is now reaching the end of its natural life, with younger people being considerably more jaundiced in their views.

The same is true here. The generation which has delivered us into the very jaws of the European superstate is now on its last legs.

When it retires to shoot duck and admire its handiwork, it will be left to the rest of us, our children and our children's children, to clean up the mess.

4. THE YEAR OF THE EUROBULLY   (April 1992)

The clear front-runner in the Eurobully of the Year Contest at the moment is the Minister for Foreign Affairs, David Andrews, for his repeated bleating about the "dangers" of non-ratification of the Maastricht Treaty and what a "tragedy" it would be for the Republic.

For those who have just joined us, a Euro-bully is not necessarily someone who is in favour of the European Community, but, more precisely, someone who speaks (usually incomprehensibly) of the EC initiatives and institutions as though they were self-evidently the only sane options, which it is unnecessary even to justify, thus suggesting that anyone failing to share this "vision" is, *ipso facto*, one or two ham sandwiches short of a picnic.

Mr Andrews, has, of course, a lot of competition. His own Taoiseach, Albert Reynolds, has been giving out stink about the "emotive and outrageous statements" being made by those who oppose Maastricht. It is interesting that Mr Reynolds has stopped short of specifying which statements are "outrageous" and which merely "emotive". I have no doubt that those responsible for such statements would be more than happy to debate their views with Mr Reynolds. If his arguments are as impressive as his outrage, he should have no difficulty in seeing them off.

And then there is Mr John Bruton, who recently declared that his party will be urging a "yes" vote because, as I understand him, the resurgence of right-wing elements in Germany and France is giving "grounds for concern" about the possible break-up of the European Community. This is a variation of the logic of closing the stable door to ensure the horse tramples us all to death. Is it "outrageous" to suggest that it might be the very nature of the EC itself which is creating the conditions for an extreme right-wing resurgence?

You see, this is one of the aspects of the Community which I happen to believe might be worth our while discussing. Which just goes to show how naive I am really. When it comes to emotive and outrageous statements, the anti-Maastricht people are only trotting after the Euro-bullies, who, by their arrogant and presumptuous attitude, have rendered impossible a proper discussion of the pros and cons of the Maastricht Treaty.

Stop me if I'm being outrageous or emotive, but I am under the impression that the ratification of the treaty was a matter for the Irish people to decide in a democratic referendum. This *should* mean that, until the completion of the count on 19 June next, the question of whether Maastricht is good or bad will, as far as the Irish Government is concerned, remain an open one, the argument to be won by persuasion and reasonable discussion.

Some hope. It is not a little sinister that the manner in which the treaty is being discussed by our politicians and in the media is such as to suggest that ratification is not alone a foregone conclusion but one to which there is no possible alternative. All the main political parties, the national newspapers, and, apparently, RTE have thrown themselves behind the pro-Maastricht bandwagon, and thus denied the public its right to a full and balanced debate.

In speaking of the Maastricht referendum, politicians use language in such a way as to suggest that the vote, let alone the debate which is supposed to precede it, is something of an inconvenience, a tedious formality which must be gone through for the sake of the constitutional niceties. They speak, for example, of ratification being "jeopardised" by the current uncertainty about abortion, and of the need to "sort out" the treaty before dealing with "peripheral issues".

This arrogant, tendentious and presumptuous language is parroted in at least 99 per cent of the media coverage of the Maastricht issue. The idea of ratification as a good thing is taken as a self-evident premise to all discussion. While the anti-ratification viewpoint is largely ignored, every fiddle-fart of a statement by the pro-Maastricht lobby is reported in full.

Far be it from me to make predictions, but I caution our leaders and opinion-formers to tread warily, to be mindful of the undoing of those who took too much for granted in the recent British general election. Or perhaps an even more salutary lesson might be gleaned from a brief study of the ongoing public discussion of the Maastricht Treaty in Denmark, the only other member-country requiring a referendum of its people on the matter. (It is an indisputable fact that Danish – and indeed French and German – doubts about the treaty are incomparably better reported in the Irish media than are the views of our native dissenters.)

In Denmark, opposition to Maastricht is not a certification matter, but a perfectly reasonable viewpoint which is held by, among many others, a large number of the moderate-minded politicians. At the moment, with six weeks to go before polling day, the Danish public is about evenly divided on the merits of the treaty. Ironically, it was the Eurobullying tactics of the prime minister, Poul Schluter, that opened up the debate in the first place. By arguing that the Danes had "no choice" other than to ratify (sound familiar?), he provoked a backlash which has now placed the question in what David Andrews would undoubtedly describe as "jeopardy".

And the funny thing is that, even if the Danes beat us to the punch in rejecting the treaty, they can never be accused by the Eurobullies of being "anti-Europe". In fact, Denmark is the only country in the EC to have political parties dedicated to European, as opposed to national or local, politics. This seems to suggest that the more knowledge and discussion there is about the EC, the more likely people are to reject it, a notion that would certainly explain the reticence of the Irish establishment to cater for a proper debate on the subject.

Already, the Danes have bought nearly half-a-million copies of the Maastricht text, a factor which, because of the incomprehensibility of the treaty, has greatly added to public scepticism. They are deeply suspicious of the idea of a German-dominated Community, and have succeeded in inserting in the treaty a protocol which allows them to prevent Germans from buying holiday homes along the Danish coast. (Perhaps the Irish Government might consider asking them for a swap.)

It is not confusion about *their* protocol that has led the Danes to be so sceptical about ratification, but the fact that they are an independence-loving people, as we once were. One of the leaders of Denmark's intriguingly named Maastricht-opposition group, Europe '92, Professor Niels Meyer, recently told the *International Herald Tribune* that one of their main arguments is about freedom. "Here, money hasn't overruled democracy," he said. "We don't want a Europe run by central bankers."

There was a time when Irish political leaders might have spoken like that. But this proud and noble argument, it seems to me, is the diametric opposite to that now being put forward by the Irish establishment. When pressed to elaborate on the nature of the "tragedy" to be unleashed if we fail to ratify the treaty, our local Euro-bullies tell us that such a "failure" would mean the loss of £6 billion in structural funds over the next five years.

So now, at least, we know the answer to the age-old question: what price Irish independence? Six billion quid. Over five years.

Let's think about that. Even if we disregard the lack of absolute commitments to these payments, fact that we're not really talking about hard cash, and the likelihood that we will have little or no say in how the money is spent (we will not, for example, be allowed to use such monies to pay off our national debt), what we're talking about is less than £2,000 per head, or less than £400 per annum. For the sake of round figures, let's say a pound a day. For five years. After all the blood and humbug of the past 800 years, that's the value we place on Irish independence.

And this thought has partly led me to make the following proposal. Such is the degree of confusion and ignorance about Maastricht, not to mention about the protocol, the addendum, the right to life and/or travel, and countless other complicating issues, that, regardless of whether we end up rejecting or passing the treaty, we will afterwards not have a clue as to what precisely we intended. I would like to suggest that, instead of the normal, restrictive method of marking the ballot paper, the Government introduce a more complex system of markings to allow for clear expression of as many as possible of the attitudes which have surfaced in the debate.

Thus, those wishing to express a wish that there be "no abortion in Holy Ireland" could mark a cross in the "no" box. The Euro-bullies, on the other hand, could mark a big, proud "E" in the box for indicating a "yes" vote. For myself, I would like to be able to mark a capital "I" (for independence) in the "no" box. And so on.

The system, as you will appreciate, has unlimited possibilities for subtlety, will enable each viewpoint to campaign without having to worry about whether their fellow-travellers are the "right" kind of people, and, moreover, will allow us to obtain a complex retrospective insight into the nature of our decision. Those who do not give an ecu for independence, Europe, protocols, addendums, zygotes or suicidal women, and just want to get their hands on the lolly, can simply adorn their ballot papers with a big fat "£".

213

5. THE SLIPPERY SLOPE TO MAASTRICHT (June 1992)

One thing that must be said in favour of our leaders is that they make no attempt to flatter the Irish public by crediting us with inordinate intelligence. At the beginning of a month in which will occur a crucial referendum pertaining to the future economic direction of this country, the unemployment figures, thanks to an act of statistical sleight of hand, are contrived to show a decrease of 7,500, rather than the tiresome increase of 2,000 which has occurred in reality. There are mild protestations, mainly of a token nature, from the opposition parties, but the net result will probably be that the exercise, for all its crudity and cynicism, will be a medium- and long-term success.

In fact, I don't see why this highly innovative approach to managing the economy shouldn't be capable of abolishing unemployment completely within a matter of months. If even half the – admittedly minimal – energy currently engaged in attempting to solve the unemployment problem were to be employed in devising further statistical renovations, I see no reason why we could not have full employment – statistically speaking, of course, but what else matters? – by the end of the year. Such is the nature of human beings that, within a short time, everyone will have forgotten about the fiddle, as we bask in the "improvement" in the jobless statistics.

Of course, if we endorse the seemingly inexorable thrust towards European integration on 18 June, those who have propelled us along this path for so long will point to the doctored statistics as evidence of our national perspicacity. If we have the temerity to vote "No", all they have to do is revert to the previous method and rub our noses in the "evidence" of our folly.

It will not be long before we beg for a second chance.

This, it seems, is the only future we can look forward to: to be bullied and conned and treated as imbeciles. In my darker moments, I have to admit, I begin to wonder if perhaps we deserve the disaster that is undoubtedly before us. For a people with such a reputation for wisdom and common sense, we are remarkably tolerant in the face of a political consensus which appears to regard us as a nation of half-wits.

The Taoiseach tells us that, in the wake of Denmark's rejection of Maastricht, a "Yes" vote in Ireland will allow us to display our "sovereignty and independence" – and *he gets away with it.* His words are faithfully reported by the media, without as much as a hint of added irony. "Four legs good, two legs bad" has overnight metamorphosed into: "Four legs good, two legs better."

But there is a fundamental sense of unreality at the heart of current discussions that goes much further than mere fibs and verbal trickery. There is some extraordinary lack in a country in which the Taoiseach, in the same week as he continues to try to dragoon us into a united states of Europe, can gain media brownie points from his involvement in the Earth Summit in Rio, the principal imperative of which is the ecological catastrophe deriving from precisely such entities as we are being asked to endorse in nine days' time.

It is the nature of media coverage to treat Maastricht and Rio as though they were two different matters; but, in fact, they are opposite sides of the same coin. The kind of policies implicit in the putative European union are the kind of policies which have already destroyed the environment in North America and placed the future of the human species in mortal danger.

The most potent symbol we have of this is to be found in the impressive stretches of motorway which have been constructed, using EC structural funds, all around this green and (thus far) moderately pleasant land. What the EC represents is the vanguard in the European leg of the drive towards the single planetary economy. What is happening is a war fought through the medium of economics, with militarism as merely a contingency option.

The implicit strategy involves the destruction of nationalities, local cultures and the transformation of human relationships into commercial transactions. In this process, work, which has been a central aspect of human expression through the centuries, is removed from the territory of personal responsibility and mediated through technologies and economic systems. The process of production, once one of the most crucial and rewarding of man's activities, is broken up into absurd divisions which make a contorted kind of "economic" sense.

In the interests of breaking down supposed divisions, we are in fact breaking up the very "mechanism" of the human being. Mankind is separated from his own activity through time and distance. Artificially maintained produce is transported vast distances in the interests of economic "efficiency", but the cost of environmental devastation is never allowed into the equation.

We feign concern about "the environment", but do not possess even the wit or the unselfishness to ensure the future of our own species. One of the buzzwords of the Rio Earth Summit – "sustainability" – says it all: what we are seeking is newer and better ways of cheating nature. In the long run, we cheat only ourselves and our descendants.

In the world according to George Bush and Jacques Delors, man is separated from his national identity, his place in nature, his cultural community, his family, and ultimately from himself. Self-reliance, the most essential element of the relationship between mankind and his environment is diminished, and environmental conservation becomes not a matter of second nature but, at best, of fad and expediency. Our leaders seek newer and better ways of disconnecting their authority from any form of responsibility; those who make the decisions are farthest away from those most affected by them. We look for guidance and they build us roads which lead away from ourselves.

It is a measure of the paralysis of the Irish debate on Maastricht that all the above will almost certainly appear to be a long way from the point. Yet this is the fundamental basis on which the other arguments against Maastricht – sovereignty, independence, neutrality, freedom, etc. – must be rested. It is equally relevant in Ireland, Denmark and Germany.

But there is now an even more fundamental reason why the Irish electorate should refuse to ratify the Maastricht Treaty on Thursday week; to do so would be to strike a blow for democracy against those who have bullied and patronised us, and insulted our intelligence.

By refusing to allow both sides of the argument to be made with equal vigour, the establishment has breached in a fundamental way the spirit of Article 40 of the Irish Constitution, which guarantees liberty of expression, but then why should we worry about the niceties of a Constitution which they are in the process of selling out?

For much of the campaign, most of the media have seemed to operate on the basis of facilitating the minimum possible dissent from the only "sane" option – a "Yes" vote. (What a moment it was, on the evening of 2 June, when they had to start to treat those urging a "No" vote as though they were not mad at all!) The man and woman in the street, have, for this reason, had little chance of achieving a measured consideration of the implications of a political and economic decision which may be the most critical of their entire lives.

In what must truly be the most comprehensive stitch-up of the democratic process since the foundation of the State, the political establishment, in concert with much of the media, has decided in advance what the outcome of this referendum should be.

6. THE DEBATE RITUAL (June 1992)

In a remarkable article, "Media Guilty of Supporting EC Consensus", in this week's *Sunday Tribune*, the editor of the paper, Mr Vincent Browne, has placed an imposing question mark over the role of the Irish media in the recent Maastricht referendum campaign.

Mr Browne who, since in his editorial pronouncements he recommended ratification of the treaty, can hardly be described as "anti-European", describes the manner in which the Maastricht debate was conducted as "amounting to a subversion of the 'equality' of political participation". I agree.

I agree also with his characterisation of the media coverage of Maastricht as a joining in with a "chorus of consensus that shut out critical perspectives". While singling out *The Irish Times* and RTE as being less blameworthy than other media, Mr Browne correctly described the media as having, in large measure, "capitulated to the consensus".

"All of us in the media", he wrote, "allowed the 'Agenda' to be set for us by a prevailing ethos, which proclaims that the European 'project' is a good thing; as is monetary union."

Mr Browne was at pains to stress that he was not

suggesting that the pro-Maastricht arguments had been false or incorrect. "Rather it is to complain that we allowed these to become almost unchallengeable assumptions, and we did so because of an economic and cultural bias which afflicts the media in a profound and disconcerting way."

While pausing for a brief spasm of regret that Mr Browne did not choose to write this article two or three weeks ago, it is vital to stress the importance – indeed the profound significance – of these statements/admissions, coming as they do from one of the most senior and respected newspaper editors in the Republic.

In Sunday's article Mr Browne put his finger on a number of key issues in relation to the role of the media and the European "project". In particular, his implicit point in relation to the distinction to be made between what the individual journalist or collective media may consider to be the "correct" choice in a political debate, and the responsibility to allow for the possibility of what might emerge as an equally persuasive dissenting argument, is one that is not widely grasped in the Irish media.

Journalists, including both myself and Vincent Browne, are members of the relatively affluent section of Irish society. Thus, there is a tendency for even the most egalitarian-minded among us to favour first of all the political and economic choices which best protect our own interests. Our public platforms give us an unfair advantage in this regard.

However, it goes further than this. The situation is aggravated by the fact that the choices which are most likely to benefit journalists almost invariably happen to be favoured also by other branches of the establishment, including political parties, banking institutions, public agencies and other powerful groupings.

Should these bodies agree to combine on a particular issue, they can create a powerful "moral" convocation which can be rendered unassailable by the additional support of the media. The fact that, by their very nature, such interests invariably have access to large amounts of money with which to purchase advertising time and space in the media is a factor which renders the entire process dangerously undemocratic. How many struggling radio stations, or newspapers with tight operating margins, can afford to go against such a consensus when it occurs?

Journalists, by their nature, are highly opinionated. This is good. They come to hold particular viewpoints in a rather extreme and passionate way. This, too, is healthy. However, the problem arises from what Vincent Browne describes as the "economic and cultural bias which afflicts the media". One of the consequences is that the views of journalists tend, for cultural and economic reasons, to gravitate towards one side of particular debates, though in a manner which causes this process to remain genuinely invisible to many of these same journalists.

And, of course, in dealing with such matters as they do, the media are instinctively remaining true to those viewpoints with which their advertisers are most comfortable. In recent years they have reflected, too, in a fairly precise manner, the drift of Irish society away from aspirations of a collective nature in the direction of a more consumerist, individual-centred model of society.

Vincent Browne remarks on the absence of a single mention of the goal of full employment in the Maastricht Treaty and the singular lack of comment which this lacuna attracted during the debate. This is indeed, as he suggests, a media failure, but more fundamentally it is a reflection of the priorities of the dominant voices of our society.

Twenty years ago, in the debate which preceded our accession to the European Community, the issue of unemployment was such a crucial issue that our leaders went so far as to seek the inclusion of – God preserve us – a *protocol*, in which the EC recognised the importance of ending unemployment in this State. The intervening years, which have been marked by a steady quadrupling of the then levels of unemployment, have also been characterised by an inversely proportionate decline in our public concern on the issue. The Irish media have provided a reasonably accurate barometer of this trend.

In all this, it is important to stress, there is never what could even remotely be described as a "conspiracy". There doesn't have to be. There is, though, what might be described as a convenient coincidence of expediency.

There is absolutely no doubt that, in debates such as that relating to the Maastricht referendum, the economic choices which are most compatible with the personal interests of editors and journalists are, by a process which is to a large degree unconscious, accorded the status of self-evident truth. The coconuts are glued firmly down at the start, and – in the interests of "democracy", of course – dissenters are equipped with carefully weighted missiles and invited to have a go.

The ensuing "debate" becomes not an equal contest between established and other viewpoints, but a ritual, in which the "correct" choices are pitted, in a token manner, against "alternatives" which have little or no chance of winning. The dice are loaded and the result becomes a foregone conclusion.

In these circumstances, perhaps the proper question to be answered is not whether, in any such "debate", it is possible to achieve an outcome contrary to the consensus, but whether, in an issue on which 90 percent of the establishment, including 100 per cent of the media, have taken one side of the argument in advance, there is any point in having a debate *at all.*

Perhaps a more sensible way of going about our national business would be to canvass in advance all the political parties, State agencies, media organisations, banks, trade unions and other potentially interested corporate parties to ascertain what the consensus on the issue was likely to be. Account would also, of course, have to be taken of the amount of money which each grouping was prepared to spend on any putative campaign on the issue. The matter could then be decided on the basis of the consensus, without the tiresome requirement of a rubber stamp from the electorate. This approach would be much easier on the public purse, much less taxing on the national nervous system and arguably just as "democratic" as the debate on European Union has been.

Many journalists, when presented with such arguments, will howl in protest. An outsider will be told that he/she does not understand how the media work. If the arguments are made by someone who is also a journalist, he or she will almost certainly be accused of hypocrisy and/or disloyalty to the profession. If one is a journalist holding such views of the media, it is as well to anticipate frequent exhortations from colleagues to the effect that perhaps the most "honourable" course would be to seek work in some other area. Thus do the modern media strive to hide their warts from themselves.

Vincent Browne has taken an honourable, courageous and important stand. The media must take positive steps to address their own inbuilt inbalances.

7. POISONING THE LOW FIELD   (May 1993)

Behind Winston's back the voice from the telescreen was still babbling away about pigiron and the overfulfilment of the Ninth Three-Year Plan. The telescreen received and transmitted simultaneously. Any sound that Winston made, above the level of a very low whisper, would be picked up by it; moreover, so long as he remained within the field of vision which the metal plaque commanded, he could be seen as well as heard. There was of course no way of knowing whether you were being watched at any given moment. How often, or on what system, the Thought Police plugged in on any individual wire was guesswork. It was even conceivable that they watched everybody all the time.

George Orwell, *Nineteen Eighty-four*

Ten years ago, as the year associated with George Orwell's doom-laden prognostications loomed large on the horizon, there was a goodly amount of self-satisfaction around Oceania and neighbouring places about the extent to which *Nineteen Eighty-four* had got it wrong. Even those who sought to "defend" Orwell almost invariably did so on the basis that he had intended the book as a critique of the nature of communist totalitarianism, which displayed, it was argued, all the hallmarks of his vision of 1984.

Of course, he had no such intention. Because the best of Orwell's books contain such a compound of the real and the seemingly fantastic, he is frequently dismissed as a writer of crude sociological polemics. In fact, like Franz Kafka, Orwell was dealing in the stuff of human nature, which is timeless, universal and unbounded by history or society. To see the concept of the *Orwellian* as a purely political notion is to misunderstand fundamentally its

223

implications for each one of us who lives in the modern world.

But even Orwell stopped somewhat short of inventing scenarios wherein, to avoid over-production of grain, farmers were not merely paid to keep land out of use but required to ensure that it was incapable of production, monitored in this regard on a 24-hour basis by a surveillance satellite, and made to spray their fields with poisonous chemicals in order to convince the watching authorities that they were behaving in the correct manner.

Yet, nine years after 1984, this is the reality of life in Europe. The EC policy of set-aside brings the Big Brother of Orwell's fiction and the hubris of communist totalitarianism into the same frame, right here in our own back gardens. What Orwell could not have foreseen was that supposedly free westerners could be persuaded to vote for such absurdities in ostensibly open referendums.

This is the reality of the European Ideal at work in the Ireland of 1993. A child tugs at its mother's apron and asks: Where's Daddy, Mammy?"

"He's working," the mother replies. "He's gone out to poison the low field."

And what do we find is the response to this latest example of the workings of the "ideal" by our normally vigilant and vocal moral guardians and interest groups? Pretty minimal, you may have noticed. The farmers' organisations, as per usual, seem happy enough as long as the money is right. A couple of environmental bodies make vague protesting noises about the dangers to wildlife. One or two newspapers carry leading articles wondering if the whole plan might not have been better considered or more carefully drafted. The Catholic Hierarchy lapses into a sudden silence.

Let us get one thing straight. Set-aside is not merely a

"poorly-thought-out" policy; it is not merely "a crude instrument"; it is not merely nonsensical. Set-aside is wrong. It is obscene. It is a crime against God and nature.

The reason this is so is not merely to do with the undoubted damage which this policy will do to the ecological balance of the environment. Nor is it simply a question of the quality of rural life. Even to speak of the absurdity of destroying the fertility of arable land while millions of our own species starve to death is only to hint at the enormity of the crime that is being committed. These are merely the symptoms of the sin, the black marks which it causes on the soul of mankind.

Set-aside is much worse than the rape of the earth. In a society laying claim to a spiritual dimension, it amounts to the attempted murder of God. Whether our notion of a higher being is of a force within nature or an elderly man sitting on a fluffy cloud, and whether we think of that being as alive, dead or merely sleeping, we must surely see that at the core of the set-aside thinking is a folly and arrogance crying out to the heavens for vengeance.

What is the nature of the sin? Václav Havel, in his essay "Politics and Conscience", wrote of the smokestack belching fumes and brown smoke being the symbol of an age "which seeks to transcend the boundaries of the natural world and its norms." Writing about the Czechoslovak experience of collectivised farming, he argued that modern science was attempting to crash through the bounds of the natural world, which it can understand only as a "prison of prejudices from which we must break into the light of objectively verified truth".

From the purely rational perspective, the natural world appears as "no more than an unfortunate left-over from our backward ancestors, a fantasy of their childish immaturity. With that, of course, it abolishes as mere fiction even the innermost foundation of our natural world; it kills God and takes his place on the vacant throne so that henceforth it would be science which would hold the order of being in its hand as its sole legitimate guardian and be the sole legitimate arbiter of all relevant truth".

For that most liberal and enlightened of modern men, "the natural world, in virtue of its very being, bears within it the presupposition of the absolute which grounds, delimits, animates and directs it, without which it would be unthinkable, absurd and superfluous, and which we can only quietly respect. Any attempt to spurn it, master it or replace it with something else, appears, within the framework of the natural world, as an expression of hubris for which humans must pay a heavy price, as did Don Juan and Faust."

Modernisation, he believes, has to be guided by humility and respect for the mysterious order of nature, and must not be "simply an arrogant, megalomaniac and brutal invasion by an impersonally objective science, represented by a newly graduated agronomist or a bureaucrat in the service of the 'scientific world view'."

Totalitarianism is not merely something that manifests itself in gulags and telescreens. It has to do with the concentration of impersonal power, the growth of bureaucracy and the tendency for these all-consuming logics to consume the human spirit to the point where it is incapable of human responses.

To our ancestors, set-aside would have seemed like the thoughts of the Devil. Such notions, of course, seem old-fashioned and superstitious to our "modern" minds, captivated as they are by the theologies of science and rationality. But the modern Lucifer wears a dark suit and speaks smoothly of the European Ideal.

How far can we be from the totalitarian apocalypse, when Irish farmers can be persuaded, for a few pieces of European silver, to poison the land their forefathers broke their backs in making fertile?

It is difficult to say which has reached the most advanced stage, western man's hubris or his stupidity. Not content with curtailing our fellow man's capacity to use his labour to reap the fruits of the earth, not content with mere indifference to the resource the earth represents, we have moved on to the final phase of our self-destruction: the deliberate defilement of the source of our life.

This argument is not about economics, social policy or environmentalism. As Havel says, it is not enough to be offended by mankind's arrogance and abuse of nature when it affects the quality of our lives – when the stench of the smokestack penetrates our apartment. We must be offended by it *metaphysically*. It is at this level that the appalling nature of the crime of set-aside must be seen. This is what is absent from even the most trenchant criticisms of this and other such EC-sponsored absurdities. We object to it, yes, but only on grounds that are utilitarian or aesthetic.

And even at these superficial levels, many of us are losing our capacity to perceive where hubris is leading us. For a people like the Irish, just two lifetimes removed from a collective death experience arising from the wrath of the natural world, such casual arrogance is doubly unforgivable.

Of course, I am not so naive as to expect our craven political leadership to rise to the intellectual or spiritual level of a Václav Havel; and I accept that our "liberal" intelligentsia is notoriously shy about discussing concepts relating to God or nature – unless, or course, these can be expressed in less embarrassing notions about environmentalism and the like. But I think we have some reason to be disturbed by the fact that, for all their bleating about the pre-eminence of the "natural law", the Catholic bishops seem utterly oblivious to its collapse in areas beyond the bedroom door. For, if the word "secularisation" has any meaning at all, it must surely have discovered the perfect synonym in the term "set-aside".

8. WATERSHED   (June 1994)

The beasts of the field shall honour me, the dragons and the owls, because I give waters in the wilderness and rivers in the desert, to give drink to my people, my chosen.
Isaiah, 43:19-20

If the World Cup were a drama written by God, perhaps the real dramatic action might not be occurring where we think it is. Perhaps we should look more to the sidelines, to the cameo scenes being enacted there and to the symbols which they are illuminating before our eyes.

Last week, for example, the off-pitch action was dominated by Jack Charlton's attempt to subvert and overthrow the dangerous and ridiculous FIFA ruling which prevented him getting sufficient water to his players on the pitch. This controversy attracted public attention for a very basic reason: all of us have an innate sense of what it might feel like to go without water, even for a short while.

The information that several members of the Irish team were deprived of water for three-quarters of an hour while they ran their hearts out in egg-frying conditions is enough to make one boil with sympathy and anger.

On the day before the match against Italy, *The Irish Times* carried a page two report entitled "US company wants to buy Galway water". The report told of a US-based multinational, Eagle Water Resources, which has applied to Galway County Council for permission to take large quantities of water from Lough Corrib for export in bulk tankers to the Middle East. The company plans to take 10 million gallons of water a day from the lake.

Nobody, it seems, feels it appropriate to boil with anger about this. Nobody has yet made any connection between this report and the World Cup. Perhaps it is time we did. A nation which is known for dropping to its knees at the merest twitch of a statue's eyelid should not find it too implausible that God might seek a more up-to-the-minute medium when he finds himself with a captive audience on which to lay his more urgent messages. Perhaps he has employed a more trendy marketing agency.

Peace and water are the two most important issues in the affairs of modern man, and they are inextricably linked. There is no doubt whatever that water will be the most precious resource of the next century. If the "resource wars" of which the European Commission President, Mr Jacques Delors, has spoken with such glib equanimity come to pass, they will almost certainly be about water.

Degradation of the world's water supply (largely as a result of the activities of US multinationals, oddly enough), is already creating innumerable pressure points around the globe. We have seen signs of this with the recent outbreak of tensions between Hungary and Slovakia about the damming of the Danube.

In this context, the sense with which we have been brought up in Ireland that water is limitless and infinitely pure begins to betray itself as a dangerous lie. It is this conditioning, perhaps, which causes us to be blasé, indifferent about reports that US multinationals are planning to export our water.

This is why we urgently need to interrogate both our own conditioning and the motives of those who now seek to take advantage of it.

The proposed Lough Corrib development, the *Irish Times* report informed us, would represent a £30 million investment which would create forty jobs. Oh, well, *then*. Forty jobs. That's *different*, isn't it? I mean, one cannot be against *jobs*! What sort of begrudger would put some airy-fairy notions about water ahead of the need to create *employment*. This is the new culture of modern Ireland – almost anything can be justified and tolerated if jobs, or even sometimes *a job*, can be hinted at as part of its consequences.

Forty jobs is pretty much the end of any argument, whether about the sale of citizenship or of our most precious life-giving resources.

There was more. A director of Eagle Water Resources, Mr David Lester-George, said that "up to 200" jobs would be created when the "facilities" were being installed in Lough Corrib. Clearly, if I wish to raise any objection to what Mr Lester-George's company proposes to do, I have to provide at least 240 jobs before I am entitled to open my mouth.

The issue is not really about protectionism or about us selfishly safeguarding our own water supply. In my view, we in Ireland should be seeking to help the destitute and water-deprived parts of the world – as a gesture of solidarity and Christian charity, yes, but also as an element of a mutually beneficial co-operative relationship. This capacity will be removed from us if we allow developments such as the proposed Lough Corrib project to proceed.

In other parts of the world, matters like this are perceived as spiritual questions. In India two years ago, for example, over 500 farmers ransacked the offices of a US multinational, Cargill Seeds, in protest at one element of the GATT package which enabled the patenting of seeds, which they describe, unequivocally, as "gene theft". They see the issue very clearly as an attack on the abundance of nature by the forces of Western capitalism.

How much more sinful, then, is an attempt to commodify the most life-sustaining resource of all? Water and life are inseparable from one another. Human beings consist almost entirely of water. As we poison the Earth's water supply, we slowly poison ourselves. The escalating crisis is not a scarcity of water, but a scarcity of *clean* water. It's later than we think.

Every other day we read about some new incident of pollution wiping out the fish stocks in an Irish river or lake, the most recent being the pollution of the River Lung in County Roscommon, resulting in the cancellation of the All-Ireland interprovincial angling competition.

This is what we are causing to occur because of our refusal to see things in other than superficial pragmatic terms. In the post-GATT world, seeds and water are not life-giving resources but commercial commodities, subject only to the laws of free trade and the capacity of people to pay their way. The market decides who the chosen people are.

It might be good to reflect on these things as we watch today's match between Ireland and Norway. This evening, as we observe water being supplied to the Irish team, we might do well to think about what it means, and what the alternative might be.

Incidentally, did anyone else find it mildly amusing that during the recent public outcry about the number of Government ministers finding themselves with official business in the US at the precise time of Ireland's World Cup matches, the accused politicians almost invariably defended themselves on the grounds that they were going to the US to "sell Ireland"?

Don't they think that they've sold quite enough of it already?

9. JUNKETING FOR THE POOR   (November 1991)

Last week I spent a couple of days in the EC. The purpose of my visit was to attend a seminar entitled "Poverty, Social Exclusion and the Media", which was held over two days at the Jean Monnet Building of the European Commission in the Grand Duchy of Luxembourg.

I had never been to Luxembourg, and in a very real sense, although I duly attended this seminar, I still cannot really lay claim to have been there. The place – or, more correctly, the entity – I visited seemed to me to be utterly unconnected to the country in which it exists, and indeed to "Europe" in any larger cultural or social sense. The place I attended, as I say, was a place called the "EC". In that strange location, it is necessary to abandon the logic which one applies to the everyday world, and allow oneself to be subsumed by a different rhythm, a different way of thinking, a different pace and a different morality.

Each of the two mornings of my visit, together with forty or so other journalists from most of the twelve member countries, I was ferried from my hotel near the airport to the building in which the seminar was taking place. Luxembourg seemed like a nice place: lots of beautiful parks with copper-coated trees and dozens of modern buildings that do not look as though they have been designed by a computer.

I peered out through the misted-up windows of the car driven by an official of the European Commission's Poverty Programme and made a mental note that I really must come sometime on a real visit.

The Jean Monnet Building is a vast black block which, although mostly made of glass, contrives to provide almost no view of the outside world. Perched in the middle of Luxembourg, it has all the appearances of an invading module from another planet, which, in a very real sense, is what it is.

On the first morning of the seminar, the official driving us had to circle the building three times before finding the entrance gate. By the end of the second circuit, I had decided that the building did not actually have a gate or a door, that it was one big window which nobody could look through, that there was nobody inside it, and that, very possibly, the "EC" had been entirely a figment of Gerry Collins's imagination.

On my second day at the conference, the security man at the entrance was unable to find my name on the list, and was utterly deaf, at first, to my protestations that I had been on that selfsame list the previous day, that he himself had been on duty and had not questioned my entry. Eventually, in a flash of inspiration, I persuaded him by asking, "Do you really think I would be going in here if I didn't *have* to?" Immediately, he snapped out of it and waved me through. Then I went to the conference room in which our conference had been conducted the previous day, and found it occupied by a completely different set of people.

Now I know why Gerry Collins makes so little sense when, from time to time, he comes home. I have always harboured deep suspicions about the EC, and particularly of people who have tried to pass off "Europe" and "The EC" as being one and the same place. Now that I have at last visited the EC, I am happy to be able to confirm all my worst prejudices about it.

It seems to me that the very basis of most of our discussion of the implications of EC membership is fatally flawed, since underlying it is the assumption that there is some stage of compromise, some happy medium, between our present state of relative sovereignty and full membership of a totally integrated Community. This is Cloud Cuckoo Land. The EC, it seems to me, is powered by a centrally driven, all-consuming logic, which it is not possible to half-believe in. You either believe in the idea of an independent Ireland, or you believe in an Ireland utterly subsumed within the logic of Europe. There is no halfway house, no plateau of peaceful coexistence; we either go on, or we start to go back.

The EC logic does not simply require a modified form of thinking; it calls for the obliteration of all existing thinking and its replacement by a self-contained, hermetically sealed form of what is wrongly called "European thinking", which, in much the same way as the former totalitarian societies in Eastern Europe, is designed to eventually kill off the possibility of logic which is threatening to it.

During the two days of the "poverty" conference, for example, I found myself being sucked into a form of logic towards which I was conscious of having a huge inbuilt resistance. Talking is one of the major growth industries in the European Community. Buildings like the Jean Monnet exist purely to accommodate the rapidly expanding talk-mountain which the EC creates.

The purpose of the poverty conference was to "encourage thought about media coverage of social exclusion", to analyse the reasons for the neglect of this topic in the media, and to provide an outline for "a productive debate" on the subject. Everyone I met at the conference was extremely pleasant and enthusiastic. Most of the journalists were people who had long specialised in the area of social affairs reporting. The officials of the European Community's Third Poverty Programme were also most agreeable, and clearly extremely well-motivated and passionate about their stated objectives.

Much of the first day's discussion hinged on technical considerations about ways to provide better coverage of what the Third Poverty Programme is about. Each of the journalists was invited to make a verbal contribution, as most of those present did. There was much emphasis on the need for greater "transparency" of the Commission's operations, and on the necessity for greater access to information and statistics. A few journalists spoke about the desirability of making poverty more "fashionable", so as to make the subject more palatable for the readers of upmarket newspapers.

I myself took copious notes of the first day's contributions, while inwardly attempting to formulate a contribution which would prove as responsible and incisive as all the others. And yet, at the back of my mind was the niggling feeling that the very idea of flying in dozens of journalists to Luxembourg, of wining and dining them for two days while they talked about poverty, had somewhere about it more than a hint of absurdity.

But, since it is not possible to sit and participate, and at the same time be constantly conscious of the absurd dimension, the first thing you abandon is your sense of the absurd. Once this has been banished, logic and common sense soon disappear through the same exit. For a time you become what Gerry Collins would undoubtedly describe as "a European".

It occurred to me that what I should say to my fellow European journalists was what I actually knew to be the *truth*. I should say that, since the EC's economic policies operate on the basis of favouring the strong at the expense of the weak, the idea of the European Commission setting about the alleviation of poverty is a bit like Korky the Cat heading up a campaign for the preservation of mice. I should also point out that the role of the journalists is not to assist the Commission's attempts at window dressing by producing articles and programmes about the more interesting and photogenic poor, but by providing critiques of the economic policies which lie at the heart of the problem.

It would also be no harm, it seemed to me, to point out that, even if the European Commission succeeded in making rich the 50 million of its citizens who are currently poor, this would not be a moral solution for as long as there continued to be beef mountains and wine lakes in a world where half of humanity does not have enough to eat.

And, on the following morning, that is more or less what I said. I am sure that if Gerry Collins had been present he would have accused me of frightening immaturity. He would have appealed to me not to burst up the party with such naive expressions of the obvious. My contribution was simultaneously translated into six languages and will undoubtedly be typed up in triplicate and consigned to the paper mountain. Nobody present so much as batted an eyelid. It made me feel better, but it will not improve one iota the circumstances of a single citizen of the European Community.

X

POST-POLITICAL POLITICS

1. THE DEVALUATION OF MISERY   (February 1993)

Within hours of the unemployment figures breaking through the 300,000 barrier, the voices on the radio were cautioning that unemployment was "on the way to 400,000". The point appears, on the face of it, irrefutable. Yet there is also a rather disquieting sense of underlying unreality about it.

I'm not talking about the predictable political point-scoring, which nobody takes all that seriously anyway, but about the undercurrents of what are mostly quite genuine and sincere attempts to articulate the gravity of the situation. All the time, there is the disquieting sense that something is being evaded rather than confronted.

This note of evasiveness has crept into much of the commentary on the unemployment situation over the weekend, by Government and Opposition politicians alike, but also by analysts and leader writers. Usually, they will have a quick tot of the 16,000 people on pre-retirement schemes and the 29,000 on FÁS training courses which, it is pointed out, bring the total unemployment figure within a shout of 350,000. This figure, while 16.66 per cent more than the 300,000 figure, is not, in a curious way, 16.66 per cent more *shocking*.

Rather, the fact that the 350,000 has yet to be reached gives the sense that the crisis point is not yet upon us. Curiously, there is an implication that, actually, nothing very remarkable has happened – the true figure has been well over the 300,000 mark for some time, so there is no need to panic just yet.

The effect of such analysis is actually to disperse the full impact of the 300,000 figure. While purporting to be an exercise in realism, it is actually an attempt at further self-delusion, at delaying the fateful day when we must face the full enormity of what is happening to us.

This approach has characterised the entire history of the growth of our unemployment figures to their present level. While unemployment was still in the five figures, the then Taoiseach, Mr Jack Lynch, told us that if it reached 100,000, the government should resign. No sooner had it breached that figure than the definition of crisis point was shifted to the 200,000 mark, and so on.

Within a few days of reaching the 300,000 mark, we have begun to accommodate ourselves to the new situation. The implication is clear: when the figures reach 400,000, we should *really* begin to be worried. It is truly remarkable how, as each new frontier is breached on the journey to our self-destruction, our sense of "normality" is restored by the simple expedient of raising the next jump.

What we are seeing is a devaluation of misery in the interests of normalisation. As a way of keeping our self-delusions afloat, it has been a remarkably successful approach, and there is every reason to believe that it will continue to work for a little longer. But, like all devaluations, it has inescapable long-term consequences.

One of the costs is that it postpones the need for any radical or profound evaluation of what is occurring. After a week or so of newspaper headlines and radio and television discussions, the old catchphrases will reassert themselves. Those who have trotted out the hackneyed clichés about "stimulating growth" and "keeping the fundamentals straight" and "creating the right environment for investment" will resume their places at the centre of the discussion, safe from any searching questions until the next milestone is reached. The possibility of a radical reappraisal will dissolve yet again.

For example, on the *Saturday View* programme on RTE Radio last weekend, Ms Mary O'Rourke, the Minister of State for Labour Affairs at the Department of Employment and Enterprise, attacked the economist Mr Raymond Crotty for criticising politicians' record on economic management while not having any answers of his own. Let us leave aside the preposterousness of the suggestion that Mr Crotty, who has written innumerable books and pamphlets on economic affairs, is lacking in ideas, and concentrate on the sub-text of Ms O'Rourke's charge.

Claiming to have read all Mr Crotty's works, the Minister went on to dismiss his analyses on the grounds that they were "weak" and "insular". What she meant, of course, was that she did not agree with Mr Crotty's views. It is reasonable to ask whether *any* politician who has presided over the recent and continuing catastrophe that is the Irish economy has the right even to disagree with, never mind flatly dismiss, the views of *anyone* with a different perspective.

As Mr Crotty pointed out on Saturday's programme, the approach advocated by Ms O'Rourke – in so far as this is in any way clear – has already failed, and failed spectacularly. In fact, given the scale of the failure of conventional approaches, it is reasonable to suppose that the correct way forward might well be closer to the diametric opposite of such analyses. In other words, the correct approach is likely to be one with which politicians most vehemently disagree. Since few people seem capable of annoying politicians as much as Mr Crotty, isn't is possible that he may be thinking along the right lines?

In a different society, such an exchange might be seen simply as a difference of opinion, but in the Ireland of 1993, it represents much more than that. It is a reminder of the imperviousness of the political system to thought from outside its own narrow assumptions.

For much of our period of alleged independence, we Irish have been caught in the most vicious of cycles. A brief respite in the 1970s apart, we have drained away the intelligence and zest that might have allowed us to function in any proper way as a society. Like mass unemployment, mass emigration should have had a traumatising effect, but we quickly learned how to accommodate ourselves.

As the society contracted, it became good at keeping up the appearance of normality, aping the responses of societies outside. We repressed the grief we should have felt at the constant loss of our brightest and best, and dressed up the mutton of our distorted and unbalanced society as the lamb of a modern European state.

This process is discernible in any number of aspects of modern Ireland, but especially so in the quality of our elected representatives. With one or two notable exceptions, our elected leaders are almost uniformly lacking in any colour, energy or radicalism. Listening to them on radio or television, one can be sure of one thing at all times: that they will not utter one word that might by any stretch of the imagination be termed surprising or interesting.

This process has become acute in recent years, and

reached its apotheosis in the recent currency crisis, on which practically every one of our public representatives was advocating the same line. By definition, politics has become an area in which one does not expect to hear anything that might in any way challenge the orthodoxies that have brought us to our present pass. The distortion and stagnation of our society has rendered us incapable of coming up with any ideas about getting ourselves out of the hole. For want of anything better to do, we continue to dig and dig.

Even though the more-of-the-same approach has failed and failed miserably, we mark each new calamity with a brief bout of breast-beating and then resume the digging with renewed vigour. Because we have learned to accommodate ourselves to almost anything, we are complacent as well as certain that the worst will eventually occur. By the time it has happened, our notions of what the "worst" is have moved on.

If we are ever to break out of this vicious cycle, we need, first of all, to accept and acknowledge that crisis-point has been reached *long since*, that we do not need the unemployment figure to reach 350,000 or 400,000 or half-a-million (which it *will*, if we go on as we are).

Then we need to begin appreciating the extent to which our condition has been self-perpetuated, that it results from the absence of vital elements in our collective thought-process, an inevitable consequence of high levels of emigration. Thirdly, we need to conceive of the possibility that almost all the assumptions that have been taken for granted up to now are not just wrong, but perhaps the antithesis of what is good for us.

We may be coming close to the last chance for our society to do what it should have done 70 years ago: to ask itself the most fundamental questions about how it proposes to sustain itself. Since it is clear that politicians are congenitally incapable of even asking such questions, it will be necessary to establish some mechanism outside politics for this purpose.

I agree with the newly elected Senator, Professor J. J. Lee, when he says that Ireland since independence has suffered from a thought-deficit. While we fondly imagine that we have, if anything, over-analysed ourselves, the reality is that much of the best thinking is done far from the corridors of power, to the minimum of effect.

The time has come to establish some form of national think-tank to deal with the most profound issues of our future survival, from a social, political, economic, cultural and psychological perspective. Professor Lee's own arrival in the Seanad, given his own brilliant contributions to our growing understanding of our plight, may be highly symbolic in this respect. But he alone will not be enough. There is an urgent need to bring into the central thought-process anyone and everyone who might have even the most unlikely idea about what is to be done.

Yes, that means asking Raymond Crotty to run that idea about rescheduling the debt by us one more time. It means exploring every idea *other* than those that continue to monopolise the present normalised public consensus. It means listening to people who, because they challenged the assumptions which are now brought into question, have remained outside that consensus.

It means politicians facing up to the extent of their own failure and particular economists staying off our television screens until further notice (for full list send stamped, addressed envelope). It means the entire political establishment admitting that it doesn't have a baldy notion how to get us out of the hole. In short, it means scrapping the present blueprint and starting from scratch.

2. The Politics of Self-delusion (July 1993)

A reader from the US writes to ask me why it is that the Irish people do not revolt. Since he has forgotten to sign the letter, I thought I might attempt a reply here. He is, he says, a US citizen who "enjoys" Ireland for about three months every year, when he comes to stay at the holiday home he has built on the west coast. He has been coming here for more than forty years, and has taken a keen interest in Irish politics and history.

My correspondent is disappointed that recent promises of "change" in Irish politics have not been fulfilled. "It always seems to be politicians behaving as usual, and the Irish people apathetically accepting it all. A bright new moment seemed to open up recently with the coalition of Labour and Fianna Fáil, but how quickly it all evaporated into disappointment as usual," he complains.

"Your scandals are constant and numerous, and pervasive. Oh yes, all other countries have their scandals too; but, in Ireland, no one is ever really reprimanded, let alone sent to jail. And the Irish people seem not to care about anything, they just go on paying the bill. The beef tribunal, Greencore, Telecom, Mespil Flats, the Davy affair, the rise in telephone rates, the environmental court affairs over the Burren and elsewhere, and other scandals I fail to remember here. Why do the Irish not rise in total rebellion?"

These are questions we frequently ask of ourselves. Because their basis is liturgical rather than political, I am beginning to think they are the wrong questions. They assume the presence of a fixed imperative at the heart of politics, and I'm not sure that we haven't long since passed the point of no return in this regard.

I know exactly what my correspondent means about the "disappointment" of the present Government. At a certain level, people *are* disappointed. They observe the almost daily wriggling of Labour politicians, on matters like the tax amnesty, hare coursing and Aer Lingus, and wonder: what ever happened to the heady promises of change.

It is indeed instructive to observe how differently our Labour Party representatives disport themselves in the comfort of the Government benches, compared with their principled outpourings from the austerity of opposition. There is something both disquieting and entertaining about their inability to answer straight questions, or even simply reiterate the straightforward stances which brought them to the dizzy heights of power.

But there are other ways of looking at it. It might be argued that, notwithstanding the air of double-standards which now pervades the reputation of the Labour Party in government, the party has actually been delivering in practice much more than public perception might allow. After a few months in office, the Government has already dealt, in a resolute manner, with a number of highly contentious issues, in particular homosexuality and condoms.

There is, behind the public perception, the possibility that the Government might deliver on a sufficient number of fronts to satisfy some other level of public expectation. The recent opinion poll results tend to support this analysis.

What "disappointment" the public feels about the Labour Party is a reflection not of its performance in government but of its sanctity in opposition. The disjunction is between perceptions rather than realities. Irish politics has recently had an overdose of priggery and piety, with Labour in opposition occupying more than its share of the high moral ground. The most unsettling thing about its ascent to office was the jolting stop to its moral crusade.

The cynical view is that Labour, having sunk its backside into the upholstery of office, is happy to forget its rhetoric and its followers. An alternative way of seeing it is as a necessary crossing of the bridge of compromise, over the river of pragmatism that runs between rhetoric and reality.

This is not as cynical as it sounds. Up until recently, the moral, quasi-religious view was sustainable in most things. The world was big enough to be compartmentalised and codified into separate blocs where different moral orders could operate with reasonable clarity. It was possible, for example, for rich countries to express sympathy for poor countries without having to acknowledge the possibility that their own wealth was a function of the poverty of others.

But such sanguine perspectives are proving increasingly unsustainable, and, consequently, a truly *moral* order is something we consider either beyond us or not worth the trouble. And so, while we continue to utilise the *rhetoric* of morality, what we express is not a truly moral outrage but a utilitarian or aesthetic outrage in disguise.

In the recent controversy about the tax amnesty, for example, it was noticeable that much of the public anger was directed at the idea that some citizens are able to get away with things that others are not. This is somewhat different to the expression of a moral imperative, which should be based on something a trifle more metaphysical than envy and greed.

Similarly with the catalogue of "scandals" listed by my American friend. Although there was indeed much public anger in each of the cases mentioned, it was not a moral anger. What most of us say in response to such revelations is: "Look what those bastards are able to get away with while I have to get along by the seat of my pants!" Never do the scandals cause us to stop and ask: "Where is the source of the rot that can be seen all around?"

We have too much to lose by opening up such profound questions; that search for a source would lead us surely to question, firstly, the immediate order of our own society, and then that of the broader world. There is no telling where such a quest would lead us, but it is certain that its rewards would not be delivered in the form of structural funds. To put it another way: beggars can't be puritans.

In the vacuum left by the departure of the moral imperative, we have adopted an essentially aesthetic view of politics, albeit couched in the language of a self-contained, localised and makeshift quasi-morality. As a consequence of our religious culture, we have come to expect our politicians to strike high moral notes, and as a rule they oblige, at least when out of power. But what passes for moral discourse is almost invariably something else.

For example, although most media commentators attack what they assert is the moral degeneracy of Fianna Fáil, it is obvious to all but the most deluded that their objections to that party are really on grounds of class and aesthetics. Basically, the Irish middle-classes don't like the idea of a Government party which they associate with Wellington boots. Most political pundits are antipathetic to Fianna Fáil on what they would claim are "moral" grounds; but when one observes their responses to scandals which do not involve Fianna Fáil, it can be seen that the most consistent object of their attacks is not *scandal*, but the idea of scandal involving parties they associate with Wellington boots.

The reason we do not "revolt" against our politicians is that, deep down, we know them to be exactly like ourselves. Irish politics has institutionalised the necessary double-standard that we developed to protect us against the contradictions of a world which the application of moral values would render unsustainable. Irish society, like other Western societies, operates quite easily on two contradictory norms at once. Irish politics acts as a kind of moral shock-absorber, dissipating many of the contradictions which would render a truly moral society incapable of functioning at all. The proceedings in Dáil Eireann act as a daily controlled-explosion of all the tensions, hypocrisies and confusions which would otherwise leave us paralysed.

As to whether there is any possibility of "change" in this situation, I have to say that this is not likely. There is a view that this Government represents some kind of milestone on the path of self-delusion which politics has been treading in recent decades, that we are approaching a political epiphany which will usher in a new era of enlightenment. For this theory to hold, you need to believe that Labour in government is a kind of Last Illusion, the final possible permutation offered by the present political slide-rule.

I wouldn't hold my breath. Firstly, it must be remembered that we are addicted to the illusions offered by politics. We have a deep need for the daily charade of the *Punch and Judy* show about "morality" and so forth. It makes us feel better about the compromises we have to make in our own lives by virtue of inhabiting a world that makes no moral sense.

A government can be a "disappointment" in terms of the big picture created by the pretend "moral" debate, and yet provide for a sufficient number of our everyday concerns to ensure its re-election. Secondly, it would be naive to assume that, because Labour's high moral tone has been muted by office, it has been permanently silenced. We need the hypocrisies of our politicians, just as we need the feelings of outrage which they inspire in us, and they show no signs of depriving us on either count.

The one thing that we should avoid underestimating more than the capacity for cynicism among our politicians, is our own capacity to forgive them for as long as they allow us to avoid the real questions. Whenever our politicians "sell out", they do so essentially on our behalf; if they did not, we could not bear the accusation which that refusal would level at us all. We go on "paying the bill" because we know that the cost of delusion is, for us, much cheaper than the price of truth.

3. THE UNFORGIVEN   (March 1993)

There is a common thread between the recent controversy over appointments by Labour Party ministers and last week's revelation that three former Progressive Democrat ministers are now benefiting from ministerial pension entitlements which, in a previous life, they dismissed as "without moral justification".

The Labour Party has railed for years against the jobbery, cronyism and stroke politics of Fianna Fáil, but in office manages to make the Soldiers of Destiny look like amateurs in each of these categories. The Progressive Democrats, seeking a niche for themselves in their start-up period, make copious hay of the pensions issue, but back in Opposition, decide to take the money and run. Both parties might, with some justification, be accused of wanting the bullfight and the bull home with them.

Both parties, it seems, have more than merited whatever unfavourable media mention they have received in respect of the two issues in question. Both have earned the anger and resentment of the public, with knobs on. What I am not so sure about it whether the public is angry for the right reasons, or whether the media comment has succeeded in getting quite to the heart of the matter.

It is interesting to examine the nature of the defences which both parties have entered in justification of their conduct. Mr Dick Spring, telling us that he has been hurt and angered by media criticism, defends the controversial appointments by isolating each one of them and putting forward a series of individual justifications.

In each case, these justifications ring true. For example, in respect of the appointment of his sister, Maeve, he says: "How anyone could believe that I should get rid of Maeve because I became Minister is beyond belief." Quite so. It is indeed unthinkable that someone who has worked as a personal assistant to Mr Spring for ten years should now be dismissed simply because she happens to be his sister. None of us could reasonably have been expected to behave any differently in a similar situation. To put it another way, there are extenuating circumstances that make it possible, in each situation, to fully justify what has been done.

Similarly with the Progressive Democrats and their ministerial pensions. One can sympathise with the three former ministers in question – Desmond O'Malley, Bobby Molloy and Mary Harney – for wishing to ensure they received the full entitlement under the regulations.

Which of us can say that we would do otherwise? And like Mr Spring, the former PD ministers have been sufficiently stung to respond angrily to criticism of their actions. Pointing out that their protest against the old system of ministerial pension had resulted in the system being changed for the better, Mr O'Malley asked: "What thanks did I get for not accepting it over a two-and-a-half-year period?"

Yet again, one can sympathise with the human beings at the heart of this matter. Contrary to conventional wisdom on the subject, our public representatives are by no means extravagantly paid, and moreover enjoy the absolute minimum of job security. Personally, I had no quarrel with the pensions they received under the old system. More luck to them, I say.

So, who precisely *did* have such a problem? That's right, the *Progressive Democrats* had a problem with pensions under the old system. When they renounced such pensions almost six years ago, Mr Molloy informed the Dáil that, in the context of high levels of unemployment and emigration, there was no "moral justification" for paying pensions to former ministers who continued to be sitting TDs.

Under the old system, the PDs argued, some former ministers received significant pensions while still in their 30s. As a result of the PD stance on the issue, the system has since been reformed, with effect from last year. Under the new regulations, ministers will not be entitled to pensions until they reach 55. However, since a significant number of former ministers has been awarded their pensions under the old system, they are allowed to choose between the two systems.

The controversy has arisen from the fact that Mr O'Malley, who is 54, and Ms Harney, who is in her 30s, have opted to receive their pensions under the old system, which they opposed, rather than the new system, which they championed. Now they are aggrieved because not only have their past sacrifices been disregarded, but they are expected to continue making sacrifices long after their point has been accepted. Mr O'Malley says he was "sneered at" for giving up his pension rights in 1987, which I can well believe.

Herein lies both the rub and the connection with the present hurt and confusion of the Labour Party. Labour and the Progressive Democrats currently stand compromised by the discrepancies between their previous rhetoric and their present actions.

Objectively speaking, neither party has, in any of the instances mentioned above, done anything to be ashamed of. It would be a mistake to hound either party on the basis of improper behaviour. In my view, it is not the behaviour, but the *rhetoric*, that deserves to come under scrutiny.

Nobody has to accuse either the PDs or Labour of wrongdoing, because they are their own accusers. They have set a standard of public behaviour which the reality of living in a human situation does not allow them to meet. This, I believe, is the real point. Nobody is accusing Bobby Molloy or Dessie O'Malley of doing anything wrong, but they stand accused by their use of the language of morality for the grubby purpose of political expediency.

Mr Molloy did not merely suggest that the old pension system should be altered, or updated, or modernised – he said it had "no moral justification". If something lacked moral justification six years ago, then it cannot have regained such justification merely because the PDs got "no thanks" for pointing this out.

Over the past decade or so, a major transformation has taken place in Irish politics. I refer not to the fallout from the Presidential election or the trend towards previously unimaginable coalition arrangements, but to the slow death of the human factor in politics that is occurring before our eyes.

Firstly, there has been the emergence of a new type of rhetoric, delivered by a hard, fundamentalist and humourless new breed of politician. This rhetoric has been responsible, as I wrote last week, for a profound abuse of language, with words like "morality", "integrity", "trust", "principle" and "credibility" being stripped of their proper meanings and dragged through the mud of political expediency and opportunism.

Not alone have these new-breed politicians removed all humour from the kind of politics they practise, but they have fundamentally threatened the survival of humour as a factor in Irish politics at all. The use of irony, for example, is now an extremely risky habit in an Irish politician, certainly much more dangerous than the abuse of alcohol or cocaine.

More to the point, perhap: they have all but succeeded in removing from politics any allowances that previously existed for the frailty of the human condition. It is interesting that many of these new politicians are lawyers, because what they have brought to politics, above all else, has been the kind of rigidity previously associated only with the law. Everything must be taken literally; everything is divided into right and wrong, black and white.

Most of this new breed have a quite appalling capacity for sanctimoniousness and self-righteousness. They allow no scope for humour, or human understanding, or weakness, or sympathy, or pity, or special circumstance. Every issue of alleged wrong-doing by a political adversary is pursued relentlessly without consideration of the extraneous factors which might be said to mitigate the matter. Individual politicians are targeted and taken out with a ruthlessness that seems quite horrific if you apply the standards of the external world. The result is a form of political charade that is totally incapable of reflecting the values of that external world in any meaningful way.

The most shameful incident of all in this regard was, of course, the crucifixion of Brian Lenihan during the 1990 Presidential election campaign. The issue of whether Mr Lenihan did or did not ring the President in 1982 suddenly became, after eight years, a matter of "principle" and "credibility".

For all the intervening period, this issue of "principle" and "credibility" had given an absolute minimum of concern, but suddenly it was a matter of absolute importance. Like Clint Eastwood in his latest film, Mr Lenihan was unforgiven for this "sin" in his political past, and the new breed was reserving the right to demand retribution at the moment of greatest advantage to itself.

One by one, they got on their hind legs in Dáil Eireann and delivered themselves of some of the most vile and spiteful utterances ever heard in either public or private life in this State. No allowances were to be made for Mr Lenihan's health or state of mind, or for the other possible explanations for his odd behaviour in the matter of the alleged phone call. No prisoners would be taken. In the end, they had their way.

So be it. Now, after several years of this form of politics, those who have practised it most relentlessly want to go back to the old ways of seeing and doing things. They talk of being "hurt" or "sneered at". When their own tactics are turned upon themselves, sometimes by the very people who joined in with their earlier moral onslaughts, they shout "foul" and plead for allowances to be made for the individual extenuating circumstances.

And yes, they have a point. It is most unpleasant to be the subject of one of these moral onslaughts, as I'm sure Mr Lenihan, Charles Haughey, Seán Doherty or Jim McDaid will confirm.

The best solution all round would be if everyone agreed to bring to an end this regrettable trend in Irish politics, to abandon the use of words like "morality" and "integrity" except in cases where these concepts, rather than party self-interest or expediency, are actually at stake, and to begin treating their fellow politicians as they would like to be treated themselves.

4. THE MORAL PREFAB   (May 1993)

(Thoughts on yet another of the periodic outbreaks of business and political scandal.)

How fascinating it is to observe the now almost unbroken coverage which the various business-related "scandals" are receiving in our media. You find yourself wondering if such scandals and such coverage can continue indefinitely, and whether there will from now on be a continuous supply of revelations and sensations relating to one thing or another.

On the other hand, if you think about these matters even slightly below their surface, you must be conscious of a certain unease on this very point. You might, for example, wonder if all these revelations are leading us anywhere other than on to the next scandal. And how many scandals is it going to take before we begin asking more fundamental questions about what is going on?

At the moment, I have this feeling that we are living in a perpetual storm, in an old house, with a crumbling, leaking roof. Every day, after a night of wind and rain, we go out to inspect the damage. We stand, in a state of mildly horrified boredom, looking up at the new holes that have appeared since the last time we looked. We shake our heads and send for the repair men to patch up the holes. So bad is the damage, however, that frequently the roofers end up putting their feet through the slates, causing even more damage than the weather.

Occasionally, when a particular large hole materialises, we set up a public inquiry to examine matters such as wind velocity and the acidity of rainwater. At no point does it occur to us that what we need is a new roof; we have total faith in the integrity of the existing roof. Meanwhile, the rain that has seeped into the beams and rafters is causing them to rot away, ever so slowly, so that one day the entire roof will come crashing down, demolishing the house and killing its occupants.

Nobody is in any doubt that things are bad and getting worse. There is no shortage of information and intelligence. We have all the facts we need. We are getting close to the point where we could well have a new scandal, comprehensively reported in the media, every new day. But there appears to be something amiss with what might be called the mind of our society, because it seems unable to make the necessary connections which would allow it to perceive that patching up the roof is no longer either worthwhile or wise.

Why is this? Largely it is because some of the most vocal and assertive of the occupants of the house are in the roof-repairing business. It is not in their interest to engage in discussion about tearing down the old roof and putting up a new one. The old roof has been good for them. In fact, the worse its condition becomes, the more they stand to gain from it. And being the most vocal and assertive of the occupants, they are able to ensure not just that their viewpoint carries the day, but that no other viewpoint is ever given more than a moment's thought.

You can observe this process in much of the media coverage which the "scandals" receive. Every day, in the newspapers, there is what amounts to a special, pull-out, scandal supplement. Every detail, every new "fact", is instantly communicated to the public in banner headlines. Even if you were never to read a word of it, the *scale* of the coverage alone would be almost sufficient to communicate the extent of the malaise.

And yet, paradoxically, when you begin to sift through the coverage itself, you become puzzled as to precisely what has been the nature of the wrongdoing. What you often find is that, although someone or other has broken the "rules" of the "game" (of business, politics, stockbroking or whatever), it is very difficult to discern where precisely the breach of *morality* or *principle* has occurred. You have this feeling that, while the issues are ventilated to the full, the conclusions inferred or drawn do not extend outside a very narrow quasi-ethical framework.

This is only partly because our newspapers represent the interests of those who wish to old roof to remain in place. There is also the question of journalistic convention, which respects "the facts" above all else. Journalism in Ireland continues to be preoccupied with information at the expense of meaning. "We just report the facts," says the journalist, "and the public can make up its own mind."

The facts, however, are only of use if they have a moral foundation. Facts, you might say, are connected to morals through meaning. In the absence of meaning, the illusion of a moral basis is provided by long and detailed pieces of analysis, usually written by lawyers, which tell you what rules have been broken and why you should feel outraged.

Then, in search of further guidance, you might find

yourself reading one of the occasional leader articles about the evolving culture of scandal. Because these are not written by lawyers, they sometimes attempt to address the issue of the scandals within the frame of morality and basic human values.

But as you read them, you become aware of something not being quite right. These editorials inevitably attempt to move the issue beyond the internalised logic of whatever the "game" is, but they invariably do so with equivocation, circumspection and circumlocution. They address the "facts" of the case and draw conclusions as to where the rules have been broken. When this appears inadequate – and because the rules have invariably been drafted by those who have broken them, it frequently does – they make up the moral shortfall with vague remarks about the behaviour in question being "dubious", "suspect" or "questionable".

There will almost certainly follow a call for more "transparency" or "accountability". Usually, too, concern will be expressed about something called "the public interest", which is intended to convey that there is some breach of trust with society, but one detects a reluctance to spell out what this means.

And always one is left with the feeling that much has been left unsaid, that no moral bottom line has been either reached or perceived, that such editorials belong to the culture of patching-up rather than of renewal. (Things become all the more difficult, of course, when some of the people at the centre of the latest "scandal" are nice People Like Us, rather than those nasty Fianna Fáil types who, as we all know, have no principles at all.)

Let us take a practical example. Suppose I get a job in a meat factory, packing meat for intervention. On my first morning at work, I am shown to a bench on which there are two pieces of meat. I am told to pack one of these in a box for intervention. I notice that one piece of meat is fresh and lean, while the other is of poor quality and starting to decay. I am free to choose which piece of meat I put in the box.

What do I know about intervention? I know that meat is stored away for several years in large warehouses so as to protect the market price of meat. I know of one such warehouse in one of the poorest areas of the city, where local people are rarely able to afford meat at present prices. I know that this warehouse is under 24-hour guard by security men whose job it is to prevent any of these local people going into the warehouse and taking the meat to feed their children.

The "rules" of the "game" tell me that the correct course is to put the good meat in the box. This is the whole point of intervention, after all: to remove from the marketplace quantities of meat in excess of what the market can dispose of at present prices. But my human instincts and sense of natural law, if I have any left, tell me that in a world where people die every second for want of food, it is wrong to put fresh meat in a box and store it away until it has become inedible.

I decide to put the bad meat in the box. By doing so, I have created yet another "scandal" and am likely to find myself in front of Mr Justice Hamilton and have my actions denounced by the leader writers of the land. I have broken the "rules" by which our society is governed.

What is the basis of this "rule"? Has it a moral basis? I think not. Surely it is simply the product of an already absurd system of logic going even more seriously out of control. If I think in moral terms, I know that it is wrong to put the good meat in the box. And yet, in our society, not to do so would result in my being branded as "dishonest".

This is why it is so difficult for leader writers to arrive

258

at the moral bottom line which undoubtedly underlies every single one of the continuing scandals: to do so would be to unleash a series of questions which, if followed through to their conclusions, would cause us to see that our society is of its essence corrupt, and that this corruption is concealed from our view only by the perpetration of countless absurdities at every conceivable level.

If you think other than superficially about the "facts", you realise that what is absent from the discussion is a sense of meaning and of morality. Instead of questioning the morality of the intervention system, for example, we spend two years on an inquiry which is partly designed to defend the integrity of that particular absurdity. Far from being an attempt to defend moral principles, it is an attempt to hide from them. It is to build a "moral" prefab inside the house with the leaking roof. Before long, we will find that it, too, has started to let the rain in.

5. THE TARMACADAM REPUBLIC   (July 1993)

If a pessimist is someone who looks at a half-full glass and declares it half-empty, what are we to call someone who looks at 98 per cent of £8 billion and is "disappointed" that it is 2 per cent "short"? A manic depressive? A begrudger? As likely as not, the correct manner of addressing the speaker will be "the Fine Gael spokesman on European affairs".

If there are any depths of sleeveenism left unexplored by Government politicians in their recent mad scramble for Euroloadsamoney, then these have been well and truly plumbed by the response of most of the opposition, and in particular Fine Gael, to the final figure announced last week.

If one was to ponder the role of political opposition, and contemplate what stances might usefully have been pursued on the Eurowads question, it is impossible to imagine any tack that might have shown the main opposition party in a worse light than the one it chose to take.

If might, for example, have asked considered questions about how the money was to be spent. It might have worried about the effect of the proposed spending on the already overly dependent Irish personality. It might have deliberated aloud upon the risk that the proposed infrastructural improvements, to be carried out courtesy of the Eurodosh, will do much more to facilitate foreign producers in penetrating Irish markets than to help Irish producers to access the European core.

Instead it chose to whinge about the – what is it? – £160 million that we *didn't* get, the 2 per cent of dogs that didn't bark. To make it even worse, Fine Gael then has either the gall or the stupidity to be baffled by its poor showing in the opinion polls.

Do the leaders of this party seriously believe that the average citizen of this State has the capacity to imagine the difference between £7.84 billion and £8 billion? Do they imagine that this is something we can succeed in getting ourselves in a state about? Most of us are utterly incapable of imagining the reality and the function of £1 million, never mind of – what is it again? – *seven-thousand, eight-hundred and forty million pounds.*

Like, how much tar are we talking about? How many miles of motorway? How many roundabouts? Perhaps some road-making contractor will oblige by giving us a meaningful figure expressed in hard shoulders.

(While we're at it, why don't we get a quote for covering the entire country, from coast to coast, in tar? This, I'm sure we'd discover, would solve most of our present problems and would vastly improve our tourism potential. We could change the country's name to the Tarmacadam Republic – motto: *if it doesn't move, we'll tar it*. Surely even the paltry £7.84 billion will buy us that amount of tar.)

At least all this talk about structural funds has taken the subject of Fine Gael off the front pages. As a former blueshirt myself, I have to say I am getting heartily sick of all this belly-aching about the "future" of Fine Gael. *What* future? A party so bankrupt of ideas that its best stab at a criticism of Government is to attack a perceived shortfall in its begging record must shortly be pronounced dead-on-arrival at the electoral clinic.

And have you noticed the rather interesting undertone of the renewed media questioning about the "futures" of both Fine Gael and the leadership of John Bruton? There is invariably a marked difference in these analyses from the character of such speculation in respect of, for example, the leadership of Fianna Fáil.

Always there is the cataloguing of the "inexplicably" sorry state in which the Fine Gael party currently languishes, followed by a testament to Mr Bruton's exemplary character and personal qualities, followed by the inevitable "unless . . . ". Unless something is done, they warn, the future is glum.

It always reminds me of Jean-Paul Sartre's Preface to Franz Fanon's classic work *The Wretched of the Earth*, about the demise of European imperialism. The word "unless", when spoken in arrogance, has a particular meaning, he pointed out. It is the sound of an alarm being set off to protect the vested interest of the speaker: "It is a threat followed by a piece of advice . . . but on the contrary, when Fanon says of Europe that she is rushing to her doom, far from sounding the alarm he is merely setting out the diagnosis. This doctor neither claims that she is a hopeless case . . . nor does he give her the means to cure herself. He certifies that she is dying, on external evidence, founded on symptoms that he can observe. As to curing her, no; he has other things to think about; he does not give a damn whether she lives or dies."

Is it not time we said publicly of Fine Gael: "We couldn't care less whether she lives or dies"? Here is a party which appears to look through the menu of possible responses on every issue and ends up always picking the most fatuous, the most ridiculous, the most perverse of the options. Why should we be expected to be in the least bit concerned, or even interested, in a party so far removed from reality?

What is Fine Gael *for* anyway? Why should we have any further need for such a party? What does it stand for, other than being opposed to Fianna Fáil? What ideas does it represent? Who does it speak for? If we were to take a leaf out of its own latest policy position on the Eurololly, we might begin to wonder if the real puzzle about Fine Gael is not why it has plummeted to an 18 per cent support level, but how it manages to get any support *at all*. How do you explain the fact that 18 per cent of the electorate can still see something in Fine Gael? Who are these people, and what ails them at all?

Every time you ask a question like that, someone or other always stands up and starts waffling about the Just Society. This is what Fine Gael stands for, they allege. The Just Society. The Just Society was a half-baked idea that arose briefly in the mid-1960s and disappeared just as quickly.

Fine Gael has had two extended periods in government since that time, and if it made any attempt to introduce a Just Society, or a Just *anything*, I'm pretty sure we would have noticed. A Just Society would, to paraphrase

Gandhi, be "a good idea".

And still, a quarter-century after it shot to obscurity, the Just Society is the best that Fine Gael is able to come up with in defence of its existence. Just as the pundits are always anxious to list John Bruton's good points, so are they ever-willing to trawl the political folk-memory in search of Fine Gael's single redeeming aspect.

My explanation for both the above-mentioned phenomena is that most of the key opinion-formers of present-day Ireland found themselves at some time or an other sitting beside John Bruton at school. At some point, they all appear to have decided that it would be a good idea for their old mucker to be made Taoiseach, an ambition they seem likely to abandon with the greatest reluctance.

Let's get it right. The Just Society was an idea that never happened, and probably never will. Its author, a Mr Declan Costello, has most recently received notice on account of a High Court judgement seeking to prevent a fourteen-year-old rape victim from travelling to England for an abortion.

The younger supporters of Costello in Fine Gael in his 1960s heyday – the so-called "Young Tigers", a motley collection of crypto-radicals which included John Bruton – have moved on to occupy influential positions in Irish life, and are no longer distinguished by any traces of radicalism. Some of them continue to be somewhat tigerish, though not in the political arena.

But old dreams die hard, which explains why, right up to six months ago, we still occasionally felt this otherwise inexplicable insistence that we put Fine Gael in government and make John Bruton Taoiseach.

Well, *we won't*.

This is not to say that he is not a nice man, with tons of ability and oodles of positive qualities. It is not a question of John Bruton being the cause of the problems of Fine Gael, but of Fine Gael being the source of John Bruton's undeserved unpopularity. Mr Bruton just happens to be leading a party that hasn't had an idea for twenty-five years, and has no direction other than down.

There is no need to wonder why this is so, no need for lengthy analyses, no need for any puzzlement. There *is* no mystery. Fine Gael is kaput. This would have happened a long time ago but for the accident of Garret FitzGerald who, pitted against *El Diabolo*, Charles J. Haughey, kept us sufficiently interested in the Punch-and-Judy tussle to ignore the fact that Fine Gael has had no real purpose for a long time.

By the manipulation of tribal loyalties and public perceptions, Fine Gael has survived for about twenty years longer than it might otherwise have expected. All its life, by virtue of the very existence of Fianna Fáil, it has been spared the trouble of having any ideas of its own.

It did not need to develop or think; it merely had to be *there* and be perceived as the logical alternative to Fianna Fáil, to point out that Fianna Fáil and all belonging to it had cloven feet. Such was the loathing for Fianna Fáil among some sections of Irish society that many leading opinion-formers have been ready to bend over backwards to justify the unjustifiable. Never in the history of politics has a party survived on so minuscule a pretext.

In the old days, the keening of Fine Gael spokesmen for the soul of the missing £160 million would have us looking for the government's blood. But since then, a few more of us have been to school, even if we didn't get to sit beside John Bruton.

The game is well and truly up for my erstwhile blueshirt compadres. Fine Gael is dying. No ifs, no buts, no unlesses. As to curing her, no; I have other things to think about. I do not give a damn whether she lives or dies. Now, could we let Fine Gael get on with dying, and let the rest of us try to get on with living in this Tarmacadam Republic.

6. IN SEARCH OF THE LEAST USELESS   (February 1994)

The ushering-in of 1987 in the Federal Republic of Germany was accompanied, as was customary, by a special New Year message on television from the Chancellor, Dr Helmut Kohl. Things appeared to proceed normally. The prerecorded message was broadcast to widespread indifference and people got on with celebrating the New Year.

Next day, however, the television company received a complaint from the Chancellor's office: it had broadcast the wrong tape. Sure enough, it transpired that the technician in charge of the broadcast had put on the tape of the Chancellor's address of the previous year. Not a single citizen of the Federal Republic had noticed anything.

Speaking of the meaning of the incident, the German philosopher and writer Hans Magnus Enzensberger said: "I don't not believe in conspiracy theories. The true explanation is much more interesting."

The truth, Enzensberger surmised, was that the technician's unconscious had whispered to him as he reached for the tape: "Who cares what's on this daft cassette? It's six of one and half-a-dozen of the other."

"At that moment," Enzensberger said, "he acted as a representative of a society which thinks exactly as he does."

Enzensberger was identifying a political condition that

utterly by-passes the conventional concept of apathy. It is an existential tedium arising from the conduct of politics and public affairs which we in Ireland would previously have been incapable of imagining. But now, I think, we can. We have reached some advanced point of development – or, more correctly, of undevelopment – at which this level of indifference is becoming the norm.

Writing for a newspaper about public affairs tends to put one out of synch with the general mood of society. Even as one attempts to grapple with the issues which affect that society, one's very closeness to the issues prevents one perceiving things in the way normal people do.

Over the past few weeks I have been engaged in something which, of necessity, tears me away from minute-by-minute obsession with public affairs, to the extent that I may, for the moment at least, have reverted to the forgotten state of being well-balanced.

So, last week, when I heard that there was another attempted putsch against John Bruton as leader of Fine Gael, I yawned. Not physically, I admit, but metaphorically, symbolically and, yes, deep within my soul – a yawn so unfathomable and intense that for a moment it seemed I might join those tax-free offshore millions in the great black hole in the sea-bed.

In these occasional periods when one is able to get on with what might loosely be called "real life", one experiences such glimpses of what it feels like to be normal. One begins to understand the looks of pity and dread that flit across the faces of normal people when one idly asks them such things as: "Who do you think will take Pat Cox's seat in Munster?" or "Is there any word of that by-election in Mayo?"

This precise form of tedium is something new here, but is rapidly gaining ground. There is infinitely less respect for politicians now than there was a decade ago. Moreover, this disrespect has reached a level of impatience which verges on intolerance. Younger people, in particular, have moved past the point of being critical or satirical of politicians; to them, politics is simply an absurd irrelevance to their lives.

Because we fancy ourselves as the equal of other western societies, we imagine such trends to be the local manifestation of a universal phenomenon. But if the symptoms are similar to those visible in other societies, the root cause is utterly different.

In the wake of the 1987 Kohl tape incident, Germany continued as before. "The Federal Republic is relatively stable and relatively successful," noted Hans Magnus Enzensberger, "not because of, but *despite* being ruled by the people who grin down from the election posters." In Ireland, precisely the opposite is true: this Republic is a total failure, not despite, but because of the people who grin down upon us.

We are, I suspect, approaching a moment when this will become obvious. For over thirty years now we have proceeded in the delusion of normality which descended during the Lemass era. We allowed ourselves to perceive the arrival of Seán Lemass as the zero-hour from which all progress was measured. This prevented us correcting mistakes which had their very roots in that moment.

Modernity had arrived, and all past efforts were aberrations, cautionary tales which reassured us all the more about our present stability, prosperity, modernity, normality. From that moment we, in effect, created a whole new Ireland, which might very well have grown to resemble the whole new Germany created after the war, except that it was founded entirely on the sands of dependency and paternalism. But the generations which emerged in this new Ireland knew or cared little about the nature of its foundations. It *was*, and that was enough. Kill another chicken, for in the long run we'll be a long time dead.

Time passed and the cracks spread through the walls and floor of the edifice. We filled them in and they opened again. New cracks appeared and the old ones became gaping holes. We stuffed them with Euro-money but it was scattered by the wind. The building began to sink back into the ground. It is not that our house is still in need of renovation. What it needs is demolition and complete reconstruction. This is the moment of realisation which may now lie ahead.

What is happening is that what might be called the "normalisers" of Irish society are, one by one, being ushered off the building site. The Lemass era spawned a single generation of delusionists who have enacted the charade of normality right up to the present moment. This generation supervised the imposition of an imported model of modernity which has now disintegrated. Because they did not attend to the foundations, what came after them was nothing but the same old story.

Looking back, it is not the distant past, the pre-Lemass era, which emerges as the aberration of Irish social and economic history, but *the Lemass era itself*. For one brief moment there was this flowering of pseudo-modernity, and then the darkness closed in once again.

Except that those who had placed themselves in charge could not, or chose not to, perceive this darkness, perhaps because the rooms in which they lived were too rarefied and well-lit. The delusion proceeded, regardless of reality.

Now is the moment of reckoning. This is the meaning of the latest Fine Gael putsch. John Bruton, for all that he belonged to an allegedly different "side", is one of the political heirs of the Lemass era. He belonged to a now almost forgotten group of student Fine Gaelers, called the Young Tigers, who for all their apparent radicalism played a critical role in the normalisation of absurdity in Irish public life.

For most of my adulthood, it has been almost impossible to turn on a television set after six o'clock in the evening without hearing one or other of them parading the same tired logic and agenda. First they papered over the cracks, then filled them in. More recently, with increasing desperation, they have been trying to block up the gaping holes in their stewardship of this Republic. Now they have begun picking one another off, one by one, and a good thing too.

It is hard for us to see what is happening, because our perceptions are dulled by a surfeit of information emanating entirely from the centre of delusion. This is why the public feels such tedium about politics; but we are confused by the din into believing that our dissatisfaction has a different cause.

For example, when we attempt to assert our desperate desire for change through a moribund party system, our stymied efforts are reinterpreted as the basis of yet another delusion. When we elect a few less Fianna Fáilers and a few more Labourites or PDs, we are told that what we have displayed, at last, is a clear desire for the modernising delusion.

What they cannot be persuaded to see is that we exercise discretion at the ballot box in the same way as, every few weeks, I find myself attempting to squeeze one last shave out of a packet of used razor blades. Because I've forgotten to buy new blades, I try out each of the old ones in an effort to make the best of the least useless. This could be a description of the electorate's response at the last two general elections. But each alleged "shift" – each different blunted option – is welcomed by the delusionists as a vindication of themselves.

Fine Gael is still caught up in this error. It still harbours a dream of returning to office, either alone or with, for example, the PDs, and delivering finally the pay-off which it still believes is possible. It will not happen, of course, but even if it did, it would make no difference.

On *Primetime* last week I heard Mr Jim Mitchell, between crocodile tears for Mr Bruton, make regretful mention of his leader's "charismatic deficit", a sad liability in a television age. Were he encouraged, I have no doubt he would have gone on to bemoan the damaging effects of television on the public's capacity to take politics seriously.

I don't know whether to laugh or cry. No, I tell a lie: I laughed out loud. The idea that what is happening to the Irish public's belief in politicians is in any way the consequence of television is only faintly more remote from reality than Fine Gael's hopes of coming up with a leader less charismatically challenged than Mr Bruton.

The effects of television on public attitudes to politics may be a growing problem in modern western societies, but Ireland is not a modern western society. This is the penny that may now be just about to drop.

7. SUPERSTITION   (February 1994)

(Thoughts on yet another attempt to depose John Bruton from the leadership of Fine Gael.)

Here is an alternative version of the main political events of recent weeks. On Monday morning three weeks ago, one hundred people set out with clipboards in search of opinions. These opinion pollsters are the invisible hand

270

of modern politics, the people whom nobody ever remembers having asked what they think about anything.

Let us follow the course of one of these and let her stand for the other ninety-nine as well. This woman has a list of ten interviews she must conduct that day. This list is called a "cluster". On her clipboard, she has a list of ten descriptions, or profiles, of the type of person she should interview. She also has a geographical starting point and a series of directions by which to proceed from that point. Firstly, she must locate in the street where she begins one of the people described in her list of ten profiles.

She knocks on a door. An elderly man wearing a cardigan and a pair of brown carpet slippers comes out. Since the man qualifies under one of the headings, she decides to conduct an interview with him. He invites her in for a cup of tea and she asks him a series of carefully worded questions. On the television as they speak is a programme called *Good Morning with Anne and Nick*. The interview takes about twenty minutes. Some of the questions relate to the performances of various political parties and party leaders.

Among these is the name of John Bruton, whom the man in the brown slippers doesn't like because his laugh is too loud. Or perhaps he is just fed up listening to Anne and Nick. Anyway, he tells the pollster that he used to vote Fine Gael, but not any more with that man in charge.

When she has finished her questions and her tea, the woman leaves the house and again consults her clipboard. It tells her, for example, to turn left when she leaves the house, take the next right turn, pass through the next street, turn right again and knock on the fifth door on the left. She does this. The door is opened this time by a middle-aged woman carrying a baby. The pollster goes through the same procedure again. And so on. Each time, she asks the same questions. Each time, she follows a precise, but different, set of instructions about her next call.

As the day progresses, it becomes increasingly difficult to locate people who correspond to the remaining profiles on her list. She knocks on a door and it is answered by an elderly woman; but because her list of profiles has no requirement for such a person, and since there is nobody else in the house, she must move on according to yet another set of instructions.

This is the way opinion polling works. Each cluster is self-contained but is interrelated with the other ninety-nine which complete the larger sample, which incorporates the demographic characteristics of the population as a whole. Through varying the sets of profiles from cluster to cluster, a "quota-controlled sample" is built up which purports to reflect the opinions of the entire electorate. When the findings of the one hundred pollsters are collated, what results is a sample that will be correct nine hundred and ninety-seven times out of one thousand.

This process, proceeding in the same manner as it did in hundreds of other such polls in the last twenty-five years, led inexorably to last week's attempt to remove Mr John Bruton from the leadership of Fine Gael. The hostility of the notional man in the brown carpet slippers, who dislikes John Bruton because his laugh is too loud or because he has a pain in his butt listening to Anne and Nick, together with the hostility of nineteen other such people whose mid-morning torpor was interrupted by a knock on the door, was, in a profound and precise way, the genesis of the issue which dominated the public discourse of the past fortnight. In all, it took twenty people to change their view of Fine

Gael's performance to produce the drop of two per cent which the party suffered. This in turn led to the gang-of-four putsch, which led to the vote of confidence.

Two years ago, some two-thirds of the Irish electorate, more than one-and-a-half million people, who had reached the age of eighteen, who were not disqualified by law and who complied with the law relating to the election of members of Dáil Eireann, went to the polls and expressed a complex set of choices in relation to the governance of this country.

Those citizens who had the right to vote in that election did not have to wait for a knock on the door, but walked proudly to the polling booth and exercised the freedom of voting on the shape of their democracy, won for them with the blood of their forefathers. One of the views expressed by the electorate at the time was that Fine Gael be returned with ten seats less than it had taken into the election.

The curious thing is that, in the wake of that democratic election, not only was there no attempt to remove Mr John Bruton from the leadership of Fine Gael, but many of those who last week attempted to remove him from his position, on the basis of the changed opinions of twenty people, were insistent at that time that he be made Taoiseach.

If you wish to gain an insight not only into the declining fortunes of Fine Gael, but also the decreasing respect for politics and politicians, I suggest you ponder the absurdity at the heart of this little fable.

The debasement of politics now under way is not occurring, as certain politicians would have us believe, because of the blanket and cynical hostility of the public to politicians in general, but because politicians themselves seem not to care about their own profession. Our leaders are frequently heard to declare that they will not be hounded out of office by opinion polls, but they themselves are the custodians of a system of politics which today places more value on the casual opinion of a thousand anonymous cyphers than on the sacred outcome of a democratic election.

Politicians use opinion polls as a means of second-guessing the electorate and as a way of scoring points off one another. When they complain about the adverse effect of opinion polling, what they mean is the adverse effects of opinion polling on their own careers. Nobody seems to be concerned about the fact that opinion polling and the depersonalised culture which it enables is having a profound effect on the metaphysical condition of modern politics.

The evidence of this change is to be seen in the preoccupation with "charisma" and television performance, the growing trend of "celebrity" candidates, the constant pandering to public perception, the growth of the spin-doctoring industry, the death of leadership and of conviction politics.

As I have observed in the past, ninety out of a hundred people do not believe opinion polls, on the straightforward basis that they themselves have never been asked to participate in one. How can the outcome of such a poll possibly accord with the real democratic view, they reasonably ask, when it does not appear to have consulted any real people?

This, of course, is nothing but mindless, irrational superstition. And, of course, the polls are indeed to a high degree scientifically reliable, being based on tried and trusted sampling techniques which have a mathematically calculable level of accuracy. (Did you know, for example, that the margin of error in any given sample is calculated by multiplying by two the square root of the result of the sample multiplied by the difference between one hundred and the result of the sample divided by the sample?)

The regrettable truth is that only a small minority has the privilege of being acquainted with the gentleman in the brown slippers, or any of the other nine hundred and ninety-nine interviewees in this or any other sample; most of us, therefore, must take the outcome of these polls on trust.

For the several hundred such polls since their introduction in 1969, only about ten per cent of the electorate has been consulted. At the current rate of polling, it would take about two hundred years for every member of the present Irish electorate to be surveyed just once. The problem with opinion polls is not that they are inaccurate or unreliable, but that they are not a democratic device.

Democracy demands not merely that the process works according to defined principles, but that it *be seen* to work in this way. We now live in a society in which the action of politics is dictated not by the ballot box but by the voodoo of statistical theory.

If Mr Bruton seeks a way forward for Fine Gael, he might profitably address himself to the kind of core values suggested by his own recent troubles. I would spell it out a little more precisely, except that the last time I offered advice to Fine Gael I got little enough thanks for my trouble.

By way of a hint, and at the risk of driving those cuddly old blueshirts mad once again, might I suggest to Mr Bruton a technique favoured by a one-time Taoiseach of this country who, having no access to opinion polls, looked into his own heart when he wanted to know what the people were thinking. The self-styled smart-alecks of the rationalist age have a great laugh at what, in their stupidity, they imagine to be Mr de Valera's pomposity and arrogance. But what he was talking about was not egoism, but empathy.

The only way any of us can know what other people think and feel is to look into our own hearts. Even the woman with the clipboard must look into her heart in order to obtain a meaning from the replies given by the man with the brown carpet slippers. The best leadership comes from those wise enough to mediate the data and information coming from outside through their own human condition.

The change in politics that we urgently need would reflect, in the broadest and most profound manner, these words of the American novelist Flannery O'Connor: "A view taken in the light of the absolute will include a good deal more than one taken merely in the light of a house-to-house survey." Mr Bruton's future – perhaps ours as well – resides in his willingness and capacity to define a politics of the absolute.

8. The Slow Death of the Irish Left   (May 1992)

It is not necessary to be someone who answers "yes" to the question "Are you now, or have you ever been, a socialist?" to be concerned about the current consensus view that there is now no alternative to capitalism, the free market and what is rather tendentiously termed "liberal democracy".

The events of recent years in eastern Europe and the erstwhile Soviet Union have not merely killed off what had been regarded as the institutional alternative to capitalism in the world, but have also silenced those who had been attempting to provide an intellectual, economic and political antithesis to the prevailing ideology in the West.

It was perhaps inevitable that, in the immediate

aftermath of the 1989 revolutions, a deal of triumphalism and ya-booing would drive the lefties into bunkers for a time. But it could not have been anticipated that the left would be unable to deal with those events other than by outright capitulation to the logic of the right.

In Britain recently, the Labour Party lost the election everyone presumed it would win, precisely because, in the final analysis, the British public opted for the party which espoused market principles as a matter of faith rather than that which had adopted them reluctantly as a matter of pragmatic necessity. What this appears to show is that the electability of ostensibly left-wing parties is predicated not on their ability to sell left-wing policies to the electorate, but on the extent to which they are prepared to move to the right.

This is a dangerous, but catching, idea. In Ireland, despite the latest opinion poll figures which show Labour's support to be on the ascendant, the absence of an alternative political analysis is more striking than at any time since Independence.

There can be little doubt that this is connected with the failure of the Irish left to engage in a full and public debate about the implications for its own future of the collapse of communism in the East. It is possible, indeed, that those events provided some people on the ostensible left with a welcome rationalisation for giving free rein to the kind of pragmatism which the more principled of their colleagues had long been uneasy about.

In any event, the net result has been that, less than three years later after the fall of the Berlin Wall, Ireland is fast becoming a virtual monolith of political thought.

Although we have a number of political parties which are ostensibly socialist, their public profiles seem to be in inverse proportion to their advocacy of a socialist perspective. Practically all the most passionate and engaging advocates of socialism have been rendered invisible.

Now, the leading "left-wingers" wear sharp suits, hold press conferences in the Shelbourne Hotel and trip across one another in their anxiety to give the least possible offence to the economic and intellectual establishment.

This would not be a cause of undue concern if we lived in a perfect world. Since we do not, it should be a matter of concern not merely to left-wingers but to all those who believe this society, and indeed the world in general, to be in need of some improvement. What is in danger of being lost is not alone the articulation of uncomfortable dissenting views, but the dialectical exchange which makes change and progress possible.

By refusing to enter into a public dialogue about the dilemmas facing it in the wake of the 1989 revolutions, the Irish left has failed both itself and the society in which it claims to be interested. To have engaged in convulsive private conscience-wrestling, however cathartic, was an insufficient response in terms of the interest of the society as a whole.

Afraid of the electoral damage which might have resulted from unseemly public squabbling, both the Labour Party and the Workers' Party chose to confine their deliberations about the future of socialism to the smoke-filled rooms, and in doing so implied that the question at issue was purely that of their own interest in electoral survival.

There was, of course, one notable exception. The then Workers' Party guru, Eoghan Harris, in his spring 1990 document, "The Necessity of Social Democracy", attempted to define the post-communist virus in terms of the threat it represented to Irish parties of the left. Providing, inter alia, an essential critique of the limits of conventional left-wing language, tradition and symbolism,

278

Harris reaffirmed his Marxist vows and argued for a three-pronged commitment to democracy, revolution and reform, while questioning fundamentally the intellectual wherewithals of socialist economics and the doctrines of the command economy.

The Harris document contained the enabling potential for major lessons, not just for the Workers' Party, but also for the Labour Party and, indeed, for Irish politics generally. But instead of providing the catalyst for badly needed debate on the likely future of left-right politics, it became the focus merely of prurient media interest in the internal squabblings of the WP.

Its author was summarily drummed out of his party, which then proceeded to engage in private convulsions behind closed doors. And, rather than face up to the implications of the Harris critique for its own future direction, the Labour Party was content to smile smugly at the discomfiture of its rival, and bury its collective head in the sand. Thus, a golden opportunity for growth was denied.

A similar attitude, it seems to me, greeted the publication earlier this year of the Japanese-American intellectual Francis Fukuyama's book *The End of History and the Last Man*, which, depending on your perspective, is either the most devastating analysis yet of the death of socialism or a threadbare intellectualisation of capitalist triumphalism.

Like Eoghan Harris's document, Fukuyama's book is deeply troubling for those who have nurtured an unquestioning belief in the viability of socialist ideas. Unlike Eoghan Harris, however, Mr Fukuyama does not have at heart the survival of socialist principles or Marxist dialectics. Crudely put, the Fukuyama thesis is that, following the collapse of communism, the world has now arrived at the final stage of dialetical history, where all the fundamental contradictions of political society have been resolved in the relative perfection of the modern liberal democracy.

The "end of history" will occur when liberal democracy has embraced the whole world, and we will all live happily ever after. (This is a grossly inadequate summation of Fukuyama's book, which comprises some four hundred closely argued pages.)

Personally, I regard *The End of History* . . . as a meretricious and contrived attempt to provide an intellectual fig-leaf for the gung-ho triumphalism of unfettered liberalism. The book is full of inconsistency, tendentiousness and distortion. For all that, it should emerge as one of the most important political books of the 1990s.

It is a book which any serious advocate of socialist ideas must read, if only for the purposes of refutation. And yet, I have not noticed a single reference to the book, on radio, television or in the newspapers, by a member of an Irish left-wing party. Indeed, apart from a handful of brief reviews and promotional features, Fukuyama's book has been ignored by the dominant discourse of this society.

A superficial analysis of what occurred in the Workers' Party following the departure of Eoghan Harris might conclude that those members of the party who left subsequently to form the Democratic Left had implicitly embraced, and thereby vindicated, the Harris analysis.

In fact, they have gone much further than that. For all the accusation of revisionism levelled at Harris, his proposal was for the continuation of a broadly socialist process. It would amount to only a minor exaggeration to suggest that both the Democratic Left and, especially, the Labour Party have now accepted the triumphalist liberal analysis, as articulated by, among others, Francis

Fukuyama, and have begun the process of abandoning the left-wing territory for good.

This can be observed in the contortions of both parties in relation to European union. Instead of responding with the trenchant critique that their traditional supporters might have been entitled to expect, they have fudged, prevaricated and, in the final analysis, fallen in with the "pro-European". This is evidence, I believe, of the extent of their intimidation by the worldwide consensus in the wake of Soviet communism.

But, more fundamentally, it is the product of an intellectual paralysis which cuts to the core of modern political thought processes. I hope to return to this subject in the coming weeks, and write about a new book with the potential to rescue the Irish left. I hope we are not too late.

9. THE MYSTERY TRAIN (January 1993)

On the day after Mary Robinson's election as President in 1990, one of her main strategists, a leading member of the Labour Party, explained to me how the war had been won. The Robinson campaign, he said, had been like a train. The challenge had been to fill each of the carriages with a different section of Irish society without allowing the occupants to become aware who their fellow-travellers were.

In one carriage were the well-heeled liberals. In another were the traditional lefties. In another, a nervous gaggle of Fianna Fáil women. In others were the allegedly "conservative" rural voters who had been wooed on Mrs Robinson's intensive tours of the countryside. And so on.

The implication of this analysis is clear: that Mary Robinson had got herself elected more or less by stealth, that irreconcilable forces had been tricked into supporting her for different sets of reasons.

If you accept much of the conventional political analysis of modern Ireland, such cynicism is unavoidable. If you see divisions defined by party political allegiance as real and meaningful, then it is understandable that you will be surprised when something happens to confound them utterly.

Moreover, if you have a vested interest in the maintenance of those divisions, you have a pressing need to rationalise away all that makes nonsense of their internalised logic.

But it seems to me that as a way of describing what had actually been a central undercurrent of the Robinson campaign – the coaxing of various diverse elements of Irish society on to a common road forward – the Labour activist's remark said rather less about the actual changes taking place in modern Ireland than it said about our politicians' inability to comprehend them.

That Labour Party man is now a Government Minister. Perhaps he regards the forces which led to his elevation to high office with the same cynical wonderment as he regarded Mary Robinson's election. Certainly, there are many others within the political establishment who see the new Government in precisely this way: as having been foisted upon the people of Ireland by a mixture of stealth and happenstance. A "perversion of the will of the people" has become the favourite phrase.

In addition to being mistaken, this is quite dangerous thinking. It would be easy to refute it simply by pointing to the unassailable arithmetic of the new Government's parliamentary support, compared to almost any of the alternatives. Or one could draw attention to the short memories of those who now complain that the new Government was not canvassed before the electorate.

But it seems to me that such analyses would be utterly superficial. There is another way of looking at it.

Let us go back to our friend's mystery train. If it is true that in order to reach new destinations in Irish politics, the occupants of each of the carriages must be kept in the dark regarding the identities of their fellow passengers, then it is time for us to pull the communication cord and make a run for it up the embankment. The implication is that reconciliation and broadly common purpose are now impossible, that Irish society has become so fragmented that we will find no united path forward except through ignorance, stupidity and/or accident. It is to say that movement forward will result only from our being taken for a ride.

To translate this into a vaguely political analysis, it implies that "progress" of any kind will come only following the triumph of one side over the other – or, more precisely, the triumph of The Rest over Fianna Fáil. It decrees that no intermingling will be permitted between the two alleged "sides" in the Irish political divide, and that consequently, no form of synthesis will ever be possible. Although criticism of the new FF/Labour alliance comes in large measure from quarters that in the past advocated an end to the "Civil War divide", the thrust of their argument is such as to justify the perpetuation of the artificial divisions which plague Irish politics.

What these people are saying, perhaps unbeknownst to themselves, is that the possibilities for freeing up Irish politics are limited by considerations which have no basis *other* than the Civil War divide.

Contrary to what they would have us believe, that conflict still divides us, not merely as a people but, more fundamentally, within ourselves. It came to define in a political context the metaphysical distinction between good and evil. We defined an aspect of our "goodness" in terms of our political allegiance and have come to perceive the antithesis in the "other" side.

Of course, for one side the concept of "goodness" was, by definition, that which the other side perceived as "bad". This is not such a difficult trick as it may appear, being a little like the ambiguity regarding whether the zebra is white with black stripes or black with white stripes. In a society that had not yet developed a single guiding intelligence, it was possible to live with such differences. It could indeed be said that such tensions fuelled the dynamic that propelled us along the tracks.

The problem has arisen as a result of our development, in common with most modern societies, of precisely such a single guiding intelligence. Crudely put, this is the collective mind of the dominant class which thinks aloud via the communications media. The voices of these media, while tolerating a marginal level of eccentricity and dissent, are pretty constant in their analysis of Irish society. They have a semblance of plurality which is largely illusory.

In party political terms, while all sides are given a fair shake in terms of space and time, this is powerless to deal with the far more fundamental quantity of prejudice which is an integral part of even the most sophisticated intelligence. Thus, the guiding intelligence of modern Ireland has internalised the fundamental division between evil and good in terms of the divide that is perceived between Fianna Fáil and The Rest.

In the same way as in the past an individual might harbour a deep-seated antipathy to the side other than his own, this society – at least in terms of its dominant discourse – has more or less institutionalised one party, Fianna Fáil, as the respository of all political evil.

This is no longer merely a complaint. I hold no brief for Fianna Fáil, and, in any event, things have gone far beyond the point where such pleas might be of any use to that party. There is no longer, it seems to me, any point in arguing on grounds of fair play. The only point still worth making about this is to ask of our central guiding intelligence the following question: which is most important, as we approach the end of the second millennium – the future of Ireland or the destruction of Fianna Fáil?

Because of the central obsession with destroying Fianna Fáil, we will shortly, as an electorate, be faced with the question as to whether it is possible any longer to channel any kind of transforming energy through Fianna Fáil, or whether we should simply bow to the superior power of the guiding intelligence.

I say this without rancour or recrimination; if the future of Fianna Fáil was all that was at stake, it might even be possible to take a neutral view of this process. I would not be surprised if we had already arrived in the Last Chance Saloon, if within a short time we are to be faced with deciding whether, in the circumstances of modern Ireland, Fianna Fáil is any longer a viable option. If it comes to that, I suspect, we will destroy Fianna Fáil to avoid our own destruction.

This brings me back to the mystery train. Far from being suckers for the three-card-trickery of politicians, the Irish electorate is, I believe, engaged in a process of making solid, rational evaluations aimed at finding a permanent escape from the present logjam. In an increasingly complex and refined way, it is delivering verdicts that put the political establishment to the pin of its collar within the inflexibilities of its own system.

It seems to me that, in an almost magical way, the electorate is sending more and more complex signal to the political process in an attempt to jump-start its atrophied grasp on reality. Get out of this one, we seem to be saying. When the system has creakily and clumsily accommodated itself to the new situation, we hit it with something equally unprecedented and relish its discomfiture.

What we have in Ireland at the moment is the best Government possible under present circumstances. This is rather fainter praise than it may seem. Because of the inability of the central guiding intelligence to understand that the changes taking place in modern Ireland are *real* changes rather than merely expedient or tactical ones (the only kind it itself understands), that intelligence is poorly equipped to guide us where we now need to go.

The obstacles to the success of the present Government arise not from any great public objection to its configuration and still less from any sense of our "will" having been "perverted" by its formation.

In the main, the public wishes the Government well and, moreover, wishes that it do something to tackle the manifold problems of modern Ireland. If such obstacles do indeed arise, they are likely to result from the obsessive insistence by the topmost elements of Irish society that Fianna Fáil be buried at the crossroads with a stake through its heart.

10. THE POLITICS OF CONTENTMENT   (May 1992)

Last week in the column I referred to a new book "with the potential to rescue the Irish left", and promised to return to the matters it deals with. I had in mind *The Culture of Contentment*, by the US economist John Kenneth Galbraith (Sinclair-Stevenson Ltd.).

For all those who, in the wake of the collapse of "actually existing socialism", have been rendered inarticulate by the triumphalist onslaught of the right,

Galbraith provides a sweet and potent antidote. Although carefully avoiding mention of the Francis Fukuyama book, *The End of History and the Last Man*, to which I also made reference last week, Professor Galbraith effectively defuses Fukuyama's central supposition that liberal democracy, by virtue of its very survival, is intrinsically the least imperfect, if not the ideal, system of social organisation.

The morning after finishing *The Culture of Contentment*, I awoke to the news of the Los Angeles riots, and immediately thumbed my way back to a passage on page 170: "The possibility of an underclass revolt, deeply disturbing to contentment, exists and grows stronger. There have been outbreaks in the past, notably the major inner-city riots in the latter 1960s, and there are several factors that might lead to a repetition . . . It has always been one of the high tenets of comfort that the uncomfortable accept peacefully, even gladly, their fate. Such a belief today may be suddenly and surprisingly disproved."

John Kenneth Galbraith, author of such classics as *The Affluent Society* and *The Nature of Mass Poverty*, is one of that rare breed, an economist deserving of being called a scientist. But he is more than that; he is also a writer of great elegance and truth. He is an artist whose medium is political economics.

Although Galbraith deals primarily with his native America, his pithy, prophetic and passionate exposition of the degradation of US democracy has profound resonances for much of western Europe, including Ireland. In an analysis that approaches poetry in every paragraph, the 84-year-old economist lays waste to the smug verities of modern capitalism and the so-called liberal democratic systems which serve its interests.

His basic thesis is that modern democracies are no

longer driven by the aspiration to equality and fraternity, but are moving rapidly in the opposite direction. In the past, he points out, the "contented", i.e. the well-heeled and privileged, were a small minority of any national citizenry. Now they represent the majority of most voting populations and are in a position to have their societies run according to their own interests. Leaders and political parties who aspire to office must on board take the agenda of the contented, and must therefore exclude from their minds all notions about egalitarianism and the common good.

The agenda of the contented incorporates demands for the lowering of taxation, the eradication of public spending and the reduction of the role of government (except in matters where this might not be in the interests of the contented). The contented are opposed to any public policy which is geared to the long term, preferring short-term action which protects their immediate well-being. Issues like unemployment, emigration, public education, homelessness, drug addiction and poverty are largely excluded from the political agenda. These are issues which affect, in the short term at least, only those of the affected underclass, most of whom can be relied upon not to exercise the democratic franchise in a manner threatening to the contented majority.

By voting strictly for such short-term interests, the contented have locked their democracies into a situation whereby the excluded, being for various reasons a minority of those who vote, can effectively be kept out of the governing process. The agenda of the contented is kept at the forefront of national consciousness by the media (run and operated by members of the contented class) and by high-profile economists who provide a constant flow of quasi-scientific rationalisation for the selfishness of the contented. "The result", Galbraith writes, "is government that is accommodated not to reality or common need but to the beliefs of the contented."

In the US the contented are represented by the Republican Party; in Britain by the Conservatives. But, more and more, the principal parties of opposition, in order to remain in the race, must align themselves with the politics of contentment. Thus, the Democratic Party in the US and the Labour Party in Britain become increasingly indistinguishable from their dominant rivals.

If we apply the filter of Galbraith's analysis to the present state of Irish politics, much begins to explain itself.

Some of us, of course, have written about the culture of contentment in Irish society under the heading of "Dublin 4", and have met with precisely the response from that constituency that Professor Galbraith expected his own book to provoke: "very angry and very articulate about what seems to invade their sense of self-satisfaction".

In the Irish system, until relatively recently, our much-derided "clientelist" model of politics had kept the culture of contentment largely at bay. Although that system was by no means perfect, at least the purpose of government was regarded as being to improve the lives of as many citizens as possible. Nowadays this is disparaged as "catch-all" politics. Today, the concept of the catch-all party has been denigrated almost out of existence. Instead, masquerading as political parties we have a growing collection of interest groups in hot pursuit of the votes of the contented.

The rot can be traced to the founding of the Progressive Democrats. Recently they have attempted to soften their message in a fudge of social concern, but they remain, essentially, the party of the well-heeled. Although self-styled the "party of integrity", they were driven from the start by interests rather than principles. And those interests were those of the contented.

The PDs manifest a positive reaction to almost every one of the criteria of contentment, as outlined by Galbraith. They are in favour of low taxation and reduced public expenditure and have a quasi-religious belief in the power of the marketplace to decide everything for the best. When asked what their policy on poverty is, they speak of the need for "incentives" (more poverty for the poor, more wealth for the rich) and expound the "trickle down" theory (if one feeds the horse enough oats, some will pass through to the road for the sparrows).

Largely through massive promotion by the contentment-driven media, the PDs have come to dictate the direction of Irish politics in a manner utterly disproportionate to their electoral strength, having arranged to force their beliefs into practically every orifice of the body politic. All Irish political parties, with the possible exception of the Workers' Party, have been forced by the PD agenda to alter direction and become more conspicuously concerned with the interests of the contented.

The politics of contentment is now almost all-pervasive. It represents the dominant agenda of Irish society, which politicians challenge at their peril.

In Ireland selfishness and short-term self-interest have become elevated to the level of high principle. Newspapers which in their marketing strategies target themselves at the contented (in marketing parlance the "ABC1s"), in their leader columns make demands for the "rationalisation" of "unviable" public services, like railways and post offices, usually in places in which their readers are not conspicuous. So-called "economic experts", who are themselves comfortable as a result of poncing off the economics of contentment, are trotted on to radio and television programmes to provide supposedly objective scientific analyses to back up the conventional wisdom.

Politicians on all sides now feel the need to make frequent calls for lower taxation, greater "incentives" and less fettering of the market mechanism. Parties which attempt to cling to the notion of "catch-all" politics are threatened with extinction. Fine Gael, for example, although it has couched its expression of concern about unemployment largely in terms of the longer-term interests of the contented (the need for tax reform, threat of crime increase, etc. etc.), has seen its support decline in more or less inverse proportion to its concern. Fianna Fáil, after some initial resistance, is learning fast. Left-wing parties seeking to achieve growth are required to stop bellyaching about poverty and inequality and cuddle up to the centre-right consensus. This they have done without undue protest.

John Kenneth Galbraith is not optimistic that, short of a major economic or social cataclysm, the politics of contentment can be reversed. "Alas," he writes, "we speak of a democracy with the least sense of urgency to correct what is wrong."

But for all its honest pessimism, Professor Galbraith's book is a sublime and essential read. It should be read by those in Irish politics who remain loosely committed to the possibility of a return to a more socially concerned ethos in public life, and especially by those on the left who remain unsure of where they stand in the post-communist 1990s. Its message is that nothing has changed other than for the worse.

11. THE THATCHERITE PLAGUE

I saw a sketch on *Spitting Image* a couple of weeks ago which showed an "average" British voter entering a polling booth. He went in determined not to vote Tory on account, one presumed, of the appalling record of that party in government over the past fifteen years. As he stood with hand poised over the voting paper, a hand reached over from one side, flipped open the top of his skull, took out his brain and replaced it with a piece of cheese. He decided, after all, to vote Tory one more time.

That sketch said just about everything I have felt about the British voting public in the era of Thatcherism and beyond. In the face of what seems like incontrovertible evidence of the social disaster which this era of Conservative rule has represented, the voters, election, after election, return the Tories to office "one more time". And so, while it is always nice to see the Tories getting a hammering, I'm not sure that there is any long-term comfort in last week's local election results across the water.

I no longer look forward, as I did in 1983, 1987 and 1992, to the electoral demise of the Tories. Even if it occurs, I am positive that it will almost certainly be for the wrong reasons. This scepticism was borne out by last week's results. As one commentator on radio put it, the result represented a disaster for the Tories, a triumph for the Liberal Democrats and a respectable result for the Labour Party. I think that's about right.

There is nothing in this result for anyone wishing to see a return to a socially conscious politics in Britain. Observing recent electoral trends there, one gets the impression that the electorate is prepared to replace the Tories only with a party which offers a "better" version of Toryism. The relative successes of the other political parties seem to pivot on how far they have been willing to adopt the broad principles of Thatcherism.

In spite of all its manifest evils and failures, there has not (yet?) been a real backlash against Thatcherism. Although the Tories have suffered the most devastating defeat in their history, there is scant sense that this has occurred because the public has copped on to the harm done in the past fifteen years. At best, it is warning to pull their socks up.

The British people, it seems to me, have not said to the ruling party, "You have done evil, now in the name of God go!" Instead, they seem to be saying to the entire political establishment, "We are still waiting for the Thatcher miracle."

This is as interesting as it is depressing, but ultimately not all that surprising. The collapse of communism merely put a full stop at the end of twentieth-century socialism, which had been in decline, in these islands and elsewhere, for two decades.

This insinuated into the public mind the idea that there is now no way forward except an improved version of the alternative "philosophy" of capitalism. In other words, if things are going badly, this can only be because the model of market-driven policies is in need of souping-up. The public, then, looks across the political spectrum for the party which advocates the purest, most streamlined version, of this philosophy.

And so, while the idea that there is but one way forward continues to hold sway, the Tories have the capacity to retain office no matter how badly they perform, unless some other party is prepared to don unashamedly the full Thatcherite outfit. Other parties enter the frame only to the extent that they are prepared to jettison emphasis on having a social dimension to policy.

As I have suggested, this is not all that surprising. In both British and Irish societies, while some slight variations are available, the essence of all mainstream prescriptions is the same. The idea is carried in virtually all media, as an irrefutable truth, that market economics is the only way forward.

The basis of this outlook is the denial of the social dimension. This is not simply an ideological position, but a particular perspective on reality. It is not simply that these societies have scrutinised the range of options and come down, on balance, on the side of market economics, but rather that they have concluded that market economics is the *only* reality. The debate is about the extent to which this philosophy should be regulated to minimise casualties.

This position is based on the assumption that each human being exists, first, foremost and only, as an individual. In general, it falls short of the full logic of Thatcher's belief that there is "no such thing" as society, but goes more than halfway in accepting that society is the *sum* of the *individuals* – as opposed to the *whole* of the community of *people* – it contains. It discounts any possibility that the society we now have is the product of interaction between people over generations, and admits only the contribution of the individual as a salient factor in public activity.

This is the logic of what we hear described as "the enterprise culture", promoted not just by all the main political parties, but by the national newspapers, the trade unions, and practically every single body which contributed to the public debate. That debate is constructed so that this idea is now almost impossible to argue against.

This is why, to give just a minor example, we now regard as an eternal, natural phenomenon the speech, the editorial, the public pronouncement, bellowing for the privatisation or "rationalisation" of this or that public service. Such calls are based on the premise that services exist only in the context of their visible realities.

They discount entirely any consideration of the culture in which a service may have developed, the public-service ethic on which it is based, the hidden benefits it provides, the unseen longer-term consequences of tampering with it, and so on. The presumption is that nothing exists except what is visible to the individualist eye.

Social benefits, because they are less visible, are hardly thought about at all, except in the sense that they can be cashed-in for the immediate profit. The future, even the future conditions in the "enterprise culture", is hardly considered.

Last week we heard Dick Spring complain about the lack of interest shown by the media in his party's social agenda in government. What he has perceived is a logical consequence of the culture I have described. The assumption of the public discourse, here as in Britain, is that the purpose of government is to create the right conditions for individual "success".

In this context, social concern is regarded as, at best, a well-intentioned "compassion" for those who are "marginalised" – on account of their own weakness, the implicit logic goes – from the enterprise culture. Mr Spring's party has, to a large degree, contributed to this climate by failing to articulate an alternative, socially based philosophy, and by broadly accepting the fundamentals of the market-driven analysis.

While socially directed policies are clearly vital, they are inadequate without a socially driven public discourse. On the basis of Britain's post-Thatcherite experience, the irony is that, in the absence of a social imperative from our political culture, the electoral prospects of Mr Spring's party may depend on the extent to which it can keep its social policies a *secret* from the electorate.

12. THE DISAPPEARING CENTRE   (March 1993)

We really should give some thought to granting our public representatives more time off. They close down Leinster House for a week and scatter themselves to the four winds to celebrate the national holiday, and what happens? The affairs of government begin to spiral dangerously out of control? The State sinks even further into the mire of despair? Well, no, actually.

What happens is that interest and inflation rates take a sharp fall and the economic picture begins to look considerably brighter than it has for over six months. The message is clear: what we need to get us back on our feet is six months without any kind of government at all.

I jest, of course, but not as much as you might think. In the first place, the above is only slightly more farcical than the kind of vaporous bluster masquerading as economic analysis that politicians indulge in all the time. When things improve, it is always because of the success of the government's policies; when things get worse, as occurs much more frequently, it is on account of "worldwide recession", or because the leader of the Opposition has talked the economy down from its dizzy heights.

In the second place, there exists at least a tentative public curiosity on the question of whether the affairs of this Republic proceed – in whatever chaotic manner they do proceed – in spite, rather than because of, the people we have elected to run it.

This curiosity, I detect, has now reached previously

unattained levels of idle recklessness. People are asking: "What is it that politicians do anyway?" "Have they any power at all?" And, perhaps even more ominously for the politicians: "Could things be any worse if there was no such thing as government?"

There was a time when these might have seemed like dangerous questions. Now they have begun to seem like an interesting area of exploration.

I am not talking about what politicians refer to as "public cynicism" (by which is usually meant any kind of criticism of the motives or performances of politicians). Nor am I referring to recent negative press comment about the salaries, allowances and privileges that our politicians enjoy. These are just superficial symptoms of a much more interesting phenomenon.

Attacking politicians as a class, however enjoyable, is beside the point. It may well be that politics, at least in the way that we have come to understand it, was always doomed to irrelevancy. There is no good reason for believing that the system of liberal representative democracy we inherited from the British should go on forever.

Liberal triumphalism has tended to depict the collapse of communism in the East as a vindication of itself, but this may tell us more about the arrogance of western liberalism than about the reality of modern politics.

Could it be that something far more fundamental is taking place? Could it be that, for all kinds of reasons (like, for instance, the effect on the human consciousness of mass communications), a change is occurring in the nature and quality of the relationship between power and people, and that this change transcends the scant borders of conventional ideologies?

It is not in the nature of power to remain satisfied or stationary. It craves movement, dynamic and expansion.

It afflicts those who pursue it in the manner of an addiction, constantly increasing both the dependency and the immunity until finally no quantity of the drug is capable of satisfying the need. Unless power has space to expand and grow, it withers and dies, like a plant in too small a pot.

Since the Second World War, western Europe has been engaged in an effort to defy the nature of power. It has attempted to curtail the expansionist tendencies of individual nations by directing their power towards a common pool. This process worked for a while, absorbing the restless energy of power which was prevented from following its natural instinct.

But by choosing to transfer power upwards rather than downwards, western Europe took the easiest but more limited of its options. We are now almost at the point of absolute inertia.

In a sense, the differences between what happened in the eastern bloc and what has been happening in western Europe since 1945 are relatively superficial. The similarities, on the other hand, are quite profound. Watching the televised reports of the French elections this past week, for example, reminded me of nothing so much as the Soviet Union in the Brezhnev era.

Almost without exception, the main contenders for leadership after the election are the same people who have dominated French politics for over a quarter of a century. All over Europe, a generation of politicians is in power which has completely lost touch with the feelings of the people, as the continuing Maastricht debacle illustrates.

Even where the personnel have been changed, as here and in Britain, the difference is at best of an aesthetic nature, with previously dominant and moderately interesting personalities being replaced by leaders who are ideologically and otherwise indistinguishable, except that they lack even a leavening modicum of charisma.

The primary impulse of post-war politics in both East and West was to refuse to hand power downwards to the people, but instead to invest it in the apparatus of government at either national or supranational level. When that power followed its natural urge to expand, it was allowed to expand upwards and outwards, but never down. In both ideological systems, the purpose of government, of economics, of social policy, was not the betterment of people's lives, but the efficient operation of the technology of power.

The result was the dehumanisation of politics, the corruption of political language and the loss of a common conscience. The differences between East and West were purely of degree and of emphasis.

But something has started to happen in the hearts and minds of the people of Europe, east and west. In much the same way that the body's immune system moves to attack invaders hostile to itself, the true democratic process has lately begun to mobilise itself against the forces of depersonalisation. This is not something you read or hear much about in the media, which by their nature are obsessed with the technology of power itself. But all the time, if you are interested in hearing, you pick up similar signals in the most unexpected places – an essay by a German philosopher or a casual remark by a Donegal mother-of-four.

People are becoming involved again in their communities, localities and societies. After a long period of believing in the good intentions of politics, they are beginning to make alternative arrangements. The relationship between state and society is changing. The most important things, the things which affect the quality of people's lives, are being taken back from the centre, independently of the political process. Even the very notion of the "centre" of power, whether it be in Paris, Bonn, London or Dublin, a concept long thought indispensable to the administration of government, is dissolving into the mists of history.

It is not so much that politicians are suddenly losing their power to the people. Rather it is that they have transferred most of their power in an upward direction – to the bureaucracy, the EC or the multinational corporation – and so have created a vacuum which a new kind of power is beginning to occupy. This power was always there, in families, communities, voluntary organisations, environmental groups, and so on, but only now has it the motivation and the necessary space to expand.

Already, the more observant among the political class have begun to sit up and take notice. They have started to acknowledge the new energy as something other than peripheral hyperactivity. They have begun to talk about "partnership" between the new politics and the old. Politicians are in danger of becoming irrelevant, they say, "unless we do something now". Perhaps they, even more than those who continue to snort in derision, are engaging in self-delusion. Perhaps that "unless" is the sign of the ultimate hubris.

The very assumption that politics as we have known it has any role at all to play in the future order may itself be mistaken. Politicians have become so conditioned to the notion of central control that they are unable to conceive of any other form of social organisation. But it could well be that one of the central characteristics of such a new order would be that it would be subject to the absolute minimum of centralised control, and possibly none.

All that we can safely predict is that the new "order" will be complex, fluid, dissipative and unpredictable, perhaps even totally acephalous. In fact, it is highly unlikely to conform to any of our current definitions of order at all, which perhaps says more about the limitations of present concepts of order than about the likely shape of our future society.

13. INEVITABLE HYPOCRISIES (August 1993)

Today's world requires us either to be hypocrites, cranks or silent. Such is the scale of our dependencies that we can survive only by entering into pacts with things that threaten to destroy us. Our philosophies and our behaviour take different routes. We are all compromised, because none of us is capable of self-sufficiency. Each of us has two faces. In a sense, each of us is *two* people: the individual and the social person.

Selfishness has become an almost mandatory condition. Suppose, for example, an awareness of ecological matters convinces one that the motor car is harmful to the environment and an unsustainable drain on the ecological balance of the planet. One may even take the view that the idea of privately owned motor cars is an absurdity which future generations of humanity will find hard to credit, and consequently believe that the motor car should be banned, or at least seriously curtailed. In as far as practicable, one may be a supporter of the idea of public transport.

However, one is also a citizen of a society in which such views are regarded not merely as minority concerns but as evidence of eccentricity. Furthermore, this mainstream view is institutionalised in the society's approach to transport issues, which give pride of place to the private vehicle and provides a minimum level of public transportation.

As a result, even the citizen who is opposed to private cars and believes in the principle of public transport must possess and run motor cars in order to go about his or her business. Thus, it is almost impossible for the citizen to behave in a manner which conforms with his or her principles.

This process not merely makes the individual in question appear hypocritical, but locks the society into its present way of doing things. The fact that I am daily to be seen driving around in my motor car tends to discredit my argument for public transport and contributes to the society's self-justification in the matter of privately-owned motor cars.

Of course, if I were to follow the letter of my own beliefs, forswear the motor car entirely and travel about on a bicycle with my socks rolled up over my trouser-legs, I would retain my philosophical integrity, while allowing those who support the status quo to dismiss all adversaries of the motor car as cranks and lunatics. There are some arguments the individual citizen just cannot win.

And so, in the end, the dissenter concludes that it is not *his* car that threatens the planet, but all the other cars, or at least that, all things considered, the contribution of *his* car to the destruction of the planet is fairly negligible and therefore far outweighed by the inconvenience and embarrassment of riding a bicycle.

The problem arises because, although an individual's response makes little difference on its own, the fact that everyone else does likewise means we are collectively heading for disaster. In the absence of a communitarian view at the core of a society, each citizen is pushed inexorably towards an individualistic perspective.

If he or she is to avoid being labelled a hypocrite or a crank, the well-intentioned citizen must remain silent or opt out. The common denominator, usually the most expedient and short-sighted of options, invariably wins the day. Individualism destroys both the collective solidarity of a society and the sovereignty of the individual human being.

Of course, this process applies only to certain aspects of our lives. It does not apply, for example, or at least not in any general sense, to income tax. Most of us dislike paying income tax and would, as individuals, welcome any opportunity of avoiding it. But on another level, as citizens of a society, we acknowledge the need for a pooling of resources for the common good and believe that income tax is a reasonably fair and efficient method of doing this. In this case, the public impulse wins out over the private, the community spirit over the spirit of individualism.

Why does this apply in some things and not in others? Clearly, it has very little to do with right and wrong, or even with self-preservation, for, increasingly, we are able to see certain aspects of our society as inherently self-destructive, and yet take little or no steps to change our ways. As a general rule of thumb, it might be said that we proceed according to some idea of a common good when this is necessary for the smooth technical running of the society *in the present and immediate future.*

When factors of time intervene, even the notion of self-interest becomes vague and unfocused, and we capitulate to that which is more immediately expedient. This conditions much of our politics and makes it reek of pragmatism, short-termism and hypocrisy. Either the model of politics we have arrived at is incapable of formulating a vision which would transcend our natural tendencies or the public mood is incapable of tolerating such a vision even if it arose.

What is it, then, that makes modern politics so hostile

to the common good? Why, for example, is there such resistance to the creation of a comprehensive system of public transport? Individually, we may be able to perceive the logic of such a system: cleaner air, less congestion, more equality of access, etc. etc.

But *collectively*, we are incapable of imagining the benefits such a system would bring, of marshalling the common-sense awareness which exists on the subject at the personal level. This is partly because the benefits remain too long-term or unfocused.

This lack of quantifiable advantage is easily exploited by the multitude of special-interest groups which have effectively hijacked the democratic process from the citizenry at large. Such groups are invariably an expression of *selfish* interests, tailored with a specificity that is indifferent to all external concerns.

This has been allowed to occur because we have no counterbalancing expression of a collective view at a political or institutional level. What is missing from us as a society is a *conscience – a common conscience.*

The formulation and development of such a common conscience is, surely, the main purpose of politics. Indeed – paradoxically? – politics depends for its own survival on the existence of something not dissimilar to a common conscience.

For why else would each citizen go out to vote if not in the belief that in this individual act of voting lay the possibility of collective expression of a common good? Other than in extreme and rare instances, one vote will not make a difference one way or another and each individual who votes is profoundly aware of this.

But, at the same time, when the individual walks into the polling booth, he or she does so in the knowledge that if everyone decided not to vote, it would indeed make a big difference, that democracy would collapse, or at least that its power would be weakened. In this sense, the voter walking into the booth is acting not as an individual but in his or her capacity as a member of society, as a communal being.

Despite the increasing tendency for voting patterns to express the vested interests of particular classes and sectors, the democratic election retains a basic function as an outlet for public-spiritedness. This symbolic function is rapidly becoming the last relic of a societal view on the political stage.

Curiously, the loss of solidarity appears to have occurred in the period – and perhaps as a result – of mass universal communication. The more we are able to communicate with the greater numbers – and the greater the distances such communication is able to bridge – the less we are able to care about the generality of mankind or take into account our role as citizens as well as individuals.

The more immediate the process of political administration, the narrower its preoccupations and capabilities. The more *touchable* our politicians, the more detached they appear to get from the needs of their society.

It is as though mass communication relates only, or at least *best*, to the individual, and politicians can use the mass media only as a vehicle for selfish ideas. Each act of communication is one-to-one, and each connection is on the basis of the narrowest advantage. There is no such thing as "television", only individual *televisions*. There is no such thing as society, only consumers of benefit.

The system we have created encourages each one of us to be selfish while hoping that everyone else will be public-spirited. And because most of us are selfish in similar ways, all we can do *collectively* is admonish the tide of selfishness which threatens to engulf us.

To attempt to reverse this process in a concerted manner would require a massive intervention by a controlling influence which we are now perhaps incapable – and probably mercifully – of generating. The way forward lies in consciousness-raising, but it is questionable whether a revolution in awareness can be developed with sufficient speed to retard seriously our present headlong rush towards a selfish self-destruction.

There are *some* signs of a new beginning. In the United States, for example, the Clinton administration has been making noises which at least hint at an awareness of the shape and size of the hole which needs to be filled.

"We need a new spirit of community, a sense that we're all in this together," Bill Clinton declared in his victory speech last November. "Without that spirit, the American Dream will wither and die." Behind the rhetoric is a sobering glimpse of reality. Without a return to solidarity and mutuality, the only dreams that will survive are the most selfish. Only the strong will have their way.

Perhaps we need to perceive first the implications of that possibility before we can grasp the kind of shift that is required.

14. REDEFINING THE HUMANLY DESIRABLES

(August 1993)

The concept of "community", in the political sense, is almost universally undervalued and misunderstood. Frequently dismissed by political establishments as an irrelevant and crankish obstacle to development, it is equally derided by conventional opposition forces, which in most western countries are quasi-leftist mirror images of the status quo they purport to oppose.

The former see community politics as little more than a nuisance, the latter, because they seek to transcend the issues of class beyond which they are incapable of seeing, as a form of false consciousness. Both objections are those of elites to the implications of true democracy.

Although there is an increasing tendency for community politics to become fashionable, as in the growth of communitarianism in the United States, what is at issue is not simply politics. Democracy, which is what we are talking about, is a political concept only as a secondary aspect. It is first and foremost a *human* ideal.

The injunction "Love thy neighbour as thyself" is perceived nowadays as platitude, but is the most radical idea in the history of politics. What it defines is not the need merely to love others; it places the role of each human being in the context of his or her inter-relationships with others, implying that a true love of self is not possible without a love of others. It is hardly possible to imagine a more refined and telling critique of the failures of recent political thinking.

Democracy is not possible without a profound love of people. Democracy is not simply a way of organising society for "productive" ends; it is a way of enabling people to live together and be as happy as possible. Both the totalitarian communism which dominated Eastern Europe before 1989, and the neo-classical simplicities which devastate the lives of millions in the West, bear witness that true democracy is not even on the menu in modern societies.

But the problem of the "democratic-deficit" is far more profound than the mere cataloguing of failed or inadequate political systems could describe. It might be argued that modern politics, in its increasing preoccupation with technocratic efficiency at the expense of the human impulse, is gravitating away from democracy.

The absence of democracy in Ireland is obscured by the vibrant prevalence of politics at personal, cultural and institutional levels, to the extent that it is impossible to think or speak publicly about the shapes of our society other than through the language and imagery afforded by politics. And yet Irish politics is, to say the least of if, an unwieldy vehicle for implementing the aspirations of Irish people.

The poverty of democracy in Ireland is largely a cultural matter, arising out of our colonial past and the effects of palliative medicines, such as an excessively pietistic form of religion, which we adopted to lessen the pain. The evidence of this legacy is still in evidence in towns, villages and communities around Ireland, where power has lain for generations in the hands of self-appointed elites and oligarchies.

This localised phenomenon has been mirrored in a very precise form in both the administration of the State and the shaping of our society, culturally and otherwise, at a central level.

What this reflects is the inheritance of a view of power as something external, as existing at a remove from each of our human selves. Politics has developed not as a means of restoring the absent democracy but as a parallel activity which aped the characteristics of democracy without bringing it an inch closer.

Politics is a sport in which everything possible is acted out, but hardly ever enacted. For us, politics is a means without an end. It divides people up without any purpose other than the division itself. Irish politics has detached Irish people from one another and the overall society from a clear connection with its own nature and means. This is true of *all* Irish politics, not just the dominant and much-disparaged mainstream form, which has actually served as an unconscious model for those who claim to oppose it.

Now, for perhaps the first time since independence, we have a population which is smarter than the elites. People are beginning to ask why it is that the power structures do not work for them. For the first time they can see clearly that this is not their fault, or their bad luck, but is because power-structures based on an externalised notion of power are, by definition, incapable of democratic application.

An additional factor is the apparent paradox that the collapse of elements of the existing economy and the accompanying structures has actually liberated communities trapped within quasi-feudal hegemonies in towns and villages around Ireland. What has occurred is a profound reorientation of people's ideas of power which, if properly nurtured and developed, has the capacity to effect a radical transformation in thinking about how we organise ourselves and our affairs.

The struggle for community consciousness is the struggle for democracy. There is, I know, an element of naivete in this assertion. There are many sensible and honourable people who believe that the notion of a truly democratic form of community-driven politics is next to impossible given the existing conditions of our alleged democracy.

There are fundamental problems of political culture and economic practice which make the ideal form of community development seem something of a pipedream. We are approaching a very dangerous point in the development of community awareness.

The danger is of colonisation by the existing power structures, which perceive that community politics could be tamed to the old ways, could be trained, for example, to depend on EC hand-outs. This would result in even less democracy than exists at present, resulting in new forms of dependency and the dissipation of the enthusiasm and energy that has so painfully been brought forth.

This would be a betrayal to exceed anything previously achieved in the sorry history of recent Irish politics. Already, there is a divide in community politics between those who are prepared to settle for short-term gains and those who want to stay in for the long haul – between the pragmatists and the idealists, if you wish. Given the antipathy of almost all forms of politics towards the fundamental idea of community, it would hardly be surprising if the overwhelming odds caused many to sell the whole effort short.

That this be avoided should be a matter of concern to every citizen of this state. The idea of community development is not simply a gimmick with a nice-sounding title. It is to do with a fundamental view of human beings and their relationship with the world and their own place. To believe in community, you need to think people first, second and last. You have to believe that people and the quality of their lives are not simply something to be weighed in the balance, but are the sole purpose of development and economic activity. That is the nature of the profound realisation that is necessary.

To this end there is a need for a programme of evangelisation to break the residual hold of the post-colonial mentality on society at large. The first, "last" and indeed *only* thing that needs to be "done" for people is give them the control which will obviate the need for "doing" things for them anymore.

But you cannot simply graft the idea of "community development" onto the existing flawed thought-process.

310

The two are opposites, inimical. One must supplant the other. The political establishment, the media, the state agencies and the bureaucracies need to be persuaded not simply that this phenomenon is a useful vehicle for creating development opportunities, but that it is an opportunity for them, as officials, opinion formers and power brokers – but more importantly as *human beings* – to contribute to a society run according to the human principles which even *they* must instinctively understand.

Community development is about finding a way forward for society which sees its value in *being* rather than *doing*, in creating rather than producing. As Father Brendan Lovett told a recent theological conference in Galway, the challenge of the coming century is to redefine our ideas of the "humanly desirable".

"Any creative way forward depends on the recovery of a more human viewpoint," he said. We must "rediscover the suppressed truth of what is truly sacred – our communal being . . . The true view of power sees it as the exercise of life (loving, working, deciding) in mutuality . . . The challenge to universal solidarity is the path to renewed community and a truly human identity for us."

There is a great paradox here in terms of the antipathy between community and individualism. You might say that *individually* the people who inhabit the power centre do not need to learn anything new in order to do this, but that *collectively* they need to relearn *everything* about visualising the world of work and activity and the purpose of human existence in the world. As human beings, they already *know*; as officials, as administrators, they are incapable of remembering.

What is required, then, is nothing less than a radical opening-up of the official mind, to make it as human as the people who staff its desks and telephones.

15. A Blueprint for Saving Ireland (June 1993)

An accusation frequently levelled at columnists like myself is that we are great at criticising the efforts of politicians but not so hot at coming up with solutions of our own. It is so very easy, the cry goes up, to sit on the sidelines and snipe and sneer and snarl, but what ideas have newspaper columnists to offer for dealing with the problems they are so fond of pontificating about? (Actually, it isn't at all easy to sit on the sidelines and snipe and sneer and snarl – it can be hard work.) This week, in response to such criticisms, I would like to unveil my Blueprint for Saving Ireland.

It's very simple really, so I won't beat about the bush. My plan is as follows. The present Government, given that it has a substantial majority in Dáil Eireann, is likely to run a full term. Barring any principled walk-outs by the Labour Party (and so far they appear to be keeping their principles firmly under control), there is no reason why it could not continue in office until, say, the late autumn of 1997. By a happy coincidence, this will also mark the end of the seven-year term of office of the President, Mrs Robinson.

Needless to say, it is a racing certainty that, should Mrs Robinson wish to avail of the option to continue as President for a second seven-year term, then this is what will happen. My suggestion is that she should be discouraged from doing so, but instead persuaded to put herself forward for the position of Taoiseach following a general election to be held to coincide with the end of the Presidency.

To do this, of course, she would need to have the support of the majority of the 28th Dáil. This should not be too difficult to organise.

312

Technically, of course, as precedent shows, Mrs Robinson would not require to be a party leader to become Taoiseach. However, this might well prove desirable from an electoral viewpoint. I have no doubt that a party – almost any party – led by Mrs Robinson would succeed in obtaining an overwhelming majority of seats. What I suggest is that, at the end of the President's current term, one or other of the party leaders would step down from his or her position before an election timed to coincide with her departure from the Presidency.

Mrs Robinson, on vacating the Presidency, would take over as party leader. The obvious choice would be the Labour Party, since she has been a member in the past, but either Fine Gael, Democratic Left or even the Progressive Democrats would be almost equally suitable. (I suspect that the cultural and aesthetic gulf to be bridged in making Mrs Robinson leader of Fianna Fáil might be too great at such an early stage. Let us not run away with ourselves.)

Mrs Robinson's party could then fight the general election on the basis of her record as President, which would undoubtedly deliver an overwhelming majority to what would be the first Irish government led by a woman. Meanwhile, the party leader who had made the ultimate political sacrifice in favour of Mrs Robinson could be elected President as a token of the people's gratitude, and would go down in history as one of the truly great Irish statesmen of the twentieth century.

I realise that the initial resistance to such an idea is likely to be great, not least from the President herself, who has argued consistently and cogently for the value and integrity of the office she now holds.

Having been persuaded of the exciting and radical nature of the potential of the Presidency, by both the rhetoric and performance of Mrs Robinson, I would be the last to attempt to underestimate the importance of the office for the present and immediate future. Mrs Robinson's achievement is consistently undervalued, I believe, by the constant barrage of platitudinous praise which is heaped upon her by an establishment which is actually incapable of perceiving the significance of what she has become. It is almost impossible, in my view, to exaggerate the profound and far-reaching nature of the change she has tapped into and led, morally and symbolically.

Symbolism is at the core of the matter. Mainstream politicians seem happy to give the symbolic nature of the President's role a rhetorical pat on the head, under the misapprehension, I believe, that "symbolic" means the same thing as "ceremonial". There is a world of difference.

All previous presidents had a largely ceremonial role; they performed official openings, shook hands and nodded their heads at the appropriate moments. Most of them did not have a *symbolic* role – or if they did, it provided a much different, *more limited*, kind of symbol than does Mrs Robinson. Mrs Robinson performs all the ceremonial functions at least as well as any of her predecessors, but it is her symbolic role that marks her apart.

When politicians say that the President has a "symbolic" role, what they usually mean is that she has no power. In a sense this is true, but in another it could not be further from the truth.

She does not have power in the executive, political sense; but she does have power in the sense of moral authority over the power that belongs to each of us citizens, which she alone among public figures has been able to recognise, and which she affirms and nourishes with every day of her Presidency. In this sense, the "powerlessness" of her office is the symbol of her power in a far more important sense. Mainstream politicians would not give you tuppence for that kind of power, which is partly why mainstream politics is on the point of collapse.

The question is: what is the limit of the process of which Mrs Robinson is such a public and powerful figurehead? The establishment's view would be that, in so far as there is anything happening at all, it is peripheral, tangential, a kind of sideshow to the important business of real politics, which, however much it can make people *feel* better, is of no real significance.

I would say – and I suspect that Mrs Robinson knows this as well – that the present reawakening will not continue indefinitely as a kind of parallel response to conventional politics, but must be seen as the beginnings of a reconstruction which will supplant the present ways of seeing and doing things.

What is happening in Ireland is just one manifestation of what is likely to become a European-wide phenomenon, as the people of the continent begin to respond to the arrogance and detachment of their political leaders. I have written many times in this regard about the President of the Czech Republic, Mr Václav Havel. Last week in Germany, we observed the conscience of the federal republic being redeemed a little by the decision of the President, Mr Richard von Weizsäcker, to attend the funeral services for the Turkish victims of racial attacks, in the wake of a further instance of the appalling ignorance and insensitivity of the Chancellor, Dr Helmut Kohl.

The German writer and philosopher Hans Magnus Enzensberger, speaking some time ago about Mr von Weizsäcker, said: "He is concerned to make the moral and aesthetic situation of the republic more bearable, as far as the limits of his office allow. He's successful in that. People understand it. He has won a kind of credibility, which other politicians have completely lost."

He could, of course, have said the same thing of the role of Mrs Robinson in this Republic. What Mr von Weizsäcker, Mr Havel and Mrs Robinson have in common is that they are democrats in the absolute sense, profoundly in touch with the moral, aesthetic and existential sensibilities of their respective peoples.

It is vital that this evolving process be seen, not as an antidote to the necessary evils of modern politics, but as an *alternative* to them. If politics is to have any future at all, then this must be it. At a certain point, not too far into the future, we will have to make decisions about how far we wish to go, whether and at what point the uncontaminated vision and moral authority of the new politics should begin to engage the apparatus of the old. An obvious and practical step would be for Mrs Robinson to move from a symbolic-cum-ceremonial role to a symbolic-cum-executive one.

When Mrs Robinson was elected, almost three years ago, we did not imagine the possibility of such questions. At the time, in keeping with the stated limits of the Presidential office, she avoided questions about engagement with the executive functions of government.

But time passes and things change. The energy she has identified and helped to increase cannot be expected to accept a peripheral role. To say that it has no future at all other than at the centre of things is not to diminish either it or her. It could, of course, grow into the mainstream without Mrs Robinson's overt involvement, but why should it have to? There is nobody else in public life who has even begun to understand it and, in four years, she will be in the prime of her public life.

I know she likes being President, but we cannot be out enjoying ourselves all the time. Anyway, it is early days yet and both Mrs Robinson and the political parties have ample opportunity to get used to the idea.

We will, of course, have to break it to her gently. It will also be important to stress that this suggestion contains no reflection on the imaginative redefinition of the meaning of the Presidency which she has achieved. What we will really be saying is that we want Mrs Robinson to be our Taoiseach *as well as* our President. I defy anyone to come up with a better solution to the problems of modern Ireland.

Also by Poolbeg

Ancestral Voices

By

Conor Curise O'Brien

In *Ancestral Voices*, Conor Cruise O'Brien illuminates the confusion and conflation of religion and nationalism in Irish history, and the enormous tensions produced by interactions between the two. He pursues this line of thought through Irish history into our own time. His interest in the general subject-matter derives particularly from his family's share in the specific Irish experiences of the workings of these formidable historical forces.

Conor Cruise O'Brien uses his life as a prism through which to view his times. He is concerned with understanding those currents of twentieth-century history that have swirled around him. O'Brien is a witness to a current of history newly relevant to the post-war world – that of nationalism, and especially its furious amalgam with religion in the force he has called "sacral nationalism". O'Brien is ever on the hunt for the lethal mixing of God with country which has spilled oceans of blood throughout this century of nationalism and which, from Bosnia to Northern Ireland, still curses the world.

Scholar, diplomat, politician, government minister, historian, biographer, anti-war activist, intellectual, playwright, newspaper editor, prose stylist, political theorist, university president, and authority on Zionism, terrorism, Ireland, Africa, post-colonialism, and nationalism: Conor Cruise O'Brien is a man of many parts.

Since the success of his most recent book, *The Great Melody: a Thematic Biography of Edmund Burke*, Conor Cruise O'Brien's international reputation has been growing. The first instalment of his autobiography was *The Atlantic Monthly's* cover story in January 1994. The editors describe him as "the only contemporary writer who can be compared to George Orwell and André Malraux."

1 85371 429 1 £7.99

Also by Poolbeg

Queueing for a Living

by

Paddy O'Gorman

Since 1984 Paddy O'Gorman's remarkable success and popularity as a broadcaster has been based on his direct approach to people. For his RTE radio programme *Queueing for a Living*, Paddy has taken his tape-recorder to dole queues, pawnshops, bookie shops, courts and prison gates in Britain, Germany, Holland and in Ireland, North and South.

Paddy O'Gorman does not trust spokespeople. Spokespeople include some social workers and any official who forces a distance between him and the people he wants to listen to. As Paddy remarks, "there is something very subversive about listening to people in queues". Paddy doesn't just listen to people. He holds conversations with them as well. It would not be true to say that Paddy O'Gorman is non-judgmental. He is opinionated, exasperated, comical and prejudiced.

This book is about people who have never previously been given the right or the opportunity to talk. Ordinary people, as well as prostitutes, criminals, victims of paramilitary discipline in Northern Ireland, drug addicts, wife beaters, beaten women, perverts and their families, all find their voices in this vivid and unsettling testimony.

Paddy O'Gorman never meets a typical person because there are no typical people.

"The best thing of its kind since George Orwell's *Down and Out in Paris and London*"

CONOR CRUISE O'BRIEN

1 85371 355 4 £5.99